Fullers

China's Gentry

China's Gentry / ESSAYS IN

RURAL-URBAN RELATIONS BY HSIAO-TUNG FEI

Revised & Edited by Margaret Park Redfield with Six

Life-Histories of Chinese Gentry Families Collected by

Yung-teh Chow and an Introduction by Robert Redfield

The University of Chicago Press / Chicago / Illinois

*This study is issued
in co-operation with the International Secretariat
of the Institute of Pacific Relations*

Illustrations based on drawings by James K. Y. Kuo

THE UNIVERSITY OF CHICAGO PRESS, CHICAGO 37
Cambridge University Press, London, N.W. 1, England

Copyright 1953 by The University of Chicago. All rights reserved
Published 1953. Composed and printed by THE UNIVERSITY OF CHICAGO PRESS
Chicago, Illinois, U.S.A

Table of Contents

[v]

Introduction

I

To Western readers Hsiao-tung Fei is known as the author of a short, illuminating book on life in a Chinese village,[1] of another and more mature work on agriculture and industry in southwestern China,[2] and of a stimulating article[3] on one of the principal themes of the present book: the gentry in Chinese society. In China he is known also as a brilliant teacher, a leader and pioneer in sociological field research, and a man who has written widely, talked much, and acted fearlessly toward the solution of the immense social problems of China. After his return from London, where he took his doctorate under Bronislaw Malinowski, and during the war with Japan he joined those Chinese students and scholars who

1. *Peasant Life in China* (London: Routledge & Kegan Paul, Ltd.; New York: E. P. Dutton & Co., 1939).

2. *Earthbound China* (Chicago: University of Chicago Press, 1945; London: Routledge & Kegan Paul, Ltd., 1948).

3. "Peasantry and Gentry: An Interpretation of Chinese Social Structure and Its Changes," *American Journal of Sociology*, LII, No. 1 (July, 1946), 1–17.

assembled to continue Chinese scientific and intellectual life in Yunnan Province. It was there that he carried on the studies that resulted in his second book. After the defeat of Japan he went back to teach in his old university, Tsinghua, in Peiping; and there (where I had come in the autumn of 1948 as a visiting professor to the same university) my wife and I resumed an old association with him.

This book is made from articles contributed by Fei to Chinese newspapers in 1947 and 1948. During that autumn of 1948 he dictated to my wife a rough translation of these articles, stopping as he did so to talk over with her the substance of the dictation and in part rewriting and enlarging the text in the course of these discussions. The work was done hastily, with enthusiasm, and in the tense anticipations of the coming of Communist control. For, while the dictation and the rewriting went on, Peiping was ringed by Communist forces, and the fall of the universities and of the city itself was expected within a very short time. In December, 1948, most of the students and many of the faculty of the university looked forward to the coming of the Communists as a relief from hardship and oppression and as new opportunity to apply intelligence to the improvement of social and political conditions in China. There was apprehension too; but, with the abundant knowledge of corruption and tyranny under the Nationalist government, the hope outweighed the apprehension. Fei, always sanguine and courageous, was then of the opinion that he could work effectively with the Communists, even though he would continue to criticize when he thought criticism was due. Like others in his university, he did not conceive the incoming government of Chinese Communists in the image of Stalinist Russia; he thought of them as Chinese like himself, as his old friends and students, whose voices he heard over the Communist radio promising all good things to the people of Peiping. So Fei spoke to us of his hope of becoming, for the Communist government, a part of "the loyal opposition." He had already fallen into the disfavor of both parties. While in Yunnan he had been threatened with arrest by the Nationalist government and was fired upon in a public meeting where he had spoken unfavorably of Chiang's regime; on the other hand, Communist voices in the North had attacked him bitterly for certain articles he had published. On the whole, however, Fei felt that his views as to developing Chinese industry and agriculture would be congenial to the interests of the new regime and that after the transition he would be able to continue to work and to speak for China. In this hope, almost a confidence, the articles here assembled were dictated.

My wife and I left Peiping in December, 1948, and for more than three years now we have had no word from Fei. From others we have learned of some bare events. At about the time when Peiping fell to the Communists, Mao Tse-tung asked Fei to take charge of a research program with regard to problems of urban reconstruction, and he accepted and began the work. Fei published articles praising the "New Democracy" of China. He accepted membership on governmental boards or committees. Later he went on an expedition to study some of the remote communities of southwestern China—where he had worked during the Japanese war. Later word tells us that he has returned to Tsinghua University.

This book is published without any participation from him in its production since the days when he dictated its substance to my wife. It is evident that he prefers it so. Communication with Westerners would embarrass or endanger him; he does not write to us, and we have ceased to write to him. My wife edited the text she had transcribed, assuming considerable responsibility in changing the order of the parts, in adding references, and even in inserting phrases or whole sentences when she was sure that Fei's meaning would be served by such additions. It is to be emphasized that the book therefore is an expression of Fei's views and judgments as he was about to step over the threshold between revolutionary China and Communist China. It was written when his students (many of whom I knew) moved in an excitement of fresh opportunity to remake their country—and moved without dogma. Few of them had read a line of Marx. Most of them saw the Nationalist government as their oppressor, the Communists as their liberators.

II

At the time he dictated a translation, Fei wanted the essays to be read by English-speaking people. Like other intelligent people of good will, he wanted China to be understood by Westerners, and he believed that he had something to say about China that was not said in other books. But, when Fei wrote the articles in the first place, he was talking to the Chinese; the present English version does not change that fact. Fei had developed a large audience for his newspaper articles; all sorts of people, mostly people neither peasants nor intellectuals, read and admired what he had to say about the problems of China.

These essays, as newspaper articles, had contributed to the extension of a sense of responsibility in the Chinese people themselves to take charge of their own affairs, and to deal with them, for their own good. Thus the book provides for Westerners an unusual and valuable light on China: a Western-educated Chinese, devoted to working to solve problems of China, analyzes some aspects of these problems so as to make them clearer to his countrymen. The essays give a Chinese point of view on China. They are not written to put a good face on things, or a dark face. They are written to help the Chinese to reach understanding of their troubles. Fei is saying to his countrymen: "Look, this is what has happened to us in recent years. This is the real revolution. This is the place where our shoe pinches. Understand; then act." To Americans, accustomed to thinking of China simply as an object of our foreign policy under the assumption that what will happen in China depends on what we do rather than on what the Chinese do, this book gives fresh insight. Problems of China are here looked at by a Chinese as problems for Chinese to solve, and to solve not by taking political sides, not by joining Russia or joining America, but by reform, by Chinese, of Chinese institutions.

Of course only some of the problems of China are considered in this book. Fei examines certain aspects of the traditional social structure and certain changes that have occurred in that structure that make difficulties for China. The changes have taken place chiefly as a result of the influence of the West. The book therefore bears on that social revolution in China which underlies the overthrow of the empire, the revolutionary republican movement led by Sun Yat-sen, and the winning of political control of China by Chinese Communists. If China is today conquered, or is to be conquered, by Russian communism, that event was no part of the transformations which Fei saw when he wrote these articles. The book does help us to understand how Chinese communism won China.

III

As the essays were written as separate articles, the threads of common idea which hold them together are not so apparent as they might be. There are two interrelated themes: the functions of the scholar and the gentry in the traditional Chinese society and the relations of the country and the city. The first theme is uppermost in the first four essays. The gentry and the scholars must be discussed together, for the scholars were chiefly (but not entirely) derived from the gentry, and the gentry carried on their functions and enjoyed their social position by virtue of the fact that some of them were scholars. The scholars were an elite; the gentry, a social and economic class. The first essay shows how the scholars, by becoming administrative servants of the imperial power, obtained security for themselves and kinsmen. In the second essay we find an account of the history of the development of this adjustment and of how the scholars reflected upon the relationship they had come to have with the centralized authority and how they explained and justified it in their philosophies. The third essay turns on the question why China experienced no important technical development. The scholars, or intellectuals, are now examined from the point of view of the exclusive concern they had with ethical knowledge: the intellectuals had no technical knowledge; they were supported by the labor of others and were unconcerned with productive work. So the governing class lacked the kind of knowledge which would have improved the material condition of the people. In the fourth essay, as in the first two, the point of attention is the function of the scholar-official in mediating the imperial power. But now the attention is directed to that educated member of the gentry who, remaining in the local community, negotiated, in a personal and extralegal way, with the formally recognized functionary who occupied the lowest position in the official bureaucracy. This critical function, exercised by the scholar-gentry, made the imperial power workable, while yet maintaining the traditional social organization of the village. This essay develops into a discussion of the *pao-chia* system (at that time recently reintroduced by the Kuomintang and later abolished by the Communists) by which it was sought to make the central authority directly influential upon the local community and shows why it was doomed to failure.

In the fifth essay there is apparently a new beginning; Fei here takes up not the administrative relations but the economic relations between country and city. The scholar-gentry are not so apparent; but they are here just the same. For, while Fei is telling us that the economic relationship between city and country works to the disadvantage of the country, because the city lives off the country by taking rent and interest from the countryman without sending to the country the products it needs and could consume, we must remember that it is these same gentry who are pocketing the rent and interest and increasingly using the money to buy Western-made products instead of Chinese-made goods. Fei distinguishes several types of towns and cities and shows how each type served the interests of the gentry (and also those of the imperial power) and did not bring advantage to the peasants. Garrison town, market town, and treaty port— all provided opportunities for the economic exploitation of the country. Thus the peasant came to pay a large part of the products of this labor to maintain the gentry class, while the gentry, coming to prefer Western goods, no longer bought the products of rural handicraft and so ruined the small manufacturing which provided the peasant with a little margin over the barest subsistence.

The sixth essay develops this theme of the unsatisfactory character of the exchange between city and country and the worsening of the situation since the introduction of products manufactured in the West. And the seventh essay continues the consideration of the dislocations of the old social and economic system brought about by the influence of the West, while it returns to the theme of the scholar and his functions in Chinese society. In these last pages we see that the modern intellectual, the man educated in Western learning, does not take the place of the old intelligentsia. He does not go back to the country where he has no social position and no career. He stays in the city; so from the country is eroded away some of its best human resources. And some of the rural people, become poorer than ever, are also detached from the rural community and become predatory rovers or—as ever in China—rebels against the government. So only a few years before the Communists began to purge by shooting, and before the fighting in Korea, this series of essays ends, a diagnosis of immense problems, a declaration of hope that the Communists would provide leadership toward solving them.

IV

To the Westerner the book sheds light on the recent political behavior of China and suggests that the failure of the West to prevent the party and power of Mao Tsetung from taking control arose out of a worsening situation among the Chinese people which the party of Chiang Kai-shek did not remedy and which many Americans did not understand. Furthermore, it offers a different construction from that which is often put forward as to the benefit so far received by China from the importation of Western technology and capital.

First is borne in upon the reader the unwisdom, in the light of this analysis, of assuming that to the Chinese the central government has traditionally the meaning to Chinese which government has had to Americans and western Europeans. We have dealt with Chinese governments as though the Chinese thought they represented the Chinese people. It might have been nearer the truth if we had begun by assuming that centralized government is, traditionally, a potentially dangerous predator upon the people—"the tiger." With the revolution of Sun Yat-sen appeared governments that promised to act on behalf of the people, limiting their own power constitutionally. However much the Communist government was itself later to become "the tiger," the credit of this promise, to Chinese, passed in the last decade from the Kuomintang to the Communist party. And the "people's assemblies," the innumerable committees and discussions, stimulated and guided by the Communists, gave Chinese, when the Communists took over, a sense of direct participation in government which they never experienced, and rarely thought was theirs to claim, during the long imperial period.

Second, we understand from what is brought forth in these pages how little prepared have been the Chinese people to assume leadership and carry on constructive and efficient national government. When many of us joined General Marshall in bidding the educated liberals of China to take the lead in constituting a government neither Communist nor corrupt, we did not understand the tradition of which those liberals are the heir. Since the time of Confucius at least, the educated man in China has been concerned with ethical advice (or "normative knowledge," as Fei calls it), not with political action. Indeed, as Fei makes quite plain, especially in the first and fourth essays, sound political policy in China has been to neutralize the political power of the emperor, not to control it. Do-nothingism, he says, has been the equivalent of a constitutional check on government. So the scholar, while being an administrator, had nothing to do with shaping national policy; and administrative effectiveness consisted not in technical efficiency, as in the West, but in skill in such personal negotiations as kept local affairs running not too much disturbed by demands of centralized power. An educated elite with this tradition, without any political power or experience in the formation of policy, separated from the peasantry by mode of life and class position, could hardly be expected to rescue China from the torments of civil war. For the Chinese who has a modern Western education is only the heir of the scholar-official of the long imperial period.

The ancient system was not based on economic justice, but it worked. It worked to the degree that, except for natural catastrophes and wars, it gave the peasant a certain amount of security. His village handicrafts provided an income supplementary to that provided by his agriculture and used the labor that was not needed in slack seasons of the farmer's year. He had to support the gentry, but the scholar-official of the class he supported was useful to him in negotiating with the representatives of the imperial power to prevent the infliction of extreme hardship; and, if the peasant was both industrious and fortunate, he might live to see his son or grandson become a scholar and an official and so experience elevation in his own status. The teachings of the ancient sages reached the peasants through these scholars and redefined again and again the sense of moral purpose which peasant and gentry had in common. The Confucian non-acquisitive ideal both harmonized the peasant's ethics with his lot in life and acted as a restraint upon an imperial power otherwise without check.

If we call this regime, from a view of its politics, democratic or authoritarian, we are likely in either case to misrepresent the facts. The participation of a good many villagers in decisions as to local matters was hardly an equal participation, and the influence of the gentry on the local life was, through their economic power alone, very great. The authoritarianism of the central government was in cases and at times truly autocratic, yet that regime was in theory based on moral authority rather than force; the teachings of the Confucians made the point again and again; the fact that an ideal other than absolutism existed influenced the facts, just as the ideal of social equality between all men influences the facts in the United States.

Thus the opposition between gentry and peasantry in traditional China was held within bounds by the real economic interdependence of the two classes, by the degree of mobility between them, by the co-operation between the two in dealing with the imperial power, and by common ethical principles. What happened to this system that made in China a genuine social revolution? Fei's book is no systematic study of this question—or of any other—but it does suggest some part of the answer. The changes that occurred in China through contact with the West disrupted this system, made it unworkable, and increased the real or apparent harshness of the inequality of life-changes between gentry and peasantry. Fei assumes but does not discuss the general effects in China of that great awakening of the ill-fed, overworked two-thirds of the human race, who live chiefly in Asia, which is such an immense event of our times: the new and growing discontent of the underdog everywhere. The special effects which he puts to the fore are the importation of goods (rather than of capital) and the new learning. Fei is plainly convinced that the benefits of Western capitalistic development in China did the common people harm rather than good. As the gentry developed tastes for Western goods, while some of them found new sources for wealth in trading with the West, they came to spend their profits realized in rent or interest on Western products. The peasant lost his market for his handicrafts and often found it difficult to move to market any agricultural produce that he might be lucky enough to have left over from his domestic wants. Whether Fei's account can stand without some qualifications or not, the visitor to China in recent years cannot fail to catch some of the bitterness with which many Chinese look upon Shanghai and the other treaty ports, where live the privileged, Chinese or Western, "sucking out the wealth of the Chinese people for their own luxuries." So the war between Nationalists and Communists is seen, against this background, not as a conquest of China by a foreign power or a foreign ideology but as a civil conflict between the traditionally privileged *rentier* class and the rural population.

And more and more did the sympathies of the Chinese with modern education turn to the rural population and against the *rentier* class. They came to take hope that the reforms promised by Mao Tse-tung would remove some of the worst of the economic injustices of China. They saw a chance that they could use the special scientific knowledge many of them had acquired in solving the problem of how the city and country might be made mutually beneficial. They attacked the question of how industrialization of China might be wisely carried on, so that the common people might benefit. They began to see how great was their own personal and professional problem: to learn to act politically, to help make public policy in rural communities, and to work with a peasant from whom tradition had separated them.

Hsiao-tung Fei, himself a member of the gentry class, at the time these essays were written was probably the leading voice among those striving to solve the problem of China with the aid of science and toward the common welfare. Through his studies and periods of residence in the West he had come to assume a position, unfamiliar to the traditional intellectual of China, that "something *must* be done to help." For this he and some few others in China like him were criticized by other intellectuals. Interested in American democracy and in English socialism, convinced that the people of China must assume responsibility for economic and social reform, he turned to the writing of the papers that now appear in this book partly because the suspicious Nationalist Chinese government would not allow him to carry on field research. The essays are in part an indirect criticism of the failures of the Nationalist government. Whether today Fei has the freedom he needs to speak and act in accordance with his convictions is not known to the writer of these lines. But those who know him are sure that he will continue as long as he is able to devote his energies, and to risk his life, to help the Chinese people.

v

The correctness of Fei's interpretations of the origins of economic and political problems in China may be open to criticism. There are other minds and other books to do this. Another aspect of the book is also open to criticism: the use and interpretation of references to classical Chinese literature. Such references occur especially in the first two essays. To me the correctness of Fei's philological and philosophical understandings is, in the general context of this work, less important than the fact that he used the Chinese classics at all. The old literati had ceased to perpetuate themselves; they are gone forever; Fei's face was turned hopefully to the Communists, whose doctrines he knew to be anti-Confucian and Marxist. Yet Fei, talking to his own people, "the plain people," elaborates and demonstrates his views with etymologies and quotations from the traditional poets and philosophers. Also he quotes Lilienthal, R. H. Tawney, and Sorokin! There is something in these pages that tells us about the forms of thought appropriate to the persuasion of literate Chinese at the turn of the revolutionary tide.

VI

Fei's seven essays are followed in this volume by six life-histories of Chinese gentry collected by Mr. Yung-teh Chow in Yunnan between 1943 and 1946. Mr. Chow has translated these into English and kindly allowed their inclusion in this book. The accounts seem to us to exhibit, in terms of the life-careers of particular individuals, some of the principal generalizations Fei offers as to the role, partly beneficial, partly predatory, of the traditional Chinese gentry. Further comment on these life-histories appears on pages 145–48.

A Chinese sociologist in this country said to my wife and me: "When a Chinese sociologist writes for Chinese, he writes very differently from the way he writes for Americans." The remark suggests something of the incompleteness with which Western social science and traditional Chinese forms of thought have become fused. It helps to explain, also, why my wife left in the text the many references to Chinese classics which Fei put there and introduced in the footnotes some explanations of some of these references. These references are entirely superfluous to the Sinologist; they are inserted to help readers who are not Sinologists to recognize the sources of some of Fei's allusions.

In the cases of Chinese who have written in English and have recorded their names with the surname in last position, we have followed this practice; in other cases we have written the names as the Chinese do: with the surname first.

My wife and I are indebted to Mr. William L. Holland and the Institute of Pacific Relations (which had previously given aid to Fei for his researches on the Chinese gentry) for guidance and encouragement in the course of the preparation of the manuscript; to Professor John K. Fairbank, Dr. Marion J. Levy, Jr., Dr. Derk Bodde, W. Lloyd Warner, and Dr. Sol Tax for their kindness in reading the work and making helpful suggestions; and to Dr. Shu-ching Lee for advice on points of Chinese language or history and in connection with the editing of the life-histories. None of the above, however, has any responsibility for the content or form of the book.

ROBERT REDFIELD

UNIVERSITY OF CHICAGO
May 1952

I / *The Gentry and the Imperial Power*

The term "gentry," *shen-shih,* refers to a class of persons with a definite position and definite functions in the traditional society of China. Here, by "traditional society," is meant the period after the breakdown of feudalism and the unification of the empire under a centralized monarchical power not long before 200 B.C. The development of the gentry class has a history; only through this history can we understand its characteristics.

The class that is here called gentry is also sometimes referred to as *shih ta fu,* "scholar-official." Actually the gentry class, although closely linked with the group of scholar-officials, should be distinguished from it. To be born into a gentry family did not necessarily insure that one became a scholar or an official in traditional China. Under feudalism the situation was different. At that time the gap between the nobles and the commoners was great. *Shih*[1] and *ta fu*,[2] although they were the bottom of the hierarchy of the ruling class, were still a part of that class and as such possessed real political power. But after the breakdown of feudalism political power was no longer portioned out but became concentrated in the person of one man, the monarch. In order to carry out his administrative functions, the monarch required assistance. This was given him by the officials. The officials then were no longer relatives or members of the ruler's own family but rather employees—the servants, or tools, of the monarch.

After the breakdown of feudalism there was another important change. The throne became the object of capture by the strong, by the hunters after power. Under feudalism, in which political power was distributed to relatives and kin, anyone not born into a noble family was a common man who had no chance of reaching the throne, of touching or even of seeing the divine paraphernalia of monarchy. No more than a woman can change into a man could a common man become royal. But, when feudalism went, anyone could become emper-

1. *Shih:* "This word is often translated 'scholar,' but this is only a derived, metaphorical sense and the whole force of many passages in the *Analects* is lost if we do not understand that the term is a military one and means 'knight.' A *shih* was a person entitled to go to battle in a war-chariot, in contrast with the common soldiers who followed on foot. Confucius, by a metaphor similar to those embodied in the phraseology of the Salvation Army, calls the stout-hearted defenders of his Way 'Knights'; and hence in later Chinese the term came to be applied to upholders of Confucianism and finally to scholars and literary people in general. The burden of most of the references to *shih* in the *Analects* is that the Knight of the Way needs just the same qualities of endurance and resolution as the Soldier Knight" (Arthur Waley, *The Analects of Confucius* [London: George Allen & Unwin, 1938], pp. 33–34).

2. *Ta fu:* lower-ranking official under feudalism.

or. Thus political power became an object of struggle. This is illustrated by the story told by the historian Ch'ien Ssu-ma of Huang Yu, who during the Ch'in dynasty (255–207 B.C.), in watching an imperial procession, said to his friend, "This I can seize." Since that time the struggle for political power has never ceased. Political power in the eyes of the people has become something precious to be sought after, an enterprise for large-scale entrepreneurs.

Unfortunately, since the breakdown of the feudal structure in China, political power has no longer been transmitted permanently in certain families, and up to the present no peaceful means of attaining it has ever been found. We continue to be convinced that the way to gain political power is through "taking up the stick' and fighting civil wars. Those few who emerge victorious in this struggle become emperors; the defeated become bandits. So we have had a succession of tyrants. A few people rule the mass. The nature of this despotic monarchy is not changed by the handing-on or relaying of power. In England, when a monarch was killed, monarchical power itself received a blow. Changes of monarchy led in time to a growth in the power of the people and to a government monarchic in name only. But, in China, blood flows from the people's veins, while those who attain the throne are but a few fortunate adventurers, like Liu Pang, the first emperor of the Han, who was born a lowly peasant, or Chu Yuan-chang, the founder of the Ming dynasty. When we study official versions of Chinese history, we find presented to us a continuous line of dynastic descent; but we should not forget that the authority of these rulers was continuously challenged by civil wars and unscrupulous adventurers.

To struggle for political power by violence is dangerous. If a man succeeds, he may become emperor; but, if he loses, he will be killed, and not only he himself but his whole family and clan. When he is challenging the established emperor, he is called a bandit and rebel, and the might of the army is directed against him. Moreover, the empire gained by violence may be lost by violence also. Twice in history, according to tradition, emperors tried to give up their power to other men who they thought would make better rulers. But those to whom the power was offered did not want it. They preferred to run away rather than to take on the responsibility. We do not know how far these two emperors were sincere in their desire to give up their power and to what extent this action was no more than a gesture or a piece of complicated political intrigue. There is no question of the fact, however, that in all of Chinese recorded history there is not a single case of voluntary abdication from the throne. Those abdications which did take place were forced. "The empire that was won on horseback will be lost only on horseback," as the popular saying goes.[3]

To seek to become a monarch is to risk one's life. The

3. [This phrase seems to refer back to the story told of Kao-tsu, the first emperor of Han, and the Confucian scholar Lu Chia. "After his [Lu Chia's] return in 196 or 195 B.C., he is said to have quoted the *Book of Odes* and the *Book of History* to Kao-tsu, whereat the latter scolded him and said, 'I got the empire on horseback; why should I bother with the *Book of Odes* or the *Book of History?*' Lu Chia replied, 'You got it on horseback, but can you rule it from horseback?' Then he proceeded to quote cases, from ancient history, of kings who had lost their thrones through their wickedness, concluding with the Ch'in dynasty, which Kao-tsu had himself overthrown" (Pan Ku, *The History of the Former Han Dynasty*, trans. Homer H. Dubs [Baltimore: Waverly Press, 1938], I, 21).]

heir to the throne must uphold his succession. The emperor, who should be merciful, may pardon all other crimes but not the crime of attempted usurpation. That is the most terrible thing that can be attempted under heaven. To anyone who reads the records of the beginnings of the Ming dynasty, the account of tortures applied to those who menaced the throne sounds like an account of progress through hell. I was told that the models of the "eighteen hells" found in district Buddhist temples are reminiscent of what was really done in the Ming dynasty. The threat of torture was the emperor's protection. I remember once as a boy calling out in play, "I am the emperor." My grandmother stopped me at once, saying, "You must never say that." This was not superstition or overcaution on her part but a recognition of a real danger in rash speaking. According to tradition at least, emperors used to have those children killed whom fortune-tellers foretold would one day become monarchs.

But this threat of violence has never really given effective protection to monarchical power. As Lao-tzu says, "When one does not fear death, how is it possible to threaten a man with death?" When it is possible to gain political power through violence, the throne is tempting. Though the brutality of those in authority may silence the majority, repression will never be entirely successful. The magnitude of the stakes, an imperial power which could be used to realize any whim, could not but make the effort attractive in spite of dangers. On the one hand, there were those who were willing to gamble with their lives; on the other, there were those who submitted quietly. One may ask, then, what it was that decided on which side a man should be.

Under monarchical rule the people had only duties without rights; the emperor's word was law. If he wanted to build a great palace, an imposing tomb, or a grand canal, he ordered it done without regard for the people. If he wanted to expand the boundaries of his kingdom, he commanded his army to mobilize regardless of whether the people liked it or not. The paying of taxes, the conscription of soldiers—these were burdens for the people to accept without compensation. Those who have lived under despotic monarchical power will understand Confucius' saying, "A brutal monarch is even worse than a tiger."[4] This policy of despotism more fearful than a tiger has had a long history in China. So we say, when the tiger comes out from his cage, the frightened people escape to the Liang hills.[5]

4. "As they [Confucius and his disciples] passed by the T'ai mountain, the attention of the travellers was arrested by a woman weeping and wailing at a grave. The sage stopped, and sent one of his followers to ask the reason of her grief. 'My husband's father,' said she, 'was killed here by a tiger, and my husband also, and now my son has met the same fate.' Being asked why she did not leave so fatal a spot, she replied that there was there no oppressive Government. 'Remember this,' said Confucius to his disciples, 'remember this, my children, oppressive government is fiercer and more feared than a tiger' " (James Legge, *Life of Confucius*, in Vol. I of *The Chinese Classics* [2d ed.; Oxford: Clarendon Press, 1895], quoted from *Li Chi*, pp. 67–68).

5. [The Liang hills are here a reference to the Chinese novel, *Ju Hu* (*All Men Are Brothers*), in which it is told how men of many sorts, fleeing from harsh punishments of the authorities, came to band themselves together and lived by defying the government and preying upon the rich and powerful. Stories of this sort had a very real basis in fact. In Pan Ku's *History of the Former Han Dynasty* we read, for example: "Ch'ên Shê was an ambitious farm boy who became one of the chiefs of a levy of men made in the present southern Honan. . . . In the later-summer of 209 B.C., a bad rain prevented this levy from reaching its destination on time. According to Ch'in laws, the officers and men of the levy would

Upon all who are unarmed, we may say, the threat of political tyranny falls with equal weight. Yet in this, too, there have always existed differences. The richer folk could afford to pay for security. In the Chinese traditional pattern conscription, for example, could be bought off. The breaking-up of a family such as is described in "Old Poem" could never have happened in a rich family.[6] Thus it was that people from this class became political adventurers.

The possession of riches or the lack of them was what was important for making some acquiesce and others rebel. "Man fears to be distinguished as a pig fears to be fat." When the political tiger attacks, the man who

---

have been condemned to death; they accordingly conspired to rebel. As a slogan they falsely called themselves partisans of Fu-su, the displaced heir of the First Emperor, and fabricated miracles to legitimize themselves. The rebellion was not thus at first openly directed against the dynasty, but was merely the act of men driven to desperation by over-harsh laws" (I, 4).]

6. "Old Poem," translated by Arthur Waley from *The Book of Songs*, reads:
"At fifteen I went with the army,
At fourscore I came home.
On the way I met a man from the village,
I asked him who there was at home.
That over there is your house,
All covered with trees and bushes.'
Rabbits had run in at the dog-hole,
Pheasants flew down from the beams of the roof.
In the courtyard was growing some wild grain;
And by the well, some wild mallows.
I'll boil the grain and make porridge,
I'll pluck the mallows and make soup.
Soup and porridge are both cooked,
But there is no one to eat them with.
I went out and looked towards the east,
While tears fell and wetted my clothes."

(Arthur Waley, *Chinese Poems* [London: George Allen & Unwin, 1946], p. 51.)

is rich will have a greater difficulty in escaping than the man without property. In such a case property becomes a burden. Propertied families developed great alertness in watching the behavior of the tiger. The poor man who has become desperate may rebel, become a bandit in the mountains, and even, in time, challenge the royal authority itself. But a man of property and family cannot easily do this. He must find some way to avoid the attack of the tiger. Unfortunately, as the old saying goes, "From the water's edge, all land is the emperor's; under the heavens all are the emperor's men." At that time travel was not easy; one could not run away to Washington or Brazil, nor was there any International Settlement in a treaty port, nor even any Hong Kong. Physically there was no escape. Perhaps this is not quite true, after all, because we know that from early times certain individuals were able to escape to Korea or Japan. But the ordinary man had to find some means of protection within the structure of society itself.

There was a weak point, however, in this centralized monarchical system. He who held power, the emperor, as I have said, could not administer the country by himself. Even though he might not wish to share his authority, he still required help in ruling and must therefore employ officials. These officials, with whom the ruling house had no ties of kinship, functioned merely as servants with administrative power but no power of policy-making. It was within the inefficiencies of this system that the ordinary man found his opportunity to carry on his private concerns.

It is true that previous to the unification of Ch'in (221 B.C.) there were attempts to establish an efficient administrative system. This was done under the influence of the *Fa Chia*, or Legalist, school of thought. Theoretically, the system proposed by this school of thought was a good one.[7] In order to have an efficient administration of the country, a legal basis must be established, with everyone controlled by the same law. Shang Yang, as prime minister of Ch'in, attempted to put this theory into practice. But the theory unfortunately neglected one small point. One man, the emperor, was left outside the law. And this omission destroyed the whole system of the *Fa Chia*.[8]

7. [Waley discusses the social situation in which the Legalist school rose to power under the title "The Realists," in *The Way and Its Power* (London: George Allen & Unwin, 1934), pp. 68–86. The *Fa Chia* system, in spite of its recognition of the importance of a "rule of law," and its effort toward greater efficiency in government, does not appeal to the Western liberal mind. *The Book of Lord Shang*, trans. J. J. Duyvendak (London: A. Probsthain, 1928), supposedly the writing of Shang Yang, otherwise known as Wei Yang or Lord Shang, expresses the extreme position of the Legalists. Duyvendak comments: "Law, having been applied theoretically only in order to enforce the observance of the standards set by natural moral law, now became the instrument for enforcing the standard set up by the state. Here came a clash between the law and moral traditions. Never had this idea of law anything to do with the codification of the conceptions of justice living in the hearts of the people; it was merely penal laws and institutions, deemed expedient for the government's centralising and imperialistic purposes; it was the expression of the state's own growing self-consciousness. It is very remarkable that, when we find the necessity for publishing the laws urged, it is not, as elsewhere, an expression of the popular wish to safeguard the people's rights and privileges for the future; on the contrary, it is government itself that desires their publication as a safeguard of its own power, as it expects that the laws will be better observed if people know exactly what punishments and non-observances will entail. Consequently, to have a deterrent effect, the laws have to be severe" (p. 81).]

8. [But, according to Fung Yu-lan, the highest ideal of the Legalist school actually was that "ruler and minister, superior and inferior, noble and humble, all obey the law." Fung quotes from Han Fei-tzu, a leading Legalist: "Therefore, the intelligent ruler carries out his regulations as would Heaven and employs men as if he were a spirit. Being like Heaven, he commits no wrong, and

Shang Yang himself lost his life on this account, for, though under the law he was able to punish the prince when he was only the heir to the throne,[9] as soon as the prince became emperor, he ordered Shang Yang killed. And the efficient system which Shang Yang himself had established prevented him from escaping.

If the highest authority were bound by law, then administrative authority would be able to cage the tiger. But in Chinese history this has never happened. As a result, the ruled, including the officials themselves, have never sought for efficiency in administration. Rather the opposite has been true. Inefficiency and parasitism, on the one hand, remoteness of imperial control and a do-nothing policy by the emperor, on the other—this has always been the ideal. Yet this ideal of government, of a "good emperor" as one who presided but did not rule, has rarely been attained. As far as the officials were concerned, the next best thing, then, could only be to protect them-

---

being like a spirit, he falls into no difficulties. His *shih* (power) enforces his strict teachings, and nothing that he encounters resists him." Fung interprets this passage as follows: "By comparing the ruler with Heaven, Han Fei-tzu means that he acts only according to the law, fairly and impartially. That he employs men 'as if he were a spirit' means that he makes use of them according to this 'method' or *shu*, secretly and unfathomably." The gulf between this conception of law and the conception held in the West may be one reason why the ideal of "Great Good Government" has, as Fung says, "never yet actually been attained in China" (Fung Yu-lan, *A History of Chinese Philosophy*, trans. Derk Bodde [Peiping: H. Vetch, 1937], I, 320–22).

9. [Even in this case the punishment was only indirect. "Then, the Crown Prince infringed the law. Wei Lang said: 'It is owing to the infringements by the highly-placed, that the law is not carried out. We shall apply the law to the Crown Prince; as, however, he is Your Highness's Heir, we cannot subject him to capital punishment. Let his tutor, Prince Ch'ien, be punished and his teacher, Kung-sun Chia, be branded' " (Introduction to *The Book of Lord Shang*, p. 16).]

selves, to keep a back door open for their relatives, and to be able to use their position as a shield against the emperor's whims. To protect not only themselves but their relatives and their whole clan from the unchecked power of the monarch, and to do this not by constitutional or by legal means but by personal influence—this is what they sought. Not by challenging the emperor's authority but by coming close to him, by serving him and from this service gaining an advantage in being enabled to shift the burden of the emperor's demands onto the backs of those lower down, did the propertied class attempt to neutralize the emperor's power over them and to avoid the attack of the tiger. Groups of officials, with their relatives, formed, thus, in Chinese society a special class not affected by the laws, exempt from taxation and conscription. Nevertheless, they had no real political power.

To escape domination while approaching the source of power takes a highly developed skill. The position of the officials was not easy. As the old sayings go, "When the emperor orders your death, you must die" and "All the blame is mine; the emperor can do no wrong." If the official relaxed his efforts on behalf of the emperor, he might lose his life. When the emperor required money or labor, he must be active in meeting these demands—a task he accomplished by shifting the burden onto the backs of the people. Yet, if the burdens became too heavy for the people to bear, they might rebel, and it was then the officials who would be attacked first and who would serve as the scapegoats of the monarch.[10] The officials

10. "We have an ancient saying that if the dragon left its water and the tiger left the mountains, even they would be insulted. Take those officers in the im-

must be two-faced: severe toward the people and compliant toward the emperor. They must know the art of going just so far and no further in order that they might not be caught either by the fury of the emperor or by the wrath of the people. Chinese officials' life has been described as the art of maneuvering on a stormy sea. Experience through the ages was the teacher. It may be noted that in Chinese the expression, "Do not speak to me officially," does not mean the same thing as in English but rather, "Speak to me sincerely."

In normal times to be an official was no direct economic advantage. From the monarch's point of view, for an official to use his position to enrich himself meant corruption of the system and a diminution of his own treasure. Thus, unless a monarch were very weak, he would not tolerate such officials. An official in ordinary times would not improperly profit from the office but would leave it with "two sleeves full of wind."[11]

---

perial court, they take in all sorts of humiliations and never dare protest; but when they reach their homes, they scold and beat their children and wife to give vent to their angers. Yet the officers dare not resign, just like the tigers dare not leave the mountains and the dragons the waters" (Liu Ê, *A Tramp Doctor's Travelogue: A Story Laid in the Manchu Regime*, trans. Lin Yi-chin and Ko Te-chun [Shanghai: Commercial Press, 1939], p. 114).

11. "A poetic expression dating back to the Ming dynasty when Yu Ch'ien as a provincial official refused to follow the custom of handing out gifts exacted without payment from the populace to the dignitaries of the imperial court but instead presented himself empty-handed. The term has come to refer to officials who hold office and retire without having enriched themselves. In spite of pressures and practices to the contrary, this type of official has always been an ideal of Confucian teaching. . . . The China of the nineteenth century still kept green the memory of past officials who had been incorruptible. Their names were household words; stories about them had been treasured for centuries. Thus, the Ancestral Hall of the Yang family was still called the Hall of the Four Knows because of what had happened there seven centuries earlier. In A.D. 1221,

Why, then, should people want to be officials? The poem of T'ao Yuan-ming expresses the feelings of one such man:

> Why should I be an official?
> I bend my back
> For only three piculs of rice.
> Why should I not go back to till the land?[12]

when a friend remonstrated with Yang Chen for leaving nothing to his sons, he replied: 'If posterity speaks of me as an incorruptible official, will that be nothing?' And when a man offered him a bribe and said: 'It is after dark and no one will know,' Yang Chen was recorded as saying: 'Not know? Why, Heaven will know, Earth will know, you will know, I will know.' There was a later Yang, Yang Ch'eng, who lived a thousand years before the time of Tao Kuang. Ordered to collect taxes during the famine, he refused, and threw himself into prison where he slept on a plank. Many other old stories of official rectitude were current" (Maurice Collis, *Foreign Mud* [New York: Alfred A. Knopf, 1947], p. 95).

12. "T'ao, who lived in the fourth and fifth centuries A.D., was our poet of nature *par excellence*. Once he served as a district magistrate. When he could not longer stand the ordeal of formality he burst out upon the occasion of the arrival of the provincial inspector, his superior, 'I cannot bow to a mean fellow from the street just for five pecks of rice.' So saying, he left his official hat hanging on the wall and went right home" (C. W. Luh, *On Chinese Poetry* [Peiping, 1935], p. 16).

> "What folly to spend one's life like a dropped leaf
>   Snared under the dust of streets,
>   But for thirteen years it was so I lived.
> . . . .
> "There is no dust or clatter
>   In the courtyard before my house.
>   My private rooms are quiet,
>   And calm with the leisure of moonlight through an open door.
>   For a long time I lived in a cage;
>   Now I have returned.
>   For one must return
>   To fulfill one's nature."

("Once More Fields and Gardens," by T'ao Yuan-ming, in *Fir-Flower Tablets*, translated from the Chinese by Florence Ayscough, English versions by Amy Lowell [Boston: Houghton Mifflin Co., 1930], p. 133.)

T'ao Yuan-ming was a typical unworldly poet. Yet, in spite of his talent and his interest in the things of the mind, even he had to "bend his back" and occupy an official position and withal receive only a small financial reward. Why did such a one accept this position instead of staying home where he was happy? The fact is that, if he had shown his scorn of officialdom by leaving office, he would probably by now be "a man without an arm."[13] The choice lay between "bending the back" or being disabled. The necessity for becoming an official was a little like the need for being inoculated. Just as one runs the risk of having a bad reaction to an inoculation, so in becoming an official one may risk having one's property

---

13. In "The Old Man with the Broken Arm (A Satire on Militarism)," *ca.* A.D. 809, by Po Chü-i, we read:

"Everyone says that in expeditions against the Man tribes
Of a million men who are sent out, not one returns.
    I, that am old, was then twenty-four;
My name and fore-name were written down in the rolls of the Board of War.
In the depth of the night not daring to let anyone know,
I secretly took a huge stone and dashed it against my arm.
For drawing the bow and waving the banner now wholly unfit,
I knew henceforward I should not be sent to fight in Yun-nan.
Bones broken and sinews wounded could not fail to hurt;
My plan was to be rejected and sent back to my home.
My arm—broken ever since; it was sixty years ago.
One limb, although destroyed—whole body safe!
But even now on winter nights when the wind and rains blow
From evening on till day's dawn I cannot sleep for pain.
    Not sleeping for pain
    Is a small thing to bear,
Compared with the joy of being alive when all the rest are dead.
For otherwise, years ago, at the ford of Lu River
My body would have died and my soul hovered by the bones that no one gathered.
A ghost, I'd have wandered in Yun-nan, always looking for home.
Over the graves of ten thousand soldiers, mournfully hovering."

(From *Chinese Poems*, trans. Arthur Waley, pp. 129–31.)

confiscated or even one's head cut off. But, once the inoculation is over, one has gained protection. This analogy is not too apt, since from an inoculation one person becomes immune, whereas if one has been an official one can protect a whole group of people. As a result, it happened that sometimes a group would join to aid in the education of one man so as to enable him to reach officialdom. "One man rises to officialdom, then all his dogs and chickens will be promoted," is the saying.

In Chinese traditional society the clan or big family naturally constituted a group which could take action of this sort, supporting one of their members until the time when he should become a scholar and be eligible for the official examinations. Once this individual attained official honors, the whole clan could rely upon him. Without any strong person at court, it was difficult to protect one's property. Ku T'ing-lin was an official during the Ming dynasty, but, when the rule passed to the Manchus, he refused to continue in an official position, gave up traveling abroad, and shut himself up at home with his books. Yet for his own protection he was obliged to send his two nephews to the Ch'ing court to serve his enemies. This was made possible by the fact that, as we have said, Chinese officials did not share in the political power of the emperor but served their monarch by neutralizing and softening down his power rather than by supporting it. With his nephews in court, the uncle was protected even in secret rebellious activities. According to Chinese tradition, officials did not work seriously for the government, nor did they like to continue as officials for a long period. Their purpose in entering the government was to gain both immunity and wealth in this order. The Chinese officials when in office protected their relatives, but, when this duty to the family had been performed, they retired. Retirement and even a hermit's life were the ideal. In retirement there was no longer any authority to be served with watchful care, while the relatives who had gained protection from their kinsman official owed him a debt of gratitude. Now he need only enjoy his social prestige and grow fat and happy. As we say in China, "To come back to one's native soil, beautifully robed and loaded with honors, is the best thing in life."[14] Such a man will not attempt to seize power; his children will not play at being emperor. Nor will he have any idea of reforming the social system, for that system will do him no harm. Once out of the way of imperial influences, he may enjoy the economic power of a landowner.

This is the sort of man I mean by gentry. The gentry may be returned officials or the relatives of officials or simply educated landowners. In any case, they have no real political power in shaping policies and may have no direct connection with politics whatsoever, yet they do tend to have influence at court and to be immune from political exploitation. And the more fearful the ruler and the more tiger-like, the more valuable is the gentry's protective covering. In such circumstances it is difficult to survive except by attaching one's self to some big family.

14. Po Chü-i thus congratulates himself on the comforts of his life after his retirement from office:

"Lined coat, warm cap and easy felt slippers,
  In the little tower, at the low window, sitting over the sunken brazier.
  Body at rest, heart at peace; no need to rise early.
  I wonder if the courtiers at the Western Capital know of these things or not?"
(From *A Hundred and Seventy Chinese Poems*, trans. Arthur Waley [New York: Alfred A. Knopf, 1919], p. 239.)

II / *The Scholar Becomes the Official*

In my first chapter I tried to analyze the position of the gentry in the political structure. My view is that, since the establishment of a central unified political power in the third century B.C., the gentry as a class have never attempted to control political power. That is, although occupying official positions, they have not exercised any decisive powers as to policy. Under the feudal system sovereignty belonged to the aristocracy; under the monarchy, to the king-emperor. The question which arises, then, is this: Why in Chinese history has there been no period in which the power of the aristocracy revived or in which a bourgeois middle class took over political power? The answer to this question leads us to a study of the political consciousness of the gentry and their attitude toward their own position. Why did they not struggle with the monarch to gain control? Why was there no movement similar to Magna Carta in England? The class who were landowners in the economic structure were gentry in the social structure. Why did they become so neutral, so negative in politics? In this chapter I shall be especially attentive to one question: What was the attitude of the gentry class toward their political position? It is true that their attitude was not cause but rather effect of the political system upon them. Nevertheless, it may be said that the attitudes of acquiescence which developed within the political system tended to reinforce the system.

Every social structure has a system of attitudes which define proper behavior and support the structure. What I am going to discuss in this chapter is the attitude of the gentry toward the monarchical power after they had come to be controlled by that power.

In the political philosophy of the traditional gentry class there was an important idea called *tao-t'ung*.[1] This idea took shape before the firm establishment of monarchical power and was probably necessary for its de-

1. [*Tao-t'ung*, literally "*tao*-series," "*tao*-succession," "*tao*-transmission," in usage something like "the orthodox transmission of the *tao* or Way." The *Chung Yung*, or Doctrine of the Mean, defines the Confucian *tao* as follows: " 'The Universal Way for all under Heaven is five-fold, and the (virtues) by means of which it is practiced, are three. There are the relations of ruler and subject, father and son, husband and wife, elder and younger brother, and of friend and friend: these five constitute the universal Way for all. Wisdom (*chih*), human-heartedness (*jen*) and fortitude (*yung*): these three are universal virtues for all. That whereby they are practiced is one. Some are born and know it; some study and so know it; some through painful difficulties come to know it. But the result of their knowing is one' " (quoted by Fung Yu-lan, *A History of Chinese Philosophy*, trans. Derk Bodde [Peiping: H. Vetch, 1937], I, 373).

Han Yu of the T'ang dynasty (768–824), in his essay *On the Nature of the Tao*, wrote: "What I will call the *Tao* is not what has hitherto been called the *tao* by the Taoists and the Buddhists. Yao transmitted the *tao* to Shun. Shun transmitted it to Yü. Yü transmitted it to Wen, Wu, and the Duke of Chou. Wen, Wu, and the Duke of Chou transmitted it to Confucius, and Confucius transmitted it to Mencius. After Mencius, it was no longer transmitted."]

velopment. In my analysis I am concerned particularly with the period before the firm establishment of monarchical power when feudalism was in process of breaking down.

I am not inclined to think that this social philosophy originated in the minds of a few scholars. On the contrary, I believe that the scholars' elaboration of the system was accepted by society because it reflected a point of view which was generally shared. The function of the scholar was to formulate, to clarify, and to crystallize this point of view into a doctrine. In the period of transition between feudalism and imperialism the school of thought which reflected the philosophic trend of the times best was that of Confucius and his followers. But the Confucian school was only one of many in this period of the "hundred schools." It was only later, after the stabilization of the imperial power, that Confucianism came to be so popular and dominating. This shows, I think, that the ideology of the Confucian school represented the point of view best adapted to the Chinese imperial system.

The conception of *tao-t'ung* developed from a set of social facts, of which one important element was that a class of socially important people had lost their political power. Confucian ideas, as formulated and organized into the Confucian system, following the concentration of monarchical power and the disintegration of the feudal system, underwent, it is true, an understandable process of change. And the writings we now have about Confucian ideas have been much modified by later scholars. I should like, however, to start here with the basic Confucian ideas and to try to trace their development to a later period. But, in discussing the influence of Confucius on the social history of China, we are not concerned with the question of whether the idea of *tao-t'ung* was that of Confucius himself but rather with the fact that this concept was selected and elaborated in his name by later scholars.

It appears to me that the development of the idea of *tao-t'ung* took place in Chinese traditional society because there had appeared a new type of person, the scholar-intellectual, one excluded from political authority but still possessing social prestige. Since he did not have political power, such a man could not decide political issues. Yet he might, through making known his opinions and formulating his principles, exercise a real influence. Such men did not try to control political power in their own interest but endeavored rather to put forward a set of ethical principles which should restrict the force of political power. The system of *tao-t'ung* which they developed came to be accepted by the gentry as the norm for their activity in politics. Eventually it came to serve the gentry not only as an ethical system but also as a protection for economic interests.

As the gentry attempted to restrict political power by ethical means, they put forward the teachings of Confucius, calling the latter the creator of *tao*, and a "king without a throne." And his spiritual descendants are those whom we now call master-scholars.

Legends which grew up concerning Confucius and his origins symbolize the separation of the ethical from the political line. In the early period of mythical history going back to such culture heroes as Sui Jen, the inventor of fire, and Shen Nung, who started agriculture, through the reigns of all *San Huang* and *Wu Ti* (the Three August Ones and the Five Sovereigns) through the recorded history of the feudal kings of Chou, Wen Wang, and Wu Wang,[2] one finds the tradition of ethics and politics united. The Confucian school upheld these ancient rulers as ideals. Here were men who both knew and followed the principles of right rulership. Following the rulers of Chou mentioned above, came Chou Kung, or the Duke of Chou, who, as uncle of the heir to the throne, ruled as regent. Much importance was attached to this individual by Confucius' school, because even under the feudal system he was able to attain high authority, being actually a sovereign. The regency itself was meaningful in that it symbolized the idea that, when the sovereign is unable to rule, the *one who knows* should take his place. Here was the beginning of the separation of the political and ethical lines. Confucius himself identified himself closely with Chou Kung. He said: "How utterly have things gone to the bad with me! It is long now indeed since I

2. [The three rulers, Yao, Shun, and Yü, the great models of virtue in Confucian tradition, are the first to be mentioned by the *Shu Ching*, or *Book of History*, most ancient of Chinese documents. There is some difference of opinion as to whether Yao and Shun, among these at least semihistorical figures, are to be included with the "Five Sovereigns," or whether they ruled later as *Sheng* or Divine Sages. Granet says: "The three first of the Five Sovereigns, Huang-ti, Chuan-hsü, and Kao-hsin, figure in the works connected with the Confucian traditions, but have a philosophic rather than an historical character. The Book of History, attributed to Confucius, only mentioned the two last, Yao and Shun. . . . In making the history of the Sovereigns and of the Three August Ones precede that of the royal dynasties, the learned men of China set out to paint a picture of an halcyon age when, with human characteristics, perfect virtue rules. The heroic figures of the early age in China preserve, however, a number of mythical features. In Yao and Shun . . . the effacement of these features is nearly completed" (Marcel Granet, *Chinese Civilization* [New York: Barnes & Noble, 1951], p. 9).]

dreamed that I saw the Duke of Chou."[3] In the legend of Chou Kung there is, to be sure, not a very marked separation between the political and ethical lines, since, as uncle of the king, Chou Kung was entitled to rule as regent. But the later followers of Confucius put him next to Chou Kung in a line of descent of noted and wise leaders. Thus Chou Kung is the starting point of the political line deviating from the ethical.

The separation of ethical and political lines was, according to the stories of the Confucian school, more clearly established by saying that this "king without a throne" was the descendant of an aristocratic family. Actually, his connection was rather remote. He was not at all comparable in this way to a Chou Kung. Confucius had no qualifications for attaining power through his kinship status. But myths which tried to find a source of authority for him in the feudal system persisted. According to the *Shih-chi*,[4] Confucius' origins were quite doubtful. He was said to be the child of an illegitimate union. His mother would not tell him where his father's tomb was, and only when his mother died did he learn from someone else where his father was buried so that he could bury his mother also in that spot. Here also is recorded the incident of a man called Chih, Baron of Lu, giving a feast to the *shih*, to which Confucius went also. But he met with a rebuff when a man called Yang Huo, a corrupt official, said, "The Baron invited *shih* (knights),

3. Arthur Waley, *The Analects of Confucius* (London: George Allen & Unwin, 1938), Book VII, No. 5, p. 123.

4. [*Shih-chi*, written by Ssu-ma Ch'ien, father of Chinese historians (145–85? B.C.). Book XLVII contains a life of Confucius. See *The Wisdom of Confucius*, edited and translated with notes by Lin Yutang (New York: Modern Library, 1943), pp. 48–91.]

not you." From this we may infer that his status as a *shih* was doubtful, although the *shih* were in the lowest rank in the feudal system. Yet such accounts are told not to demean Confucius but to raise him still higher, as when an account later on in the same book adds that Confucius was born after his mother had prayed on a hill—the implication being that Confucius was of divine, not merely mortal, origin.

The importance of all these myths was not so much to establish the origins of Confucius as to set up divine authority for the ethical line which he represented. Thus, if Confucius derived his power not through his kinship with a feudal lord but from divine sources, his spiritual throne must be as high as the actual kingly throne. So from Confucius there derived a line of important and authoritative figures of those who followed the *tao-t'ung*. These people might lack political power, but in the society about them they were as important as the actual monarchs in that they ruled the people by ethical and social influence.

The separation of political power from ethical power is one of the fundamental ideas in Confucian philosophy and is also an important factor in the Chinese power structure. It may be compared to the separation of church and state in the West but is not exactly the same. Theoretically, when Jesus said, "Render unto Caesar those things which are Caesar's," he recognized a duality of power. When the priests asked Jesus what authority he had in doing the things he did, he countered with, "The baptism of John, whence was it? from heaven or of men?" And the priests were in doubt what to reply and at last answered Jesus, "We cannot tell." And he said to them,

"Neither tell I you by what authority I do these things."[5]

We see clearly that to Christ there were two possible sources of power, worldly and divine. But these two powers were not on the same level. Rather, one was subordinate to the other. So in European medieval history worldly power submitted to divine power, monarchical power submitted to religious power. When, in a later period, these two powers became separate as the powers of church and state, the civil rights of the people came to be recognized. In Western political thinking it came to be accepted that the power which does not come from heaven could come only from the people, the common man. So long as the monarch derived his authority from his divine origin, he might slight the popular will. But once the throne was separated from the church, and it was recognized that the king's power was secular, it was quite natural that the people should be allowed to have their say and to share in government. It seems to me that in the Western political system power was never entirely independent and self-justified but was always based on an authority derived from either divine or popular sources. The situation in China was somewhat different.

In China, Confucius also recognized a duality of power, but for him the two systems were not in the same order. One was not necessarily subordinate to the other; rather they were seen to be parallel. In China political power was like Caesar's, but the other type of power, in contrast to the West, was not viewed as having a divine origin. Some people think that Confucianism is a system of religion, yet it recognizes no supernatural force. This

5. Matt. 21:23–27.

is not the only way, however, in which it may be distinguished from Western religions. Another aspect of Confucianism in which it differs from the West is its relation to action. Jesus Christ was using his power in the same domain to control human affairs. As a result of this conflict, one power became subordinate to the other. But the Confucian *tao-t'ung* stands not for action but for the upholding of a standard or norm which defines the Way of a good emperor (and a good citizen). It is one thing whether the monarch acts according to the Way or not. It is another whether we have made clear the Way to be a good ruler. Christ made clear the good and wanted action toward that good. But Confucianism is divided into two parts: (1) the knowing what is good and (2) the doing what is good. Thus the man who knows what is good does not necessarily have an obligation to carry it out. In fact, he may not be able to do so, since what he is able to do depends upon his social position. So we have the differentiation into separate categories of the scholar who knows and the monarch who does. The following quotation explains the psychology of Confucius. Confucius said to his student: "Hui, the poem says that tigers and wild beasts are running wild in the fields. Is my Way wrong? Why should I become so poor?"

Then the student Yen Hui answered: "The Way of my master is very great—the world cannot accept it. But, my master, try to carry out your Way. If others don't accept you, it shows that you are a gentleman. If we don't work out the Way for doing things, that is our shame. If those who have the power don't follow the right Way, that is their shame."

Then Confucius smiled and said: "You are right. If you were rich, I should become your secretary."[6]

This quotation explains how even in a world in which brute beasts are running wild it is still possible for scholars to work out the Way. For the *tao*, or Way, is detached from worldly events. The Way can be perfected irrespective of actual happenings in the world. To make this Way effective, to practice it, is not the duty of a man who is not in a position to do so; in other words, of the man without political power. The man who has control of political power may administer his affairs according to the Way or may utterly disregard it. Those who are not in his position of authority may themselves maintain the Way, and they may "push it and try to make it work," so that the Way will be followed by the man who controls the country. But they must not try to usurp the position of the man in power. What Confucius means when he speaks of "push it and make it work" is simply the use of persuasion. Confucius never assumes the authority assumed by Christ. As a result, in the Chinese scheme, the political line is active, the

6. "Tzu-kung came out and Yen Hui went in, and Confucius said, 'Ah, Hui, it is said in the *Book of Songs*, "Neither buffaloes, nor tigers, they wander in the desert." Are my teachings wrong? How is it that I find myself now in this situation?' And Yen Hui replied, 'The Master's teachings are so great. That is why the world cannot accept them. However, you should just do your best to spread the ideas. What do you care if they are not accepted? The fact that your teachings are not accepted shows that you are a true gentleman. If the truth is not cultivated, the shame is ours; but if we have already strenuously cultivated the teachings of a moral order, and they are not accepted by the people, it is the shame of those in power. What do you care if you are not accepted? The very fact that you are not accepted shows that you are a true gentleman.' And Confucius was pleased and said smilingly, 'Is that so? Oh, son of Yen, if you were a rich man, I would be your butler!' " (Lin Yutang, *op. cit.*, pp. 74–75). (This episode is apocryphal.)

ethical line passive. Those who follow the ethical line will behave according to the popular saying:

> When wanted, then go;
> When set aside; then hide.[7]

To employ and to discharge belongs to the man who has power; to work or to hide is the role of the man who has the Way. According to this system, there will be no conflict. From the point of view of the person who upholds the norms, practical politics may sometimes coincide with the norm and sometimes not. One may distinguish those nations which have *tao* and those which have not. Yao and Shun are examples of those who ruled the nation according to the *tao*.[8] Yü and T'ang are other examples. So also monarchical power may lose its Way, and, when this occurs, the man who knows it, and through this knowledge possesses it, should guard it and keep it safe from harm. Such a man must work hard to cultivate himself so that the norms will not disappear entirely. But he will have no idea of trying to correct the conduct of the monarch. This, then, is the Confucian view: the one who knows should be ready to present his views when asked but when not asked should keep them hidden. These scholar-masters do not desert the Way in time of difficulty, but only when the monarch in his behavior approaches the Way will they come forth and act as officials.

The Master said, "Be of unwavering good faith, love learning, if attacked be ready to die for the good Way. Do not enter a State that pursues dangerous courses, nor stay in one where the people have rebelled. When the Way prevails under

7. Waley, *Analects*, Book VII, No. 10, p. 124.
8. See n. 1, p. 34.

Heaven, then show yourself; when it does not prevail, then hide. When the Way prevails in your own land, count it a disgrace to be needy and obscure; when the Way does not prevail in your land, then count it a disgrace to be rich and honoured."

"A gentleman indeed is Ch'u Po Yü. When the Way prevailed in his land, he served the State; but when the Way ceased to prevail, he knew how to 'wrap it up and hide it in the folds of his dress.' "[9]

The real problem, then, is the link between the political and the ethical lines. The ideal of the Confucian school was that of the kingly Way—*wang-tao*—in which both political and ethical lines coincided. But how could that ideal be realized? Here we find the conflict in Confucius' ideas. Since he had been brought up under a feudal system, he valued a social order of this sort, one in which a stable society was ruled according to well-established traditions. The feudal tradition prevented him from breaking the connection between the political line and kinship; the static ideal made him abhor social changes. This is the first point to be noted with regard to Confucius' attitude. He took for granted the political system and did not wish it to be changed. At the same time, he was living when the system was actually disintegrating; men in a certain position no longer behaved according to the norm set up for them. To meet this difficulty, Confucius detached the norms from actual practice and set them up as an ideal type of behavior which was not to be deviated from. In this he was very stubborn and persistent. The student Tzu-kung said to him: "The Master's teachings are too great for the people, and that is why

9. Waley, *Analects*, Book VIII, No. 13, p. 135, and Book XV, No. 6, p. 194.

the world cannot accept them. Why don't you come down a little from your heights?"

Confucius replied: "Ah Ssu, a good farmer plants the field but cannot guarantee the harvest, and a good artisan can do a skillful job, but he cannot guarantee to please his customers. Now you are not interested in cultivating yourselves, but are only interested in being accepted by the people. I am afraid you are not setting the highest standard for yourself."[10]

We may wonder how, in such a case, the norms are ever to be brought into close contact with reality. It seems that this must depend largely on chance, since, on the one hand, one is bound to wait with patience and, on the other, to retire and let others seek one out. But Confucius did express himself on this matter of chance. The student Tzu-kung said: "Suppose one has a lovely jewel, should one wrap it up, put it in a box and keep it, or try to get the best price one can for it?"

The Master said: "Sell it! Most certainly sell it! I myself am one who is waiting for an offer."[11]

Confucius actually did go about and offer his services to more than seventy lords. The following quotation makes this point even more clear. When Confucius was fifty years old, Kung-San Po-niu started a rebellion against Baron Huan in the city of Pi. Baron Huan sent for Confucius, and Confucius was eager to go. He said: "The kings Wen and Wu rose to power from the small cities of Feng and K'ao and finally established the empire of Chou. Pi, I know, is a small place, but perhaps I may try." But Confucius' student, Tzu-lu, was displeased

10. Lin Yutang, *op. cit.*, p. 74.
11. Waley, *Analects*, Book IX, No. 12, p. 141.

and tried to dissuade him from going. Confucius said, "Since the Baron asks to see me, he must have a plan in his mind, and if he would put me in power, we might achieve something resembling the work of Emperor P'ing."[12] But after all he did not go. Confucius felt the urge to be employed, and, when he was, he endeavored to carry out good projects. At the age of fifty-six he was pleased when in a certain principality he was made chief minister. His disciples said to him, "I hear that a gentleman is not afraid at the sight of disaster and not delighted at success."

"Is that so?" remarked Confucius. "Is it not said that one is happy because he rises to a position above the common people?" But he stayed in office only about three months, during which time he had executed a minister who opposed him. But it was said that during the time of his office there was no cheating in the markets, men and women did not walk together, people did not take things which belonged to others, and there was no litigation.

But, although Confucius waited patiently, he had little real chance to enter politics. Even when he did get his chance, there was no assurance that his way of merging ethics with politics would be continued. So at last Confucius left Lu and said, "How free I am. I can now spend my life in a leisurely way." Yet he still felt disheartened at times, saying, "The Way makes no progress. I shall get upon a raft and float out to sea."[13] Actually, as far as a practical career was concerned, he had accomplished nothing. But we may imagine that if

12. Life of Confucius, from the *Shih-chi* (Lin Yutang, *op. cit.*, p. 56).

13. Waley, *Analects*, Book V, No. 6, p. 108.

he had had a chance to remain in office for three years, as he wished, he might have accomplished some of the great results he had hoped for. Yet, in such a case, Confucius' death might have been like those of Tu Ming-tu and Shun Hua, two officials who attained high office but were later killed by their lords. When this news came to Confucius, he sighed. He was standing at the time near a stream and said: "How beautiful is the water! Eternally it flows! Fate has decreed that I should not cross this river."

"What do you mean?" asked Tzu-kung, coming forward.

And Confucius replied, "Tu Ming-tu and Shun Hua were good ministers of Chin. Before Baron Chien Chao got into power, he said that he would insist on taking these two men, should he get into power, and now that he is in power, he has killed them. I have heard that when people disembowel embryos or kill the young, the unicorn refuses to appear in the countryside, and that when people dry up a pond in order to catch fish, the dragon refuses to bring the *yin* and *yang* principles into harmony (resulting in famine and flood),[14] and that

14. "Yang, the positive principle, is associated with all that is bright, beneficent, active, masculine: symbolized by Heaven and the Sun. Yin, the negative principle, with darkness, passivity, the feminine in nature: symbolized by the Earth and Water.

"The Yang is said to transform, the Yin to unite. By these processes they brought into being the five essences, water, fire, wood, metal, and earth. . . .

"In no sphere of Chinese life and thought can the Yang and Yin be lost sight of. Their nearest Western parallel is what we call 'the mysterious causes underlying the operations of Providence' " (G. Willoughby-Meade, *Chinese Ghouls and Goblins* [New York: Frederick A. Stokes, n.d.], p. 4).

"In Zoroastrianism, Darkness is essentially evil; the principle of Light, essentially good. The fundamental conception of *yin* and *yang* is quite different. They are two interdependent and complementary facets of existence and the

when people snatch birds' nests and break birds' eggs, the phoenix refuses to come. Why? Because a gentleman avoids those who kill their own kind. If even the birds and beasts avoid the unrighteous, how much more should I do the same?"[15]

These remarks show Confucius' recognition of the difficulty of applying his Way in practical politics. Let me quote another passage from the *Shih-chi*. The lords of Lu had a hunting party and caught a strange animal which Confucius declared was a unicorn. Then Confucius said: "This is the end of it all. There is no one in this world who understands me."

His disciple Tzu-kung said, "Why do you say that there is no one who understands you?"

And Confucius said, "I don't blame Heaven, and I don't blame mankind. All I try to do is my best to acquire knowledge and to aim for a higher ideal. Perhaps Heaven is the only one who understands me! Po-yi and Shu-ch'i were two sages who loved their ideals and their self-respect! (These persons and the following were famous scholars living as recluses.) Liu-hsia Hui and Shao-lien lowered their ideals and lost their self-respect. Yu-chung and Yi-yi remained active and outspoken, but their conduct was clean and they had good judgment. But I am different from all of them. I will insist on nothing." Then he added: "A gentleman will suffer pain to die without having lived up to his name. My Way will not be carried out. What can I do to explain myself to those

---

aim of *yin-yang* philosophers was not the triumph of light, but the attainment in human life of perfect balance between the two principles" (Arthur Waley, *The Way and Its Power* [London: George Allen & Unwin, 1934], p. 112).

15. Ling Yutang, *op. cit.*, p. 68. (This is another apocryphal incident.)

who come after?"[16] He chose to compile the book of *Spring and Autumn Annals* from historical sources.

The *Spring and Autumn Annals* is a Chinese grammar of politics. It reveals the norms of good government but does not necessarily give any practical advice for realizing them. From this work one may learn the *tao*, or Way, which runs side by side but does not merge with practical politics. The title given to Confucius of a "king without a throne," that is, a king without any political position, makes clear this peculiarly Chinese concept.

If the ethical line cannot control the political line, though scholars may repeatedly criticize the government as not acting according to the *tao*, in actual everyday politics the emperor, or the man who possesses political power, will not feel shame and will disregard them. In a state which is misgoverned, in which the scholar folds up his norm and hides it in his bosom, what happens to the people? Scholars may say, as Confucius once did, "If Heaven will not destroy this work what harm can my enemy do to me?" But Confucius also said, "Heaven may destroy this work, and those who come later will never again have a chance to learn the Way." Scholars may die, for they are men of this world, not of another. How can they hide when the imperial power rules the entire land? The imperial power may burn the books and

16. [Fei's translation. See Lin Yutang, *op. cit.*, p. p86–87. The significance of catching the unicorn was that, although this creature in itself symbolized the coming-to-power of a sage and of general peace and prosperity, the fact that in this case the unicorn had been hunted down was rather the sign of something unusually disastrous, in this case of the death of the great scholar Confucius. Fei's repetition of the tradition that Confucius composed the *Spring and Autumn Annals* would be repudiated by most scholars.]

bury the scholars alive.[17] It may kill students because of some writing which injures the emperor. It may block the ethical line entirely for a time. Confucius was not able to solve this difficulty, namely, that, living together in the same world, the two lines, ethical and political, cannot let each other alone. Although the ethical line of the scholars may be willing not to struggle against the political line, the political line can, and often does, suppress the ethical. When this happens, what can scholars do? The positive way to meet this dilemma is, as was done in the West, to conquer the imperial power and subordinate practical politics to the socially accepted norms. But positive measures of this sort are not in accordance with the feudal tradition, and we find very little in Chinese history of this sort of positive resistance. Another line was taken.

When Confucius appealed to Heaven, that Heaven was an indifferent abstraction which would not interfere with worldly events.[18] But when the ethical line of the scholars was suppressed by the emperors to such a degree that there was no possibility of their gaining any power in politics, they tried to convert Heaven into a really

17. [These events took place under the harsh Ch'in empire, in 212–13, as a means of enforcing intellectual conformity. All books throughout the empire, with certain important exceptions, were collected by the government and burned, and over 460 scholars were allegedly buried alive.]

18. [The substance of this and the following paragraphs as set out here by Fei would be disputed by many scholars in certain respects. That Heaven to Confucius was an indifferent abstraction is not the view of others (cf. Fung Yu-lan, *op. cit.*, I, 58: "For Confucius, Heaven was a purposeful supreme being"). Second, it is more widely thought that the theory of the Will of Heaven here attributed to Tung Chung-shu antedates him by almost a thousand years (see the chapter on this subject in Herrlee G. Creel, *The Birth of China* [New York: Reynall & Hitchcock, 1937]).]

active force. Confucian *tao* has no inherent power. It cannot *do* things, for doing things is the emperor's task. In the Han dynasty, however, the conception of a realistic God who would interfere in human affairs gradually took shape. Tung Chung-shu (179?–104? B.C.), a scholar of the Han dynasty, interpreted the *Spring and Autumn Annals* in such a way as to threaten the royal power with heavenly anger. In a statement addressed to the emperor Wu he said: "Your servant, in reading the *Spring and Autumn Annals*, has come to see that, in this work done by previous generations, there is presented a relation between Heaven and Man. I realize the awfulness of this relation. When a nation loses its *tao*, Heaven will first warn the people by famines and disasters. If the emperor does not look back upon himself to criticize himself, then Heaven will warn him by portents. If he still does not change his way, then he will court real disaster. This shows the benevolence of Heaven, which wishes to stop disturbances in the world."

In Tung's formula Heaven comes first, the emperor second, the scholars third, and, at the bottom, the people. Following this formula, the emperor should no longer be repressive but should be awed and restrained by the behavior of Heaven. But the question is: Since Heaven expresses approval or disapproval through natural phenomena, who knows the meaning of the heavenly signs? Who is able to interpret these signs but the scholar? Thus Tung really emphasizes the importance of the scholar, in that he alone could interpret Heaven. The first part of this conception was different from the usual Confucian point of view and especially that developed by Mencius, according to which the will of Heaven is to be expressed in the will of the people. According to this new idea, scholars should interpret the will of Heaven as expressed in natural phenomena. It was not an attempt to control political power democratically but rather, indirectly, through religion. The role of the scholar was simply to help the monarch to meet Heaven's demands; and the punishment of the emperor, if it came, would be through natural disasters and not by the people. Theoretically, monarchical power was thus subordinated to religious power, and the scholar given a position of some independence. In other words, the scholar's ethical line was no longer to be held down by the political line of the emperor.

If Tung Chung-shu had advanced a step further, perhaps he might have gone so far as eventually to transform the scholar from an interpreter of Heaven into a priest. Then the scholar-priests might have formed an organized church, which, with divine sanction, might have been strong enough to check the unlimited monarchical power. If this had taken place, we might have had in China something similar to the relations between church and state in the West. But when this theory came to challenge the supremacy of the monarchical power, it was suppressed at once. Tung Chung-shu developed a theory of omens and could even predict natural disasters from the *yin* and the *yang*. "When you want rain," he said, "stop the *yang* and open the *yin*. If you want the rain to stop, reverse the process. Practice this throughout the nation, and it will not fail." Once in Liao-tung, a hall in the tomb of the emperor caught fire. Tung interpreted this to mean that the emperor had done something wrong. A friend of his called Yen Chu-fu, who knew of this and who was jealous of Tung, stole the writings which made clear this interpretation and showed them to the emperor. The emperor called together all the scholars and showed the writings to them. A student of Tung's called Lu, who did not know the writings were his master's, said it was all "nonsense." Then the emperor was relieved. He put Tung into prison and condemned him to death. Later Tung was pardoned but never again dared to interpret in this way.

The theory of heavenly anger expressed through portents did not succeed in controlling monarchical power. But it encouraged the people in that it destroyed the theory of imperial absolutism. If Heaven dislikes the ruler, then the ruler must be changed. During the Han dynasty, and afterward, whenever there were social disturbances, this theory was used to justify the rebellion of the people. But, although as a popularly accepted theory it might be a justification for revolt, it did not change the nature of the imperial power.

At the same period as Tung, under the Han emperor Wu, there was another scholar who had also studied the *Spring and Autumn Annals*, namely, Hung Kung-sun. This man, who took part in the persecution and exile of Tung, presents another form of adjustment to the imperial power. That is, to become an official and serve the emperor. Orthodox Confucianists scorned Hung Kung-sun because he sold out the spirit of Confucianism, the keeping of the *tao*. An old scholar, ninety years of age, Yuan Kung-sun, who had retired because he would not modify his opinions to please the emperor, looked askance at Kung-sun, and said: "You, Kung-sun, should say what you have learned. You should not bend your teaching to please the world." This meant that it was the duty of the scholar to hold to the ethical line and not to be an opportunist. Kung-sun had come of humble origins; he had been a jailer and at one time had even herded pigs. Yet he came to be prime minister, the first who had reached this position without being related to the emperor. He thus, very well, saw the advantage of selling out the ethical line to the emperor and of subordinating the Confucian norms to the monarchical power. Actually, unless one retired from the world entirely, there were, practically speaking, only two alternatives: either to subordinate ethical power to political power or to become unpopular. Yuan Kung-sun, the old scholar, and Tung Chung-shu did not submit and were exiled. But Hung Kung-sun submitted and became prime minister.

As prime minister, Kung-sun advocated the principle that monarchy should rule the people through the scholars of his ilk. He said: "The leopard, the wild horse, the untamed ox, all wild beasts and birds are difficult to control. But, when they are domesticated, they may be used for human purposes. To bend wood takes less than a day. Gold and other metals can be melted in less than a month. A man who has a mind of his own and can judge the good from the bad, advantage from disadvantage, must be more difficult to handle than animals, birds, wood, or metal. But in a year's time he too may be molded." Kung-sun developed the technique of how to serve the emperor as a good official as follows: Each morning, when there is a conference, he will present the choices of action to the emperor and let him make his selection. He will not argue or insist upon anything.

Then the emperor will see that he is discreet and understanding and that he knows administrative work and is an expert scholar. The emperor will be glad to have him near him. When the emperor grants him an audience, and he finds that they are not in agreement, he will not argue but will go back and find someone else to mediate. This man will present the case first to the emperor, Kung-sun following him. For this tactful approach the emperor will be very pleased with him. Moreover, even when a conference of ministers has decided a matter, the man who is wise will not speak according to the agreement but will fit in with the emperor's mood.

For following the latter precept, Kung-sun was attacked by other officials. They said: "This man is most treacherous and unfeeling. He turns his face against his friends. He suggests the idea himself first and then abandons it; he isn't loyal." The emperor asked Kung-sun if this were true. He replied: "Those who understand me will think that I am loyal. Those who do not understand me will think that I am not."

Another critic of Kung-sun said: "Hung Kung-sun has a high position among the top men. His salary is very high, but still he affects cotton gowns. That is not honest. He gives the impression of being modest and frugal when he really is not. Kung-sun started from a lowly position but in only a few years has climbed so far that he has become a minister and a lord. Outwardly his personality seems that of a temperate and hospitable man. He has built a guest house and filled it with guests whom he invites to participate in his work. While he himself takes only one piece of meat, they are entertained lavishly, and even his family neglected on their account.

But, in spite of all this outward good will, inwardly he is jealous of everyone. He makes up to those officials who are not on good terms with him and then finds some way to hurt them. He killed Yen Chu-lu and exiled Tung San-tzu. These are his plots."

From these old quotations we can see that here was a man without principles, one who merely tried to follow the emperor's whims, did not keep his word, sold out his friends, and formed his own party to help maintain his high position in the government.[19] This is a type of official which has often been seen in China.

Following the example of Hung Kung-sun, the ethical line which had been maintained by Confucius and his followers no longer was the norm. Scholars took to supporting monarchical power. This transformation was completed in the person of one Han Yü who, though considering himself directly descended from the ethical line, converted his position not into that of a critic but into a way of showing the emperor's tolerance. Han Yü was a man without academic honors, a hermit, but the emperor liked his conduct so well that he took him out of obscurity and created for him the office of imperial censor, an official who should tell the emperor what was wrong throughout his domain. His role was to convince the world at large that in the court people were allowed to speak freely and honestly, to make it evident that the emperor did not confer rewards unjustly, and to show

19. [But Dubs says: "Kung-sun Hung proved to be admirable in personal conduct, able in disputation, capable in legal matters, and an ornament to scholarship" (Introduction to Pan Ku's *The History of the Former Han Dynasty*, trans. Homer H. Dubs [Baltimore: Waverly Press, 1938], II, 23). For discussion of the reign of the emperor Wu and his attitude toward Confucianists see also Herrlee G. Creel, *Confucius, the Man and the Myth* (New York: John Day Co., 1949), pp. 233–43.]

that the emperor had the great virtue of being willing to follow suggestions disagreeable to him.[20] This, it was thought, would make the "people in the caves," the common people, "put on their finery and come to court to tell their wants." And this would make the emperor approach in virtue Yao and Shun, and his name would go down in history for ever and aye.

Han Yü no longer asked whether the imperial power followed the *tao* or not. To him this was no longer a problem, for he believed that the political line must be the same as the ethical. The emperor could do no wrong. Moreover, the emperor had the obligation to use the scholars, and the scholars, in turn, had the obligation to present themselves in court. His reasoning went thus: "In ancient times scholars were sorry for one another if one or another of them went as long as three months without being in office. Such a one, leaving his own country, would go to bear gifts to the court of another lord. He would feel so anxious to find an opportunity to serve in government that, if he could not find a job in Lu, he would go to Ch'i, if not in Ch'i, he would go to Sung and Chien [Cheng?]. . . . But now we have a centralized government. Within the four seas there is but one rule. If a man is to leave, he must go live with savage tribes,

20. "Since the fourteenth century, there has existed a definite organization known as the Censorate, the members of which, who are called the 'ears' and 'eyes' of the sovereign, make it their business to report adversely upon any course adopted by the Government in the name of the Emperor, or by any individual statesman, which seems to call for disapproval. The reproving Censor is nominally entitled to complete immunity from punishment; but in practice, he knows that he cannot count too much upon either justice or mercy. If he concludes that his words will be unforgivable, he hands in his memorial, and draws public attention forthwith by committing suicide on the spot" (H. A. Giles, *The Civilization of China* [New York: Henry Holt & Co., 1911], pp. 158–59).

leaving behind the country of his father and mother. The scholar who wishes to practice his *tao* must do so at court or else go off to the wilds. In the mountains and forests he can do nothing but cultivate himself; this is a way out only for those who care very little for the world, not for those who care for people."

From Han Yü on, Chinese scholars ceased to bother themselves about whether the emperor was good or not. Their function as scholars they now saw was to uphold the emperor. As people who simply read the orders of the emperor, they became caricatures of the real scholar.

Thus the relation between the scholar and political power changed in the course of history. In the beginning they were separated from practical politics; they were regarded as maintainers of the ethical way but not as positively effective in government. In the process of concentration of monarchical power this same class was unable to protect its own interest; its members turned to religious sanctions in the hope that divine authority, in controlling the monarch, would at the same time offer them protection. But the divine sanctions were not effective, and thus the only alternatives came to be either to rebel or to surrender. Since the scholar class were never in any sense revolutionary, they chose the latter course, becoming officials. And they even degraded themselves by becoming utterly subservient to the emperor. This is the historical process which determined the later position of the gentry in the social structure. They did not themselves attempt to take over political power but found security by subordinating themselves to the mercy of the imperial court. In the power structure of traditional China the gentry were a distinctly noncombative element.

III / *The Gentry and*
Technical Knowledge

The Chinese term for "intelligentsia," *chih-shih fen-tzu*, "they who know," indicates that in Chinese society there was a differentiation based on wisdom. The questions arise: What kind of wisdom was it upon which this social differentiation was based? What was the mechanism by means of which it was monopolized by one class in society? We should like to ask further: How did this class maintain its position in the traditional scheme, and what changes are taking place in it through contact with the West?

The characteristic of the members of this class has always been not only that they knew something but that they had a special kind of knowledge. What this special knowledge or wisdom was is made clear in Confucius' work. The word *chih* has a restricted meaning. For example, the student Fan Ch'ih asked Confucius about the meaning of the word *chih*. Confucius said, "He who devotes himself to securing for his subjects what it is right they should have, who, by respect for the Spirits, keeps them at a distance, may be termed wise."[1] Confucius also said: "There may well be those who can do without knowledge; but I for my part, am certainly not one of them. To hear much, to pick out what is good and follow it, to see much, and take due note of it, is the lower of the two kinds of knowledge."[2]

From these quotations it is clear that Confucius did not use the word "knowledge" to mean merely cognition but implied knowledge of the right thing. Again, when Fan Ch'ih asked what it meant to be wise, the Master said, "Know men." Fan Ch'ih did not quite understand. The Master said, "By raising the straight and putting them on top of the crooked, one can make the crooked straight."[3] Confucius described the process of knowledge as, first, perception—the gathering of information—but, following upon this, the drawing of distinctions and the making of a choice. Knowledge is more than mere gathering of information, since it involves choice, and this choice is based on the ability to distinguish the good from the bad. Knowledge in this restricted sense, and based on a standard or norm, is designated by the word "straight." When you know what is straight, you must act upon it. And by so doing you will make the crooked straight. Thus Confucius explains the word *chih* as wisdom or knowledge of right behavior. Those who work

1. Arthur Waley, *The Analects of Confucius* (London: George Allen & Unwin, 1938), Book VI, No. 20, p. 120.

2. *Ibid.*, Book VII, No. 27, pp. 128–29.

3. *Ibid.*, Book XII, No. 22, p. 169.

for the people and those who respect the spirits are the people who know what they ought to do, and they are therefore "those who know." To know in this sense is not only to be intelligent but also to be virtuous. Knowledge of this sort goes with *jên*[4] and courage. The wise man not only is an intellectual but also knows the Way, the norm, the things he ought to do.

We can differentiate knowledge into two categories: first, understanding of the nature of the physical world and, second, understanding of what constitutes right conduct. In the Confucian classics *chih* refers to the second type of knowledge. Confucius even believed that the man who knew the moral norms did not necessarily need to know about nature. In fact, he was himself represented as that sort of man whose "four limbs are unac-

---

4. [Referring to *jên*, "man," and continuing to show its relation to *jên*, "goodness," Waley says: "This word, in the earliest Chinese, means freemen, men of the tribe, as opposed to *min*, 'subjects,' 'the common people.' The same word, written with a slight modification, means 'good' in the most general sense of the word, that is to say, 'possessing the qualities of one's tribe.'. . . Finally, when the old distinction between *jên* and *min*, freemen and subjects, was forgotten, the *jên* became a word for human beings, the adjective *jên* came to be understood in the sense 'human' as opposed to 'animal,' and to be applied to conduct worthy of a man, as distinct from the behaviour of mere beasts.

"Of this last sense (human, not brutal) there is not a trace in the *Analects*. . . . *Jên*, in the *Analects*, means 'good' in an extremely wide and general sense. . . . It is a sublime moral attitude, a transcendental perfection attained to by legendary heroes such as Po I, but not by any living or historic person. It appears indeed that *jên* is a mystic entity not merely analogous to but in certain sayings practically identical with the *Tao* of the Quietists. Like *Tao*, it is contrasted with 'knowledge.' Knowledge is active and frets itself away. Goodness is passive and therefore eternal as the hills. Confucius can point the Way to Goodness, can tell 'the workman how to sharpen his tools,' can speak of things 'that are near to Goodness.' But it is only once, in a chapter showing every sign of lateness, that anything approaching a definition of Goodness is given" (*ibid.*, Introduction, pp. 27–29).]

customed to toil" who "cannot distinguish the five kinds of grains."[5] Fan Ch'ih asked the Master to teach him about farming. The Master said, "You had much better consult some old farmer." He asked to be taught about gardening. The Master said, "You had much better go to some old vegetable gardener." When Fan Ch'ih had gone out, the Master said: "Fan is no gentleman! If those above them love ritual, then among the common people none will care to be disrespectful. If those above them love right, then among the common people none will dare to be disobedient. If those above them love good faith, then among the common people none will dare to depart from the facts. If a gentleman is like that, the common people will flock to him from all sides with their babies strapped to their backs. What need has he to practice farming?"[6] This quotation explains that, to Confucius, a knowledge of nature was not so important and also shows his conception of his own social position. Men such as he are at the top; the ordinary people are at the bottom. The people must work on the land, but those at the top need only acquire and keep the respect of the people through upholding the *li*[7]—justice and faith. The man who

5. *Analects of Confucius*, free translation by Fei. "The five grains are paddy, millet, panicled millet, wheat, and pulse" (James Legge, *The Works of Mencius* in *The Chinese Classics* [2d ed.; Oxford: Clarendon Press, 1895], II, 251 n.).

6. [Waley, *Analects*, Book XIII, No. 4, p. 172. See Legge's version of the Confucian analects for a somewhat different translation. Although somewhat less literal than Legge, Waley's text of the *Analects* has been employed as being closer to Fei's usage. For example, Fei uses the term "gentleman," as does Waley, rather than "superior man," "man of the higher type," "wise man," as do Legge and Soothill.]

7. *Li:* "Ceremonials, customary morality, *mores*, rites, rules of good manners, proper conduct, propriety" (Fung Yu-lan, *A History of Chinese Philosophy*, trans. Derk Bodde [Peiping: H. Vetch, 1937], I, 439).

knows about the norms of conduct need not work for his living.

In Mencius this social structure becomes still clearer. A man called Ch'en Hsiang spoke to Mencius about Hsü Hsing's idea that a worthy prince would till the land with the people. But Mencius did not agree with him and put forward arguments to show that a division of labor was both natural and right.

When Ch'en Hsiang saw Hsü Hsing, he was greatly pleased with him, and, abandoning entirely whatever he had learned, became his disciple. Having an interview with Mencius, he related to him with approbation the words of Hsü Hsing to the following effect: "The prince of T'ung is indeed a worthy prince. He has not yet heard, however, the real doctrines of antiquity. Now, wise and able princes should cultivate the ground equally and along with their people, and eat the fruit of their labour. They should prepare their own meals, morning and evening, while at the same time they carry on their government. But now, the prince of T'ung has his granaries, treasuries, and arsenals, which is an oppressing of the people to nourish himself. How can he be deemed a real worthy prince?"

Mencius said, "I suppose that Hsü Hsing sows grain and eats the produce. Is it not so?" "It is so," was the answer. "I suppose also, he weaves cloth, and wears his own manufacture. Is it not so?" "No. Hsü wears clothes of haircloth." "Does he wear a cap?" "He wears a cap." "What kind of a cap?" "A plain cap." "Is it woven by himself?" "No. He gets it in exchange for grain!" "Why does Hsü cook his food in boilers and earthenware pans, and does he plough with an iron share?" "Yes." "Does he make those articles himself?" "No. He gets them in exchange for grain."

Mencius then said, "The getting of those various articles in exchange for grain is not oppressive to the potter and the founder, and the potter and the founder in their turn, in exchanging their various articles for grain, are not oppressive to the husbandman. How should such a thing be supposed? And moreover, why does not Hsü act the potter and founder, supplying himself with the articles which he uses solely from his own establishment? Why does he go confusedly dealing and exchanging with the handicraftsmen? Why does he not spare himself so much trouble?" Ch'an Hsiang replied, "The business of the handicraftsman can by no means be carried along with the business of husbandry."

Mencius resumed, "Then, is it the government of the kingdom which alone can be carried on along with the practice of husbandry? Great men have their proper business, and little men have their proper business. . . . Hence, there is the saying, 'Some labour with their minds, and some labour with their strength. Those who labour with their minds govern others; those who labour with their strength are governed by others. Those who are governed by others support them; those who govern others are supported by them.' This is a principle universally recognized."[8]

We may see here how a recognition of the obvious need for an economic division of labor was used to support class distinctions and to justify the privileges of the ruling class. But I quote the two passages given above in this context to show the difference in attitude under the traditional system toward knowledge of the natural world and ethical knowledge. Knowledge of the natural world was knowledge for production and belonged to farmers, craftsmen, and others who depended upon it for earning their living. Ethical knowledge, on the other hand, was an instrument in the possession of those who used their minds to rule the people. To rule others means that one is superior and should be able to be maintained

8. Legge, *op. cit.*, Vol. II, Book III, Part I, chap. iv, pp. 247–50.

by others, if not exploit them. Because such men do not deal with the material world, they form the habit of "not using their four limbs" and "not distinguishing the five grains." It is this which Confucius suggests by his question as to why he should till the land.

Although Mencius laid down the distinction discussed above as a universal principle, he did not explain why those who work with the mind, those who possess ethical knowledge, should stand above the people and rule them and be entitled to be supported by them.[9]

This leads us to the question: How did the intelligentsia acquire their social position? Much of their authority was derived from the nature of the knowledge they possessed, a knowledge not, as we have seen, of practical affairs but of something other, of recognized social value.

In order to satisfy the basic needs of existence, such as food, clothing, and shelter, we must use material goods and have some real acquaintance with the world about

9. [Mencius did say: "The Minister of Agriculture taught the people to sow and reap, cultivating the five kinds of grain. When the five kinds of grain were brought to maturity, the people all obtained a subsistence. But men possess a moral nature; and if they were well-fed, warmly clad, and comfortably lodged, without being at the same time taught, they become almost like the beasts. This was a subject of anxious solicitude to the sage Shun, and he appointed Hsieh to be the Minister of Instruction, to teach the relations of humanity:—how, between father and son, there should be affection; between sovereign and minister, righteousness; between husband and wife, attention to their separate functions; between old and young, a proper order; and between friends, fidelity. The highly meritorious sovereign said to him, 'Encourage them; lead them on; rectify them; straighten them; help them; give them wings:—thus causing them to become possessors of themselves. Then follow this up by stimulating them, and conferring benefits on them.' When the sages were exercising their solicitude for the people in this way, had they leisure to cultivate the ground?" (*ibid.*, Book III, Part I, chap. iv, pp. 251–52).]

us. We must know how to deal with material objects in the right way. For instance, the knowledge that friction will produce fire was an early-discovered principle and an important addition to civilized knowledge. But one cannot make fire simply by rubbing something together. The knowledge of how to make fire must include a knowledge of what materials to use and of how long friction of these materials must be maintained. Only under certain conditions is the principle of making fire through friction realized. A technique prescribes a definite procedure by which one reaches certain desired consequences, and a knowledge and proper use of it determine whether one achieves the desired result or not. But in human life we do not use techniques for their own sake but rather as a means toward an end. We make a fire in order to cook, to warm a house, or to worship the gods. Thus making a fire brings not only the problem of *how* but also of *when*, *where*, and *by whom* to make *what kind* of fire? Making a fire is not an isolated activity but part of a social institution. And social institutions always involve not only efficiency but also values. The problem is whether we ought or ought not to make the fire. This is part of what Confucius called the *li*. Thus the same action may be right in certain contexts and not right in others. When someone asked Confucius if Kuan Chung knew about the *li*, he said: "Only the ruler of a State may build a screen to mask his gate; but Kuan had such a screen. Only the ruler of a State, when meeting another ruler, may use cupmounds; but Kuan used one. If even Kuan is to be cited as a expert in ritual, who is not an expert in ritual?"[10]

10. Waley, *Analects*, Book III, No. 22, pp. 99–100.

That which decides what we ought to do is not the technique but a norm of conduct.

In dealing with nature, it is a question of doing what is practically right. If we work according to principles inherent in nature itself, we will reach our desired end. If we do not do so, we will not succeed in making the fire burn. Thus no extra authority is needed to reinforce knowledge of the natural world. If one does not act according to social norms, the consequences may be bad for society as a whole, if not for the individual himself. To protect the common good, we need sanctions which will make the nonconformist respect the norms. In this way, we turn *ought to be* into *dare not do so*. Social sanctions require authority from society at large. But this authority cannot be given to everyone; society must delegate someone to be its agent. In China such persons have been those whom we referred to above as "the men who know."

In a static society those norms of conduct which are developed through and accumulated by practical experience are usually effective directives for a successful life. Their effectiveness is their *raison d'être* and their justification for their support by social authority. In such a society the other side of the coin is the fact of willing conformity by the majority, because conformity to these norms of conduct gives satisfaction in daily life. Norms of conduct in a stable society are traditions handed down over the years, crystallized experience in dealing with the world. Confucius achieved his social authority not so much from his own wisdom or learning as from his profound knowledge of the traditional way. In a stable, traditionally organized society a man does not need to question, to rationalize, or to justify. What he needs to do is to find out what the custom is. When Confucius speaks of "finding out," he is not seeking to explore something new but to rediscover the past.[11] In a society in which historic traditions have the only real validity influence lies not with the innovators but with those who can guide along established paths. As apprentices learn their techniques from their masters, so the common people depend upon the students of traditional values to teach them the way in which they must go. And these teachers are those who possess social authority and prestige.

Social authority is, however, different from political power. I emphasized the fact that the Chinese gentry did not possess real political power. In fact, in China, political power has always been quite different from social authority. Political power is attained by violence and imposes the relationship of conqueror to conquered, while social authority is a rule of society over the individual which is based on consent and common understanding. Confucius' school hoped that political power and social authority might be made to coincide. When a ruler rules his country by political power alone, he will be called a despot, or *pa*. When political power and social authority coincide, he will be called a king, or *wang*. In actual fact, in the history of China, the combination has never been achieved. Confucius was revered as a "king without a throne," *su wang*, a man with social authority but without political power. The result of having two

11. "The Master said, 'I for my part am not one of those who have innate knowledge. I am simply one who loves the past and who is diligent in investigating it' " (*ibid.*, Book VII, No. 19, p. 127).

parallel sources of authority meant that, in Chinese society, order was established on two different levels. The daily life of the masses was regulated by social authority, while political authority was usually confined to the activity of the *yamen*.[12] The court, except in the case of a few tyrants, did not interfere in the going concern of society. In general, a good monarch collected a definite amount of taxes and left the people alone.

In a simple society the norms of conduct are known to most of the people and are not specialized knowledge. Anyone may follow the norms and receive recognition. A student of Confucius', Tzu-hsia, once said: "A man who treats his betters as betters wears an air of respect, who in serving father and mother knows how to put his whole strength, who in the service of his prince will lay down his life, who in intercourse with friends is true to his word—others may say of him that he still lacks education, but I for my part should certainly call him an educated man."[13] The reason for the lack of special qualifications for the person who knows the norms is that for most of the people ethical or normative knowledge is accessible. In a simple society this kind of knowledge is handed down orally and learned by repetition. Confucius used the word "exercise" in writing of acting upon knowledge gained by hearing rather than by the study of books. Literacy had not yet become so all-important. It is said of Confucius that, "when the Master entered the Grand Temple, he asked questions about everything there. Someone said, 'Do not tell me that this son of a

12. [*Yamen:* The habitat of or the official and private residence of a mandarin, i.e., the bureaucracy itself.]

13. Waley, *Analects*, Book I, No. 7, pp. 84–85.

villager from Tsou is expert in matters of ritual. When he went to the Grand Temple, he had asked about everything.' The Master, hearing of this said, 'Just so! such is the ritual.' "[14] And when the disciple Tzu-kung asked, "Why was K'ung Wên-tzu called Wên ('The Cultured')?" the Master said, "Because he was diligent and so fond of learning that he was not ashamed to pick up knowledge even from his inferiors.[15]

But, when life becomes more complicated, the transmission of norms of conduct can no longer depend entirely on oral transmission. There come to be different versions, and the decision which is right requires verification through the study of documents. Confucius said, "How can we talk about the ritual of the Hsia? The State of Ch'i supplies no adequate evidence. How can we talk about the ritual of Yin? The State of Sung supplies no adequate evidence. For there is a lack both of documents and of learned men."[16] When ethical values are no longer transmitted by word of mouth but mainly through written documents, they no longer are accessible to everyone, and literacy becomes very important. Then there develops a special group of people who know how to read books—the *chih-shih fen-tzu*, or intelligentsia.[17]

14. *Ibid.*, Book III, No. 15, pp. 97–98.

15. *Ibid.*, Book V, No. 14, p. 110.

16. *Ibid.*, Book III, No. 9, p. 96.

17. [Giles wrote of the China of 1911: "The Chinese, recognizing the extraordinary results which have been brought about, silently and invisibly, by the operation of written symbols, have gradually come to invest these symbols with a spirituality arousing a feeling somewhat akin to worship. A piece of paper on which a single word has once been written or printed, becomes something other than paper with a black mark on it. It may not be lightly tossed about, still less trampled under foot; it should be reverently destroyed by fire, here again used as a medium of transmission to the great Beyond; and thus its spiritual essence

At the folk level in traditional China there has always been an oral literature.[18] Classical literature, the only literature officially recognized, which developed from the writing-down of sacred rituals and songs, systems of divination, dynastic histories and genealogies, remained always something apart from the common man. Official historical records of the teachings of the sages may serve to instruct but are of little practical value to the struggling farmer. Not only is the content of what was written difficult to grasp, but the (classical) written language itself is quite distinct from common speech. And since the very structure of the written language differs from spoken, even a literate man who can speak well will not

---

will return to those from whom it originally came. In the streets of a Chinese city, and occasionally along a frequented highway, may be seen small ornamental structures into which odd bits of paper may be thrown and burnt, thus preventing a desecration so painful to the Chinese mind; and it has often been urged against foreigners that because they are so careless as to what becomes of their written and printed paper, the matter contained in foreign documents and books must obviously be of no great value" (H. A. Giles, *The Civilization of China* [New York: Henry Holt & Co., 1911], pp. 231–32).]

18. "So long as men seek illusion, the story-teller will remain a feature of Chinese life, invited to wealthy homes to amuse those of the 'inner chamber,' welcome in the village tea-shops on the summer evenings where he is the peasants' living book of history, drawing his audience at fairs and wringing hard-earned coppers from the pockets of the crowds by the same device our up-to-date magazines use for serial stories, demanding a new outlay for a new installment. The story-tellers belong to an organization. Novices sometimes start their careers under an experienced teller of tales, but, usually, in the old days, they were unsuccessful students" (Juliet Bredon and Igor Mitrophanow, *The Moon Year* [Shanghai: Kelly & Walsh, 1927], pp. 152–53). [Even fairly recently, during the war with Japan, the management of a factory in Free China hired an old-fashioned storyteller to tell stories of "The Chinese Robin Hood." This was entertaining for the less sophisticated local workers, but the nonlocal workers did not care for it (Kuo-heng Shih, *China Enters the Machine Age*, ed. and trans. Hsiao-tung Fei and Francis L. K. Hsu [Cambridge: Harvard University Press, 1944], p. 110).]

necessarily be a good writer. Literary composition cannot be picked up but requires great application. The pictorial characters are hard to learn, and, if one does not use them constantly, one forgets them. In an economy of scarcity very few can enjoy sufficient leisure to learn.[19] Agriculture is the main occupation of China. Farmers engaged in the work of the fields expend their energies in long hours of grinding labor and enjoy small incomes. Such men cannot hope for long periods of leisure. As I described the situation in *Earthbound China*, production and leisure are mutually exclusive; unless one can be supported by others who produce, one cannot leave manual labor. Thus those who have leisure must be big landholders, so big that they can live entirely on their rents. In this way the class of people who are trained in an understanding of values is limited to an economic group who do not represent the interests of the common people.

Mencius said that those who use their minds should be supported by those who use their labor. It appears to me true that only those who are supported by someone else can enjoy literary work. But this does not mean that all

19. "The 'bridge of learning' is a long one. From the primary school to the upper grades of the middle school takes nine years. And during these nine years parents must pay not only for the food but also for the other expenses of their children. . . . Moreover, while the children are in school, they cannot help on the family farm. This means that only the rich can afford to send their children to school. The young men of the poorer houses can have no chance to pass over this bridge; so they must find another way out. None of those from the middle, poor, and landless classes, who left the village, had had a middle-school education. Among the ten persons who went out from the rich houses of the village, seven of them had received a middle-school education" (Hsiao-tung Fei and Chih-i Chang, *Earthbound China* [Chicago: University of Chicago Press, 1945], p. 274).

those who are supported by others and do not work with their hands necessarily are capable or willing to work with their minds. Those who are privileged to be supported by others have no need to learn technical knowledge, but they also need not learn norms of conduct; they may merely live parasitically. However, in this case, their privileged position may not be secure. Privilege must be supported by some force, either by political power maintained by physical force or by social authority. The class of people who enter officialdom not only can afford to become educated but must do so in order to acquire prestige. The prestige of literacy combined with the power of political authority to support a privileged class distinguished from the laboring class by their higher economic position, their greater opportunity for education, and resultant greater social authority, and, last but not least, their separation from all practical technical knowledge.

As I have shown above, technical knowledge should be related to ethical values. But, once the knowledge of values became so closely linked with literacy that it became the monopoly of one class, it became separated from technology. And, once this link was broken, technological development was arrested. I have said that knowledge of the natural world must be incorporated into a social institution to become "useful," that is, a technique which improves the life of the people. If, however, the governing class, who are responsible for the life of the people, completely lack technical knowledge, they will not be able to order human affairs by technical means. For example, if those who "do not move their four limbs and who cannot distinguish the five grains" have the power of deciding techniques of land cultivation, they will not be willing or able to improve production by introducing improved techniques which may disturb existing traditional ways. Progress in modern techniques comes only when the producers themselves have the power to decide. Once this power is separated from the real producer, technical improvements will cease.

In Chinese traditional society the intelligentsia have been a class without technical knowledge. They monopolized authority based on the wisdom of the past, spent time on literature, and tried to express themselves through art. Chinese literary language is very inapt to express scientific or technical knowledge. This indicates that, in the traditional scheme, the vested interests had no wish to improve production but thought only of consolidating privilege. Their main task was the perpetuating of established norms in order to set up a guide for conventional behavior. A man who sees the world only through human relations is inclined to be conservative, because in human relations the end is always mutual adjustment. And an adjusted equilibrium can only be founded on a stable and unchanging relation between man and nature. On the other hand, from the purely technical point of view, there are hardly any limits to man's control of nature. In emphasizing technical progress, one plunges into a struggle in which man's control over nature becomes ever changing, ever more efficient. Yet these technical changes may lead to conflict between man and man. The Chinese intelligentsia viewed the world humanistically. Lacking technical knowledge, they could not appreciate technical progress. And they saw no reason to wish to change man's relations to man.

IV / *Basic Power Structure in Rural China*

THE DO-NOTHING POLICY OF THE IMPERIAL POWER

A centralized political system has had a long history in China. Since the time (221 B.C.) when the First Emperor abolished feudalism and created the provinces and districts, local officials theoretically have always been appointed by the central government, the custom being that local men should not be named as local officials. It would appear from this that the Chinese political system was one controlled completely from the top, one in which the people were entirely passive and in which local interests had no voice. If this had been really true, the Chinese political system would have been the most authoritarian known to man. Yet it is obvious that, unless the people were completely enslaved, a centralized control of this sort would be very difficult to maintain, particularly in a huge country in which the system of communications was not comparable to that of the Roman Empire, for example, and which was without many strong garrisons. Any political regime which wishes to maintain itself for long, if it cannot win the active support of the people, must at least gain their tolerance. In other words, the political system cannot be developed on a single track from the top downward. Under any kind of political rule the people's opinion cannot entirely be ignored. This means that there must be, in some way, a parallel track from the bottom up. A sound system which will endure must thus be "double track." This is clearly seen in modern democratic institutions, but in fact it may also be traced in the so-called absolutistic governments. When under this sort of rule the track from the bottom up is broken, we have a tyrant, and the result is disaster. The fact that in China, even under the absolutistic system, despotic tyrants have not always ruled indicates that there has been some informal type of track by means of which the people's opinion has penetrated to the top levels.

In the Chinese traditional political system there have been two lines of defense which prevented an absolute monarchy from becoming intolerably tyrannical. The first defense was Chinese political philosophy, the theory of do-nothingness. Years of experience shaped this. In Chinese history there has been little theory or practice to encourage political power to interfere with the social life of the people. It is true that the realistic and materialistic Legalistic Han Fei-tzu (*ca.* 280–233 B.C.) did advocate reforms in the government to strengthen it and to make the nation rich. He and his followers worked out the Legalist theory of rule by law. But in the eyes of traditional scholars throughout Chinese history, Han Fei-tzu has been poorly regarded, and his tragic end[1] has been pointed out as a warning to those who would have liked to follow the same path. Two other well-known reformers, Wang Mang in the Han dynasty (who usurped the throne A.D. 9–23), and Wang An-shih (1021–86) in the Sung dynasty, wished the government to carry out social reforms and were against the do-nothing policy. But both failed. It may be said by those who sympathized with them that they were prevented by reactionaries from attaining their goals. And yet none of these reformers went so far as to attempt to restrict the monarchical power by law. Nor did any of them make any effort to learn whether their reforms would be acceptable to the people either in whole or in part. In fact, there was no evidence that the policy they urged upon the government, coincided in any way with the people's desires.[2] The policy of maintaining the monarchical power unrestricted and enforcing the government's will upon the people naturally resulted in conflict with the latter. In the political history of the West the tendency has been increasingly to give up the responsibility for, and control of, political power to the people. In China political policy throughout the ages has been rather to neutralize political power in such a way that the people did not become restless (while the few would-be reformers of this system have tended toward more authoritarianism than those whom they opposed). Do-nothingism is a way of

1. Han Fei-tzu, slandered and unable to plead his case, ended his life by taking the poison sent him by his slanderers, according to Ssu-ma Ch'ien's *Historical Records* (see *The Complete Works of Han Fei Tzu*, trans. W. K. Liao [London: A. Probsthain, 1939], I, xxii–xxix).

2. See chap. i, n. 6.

dealing with political problems which is different from the positive check of a constitutional government but which serves as the "first defense" against political absolutism.[3]

We recognize now that such a system is not effective in modern life, since we depend upon central governmental power to take action with regard to those things which concern the people as a whole. But in economically self-sufficient communities it is not necessary to employ authority beyond that found in the local community. Constitutional government is a modern achievement. Before it developed in the West, political power was there as elsewhere restricted by traditional morality, in this case reinforced by the supernatural authority of the church.[4]

3. " 'But it is a pity that a talented person like you is unwilling to serve the government. Those who are not talented wish to become officials but those who are, only wish to escape it. This is indeed a most regretful matter.'

" 'You are not right,' argued Lao-t'an. 'It is a matter of no importance whether the common clay wish to become officials or not. The regretful thing lies in the fact that the talented wish to get such posts. As you can see, Mr. Yu is a talented person, but he is too hasty—hasty for promotion, for becoming a big shot. Therefore, he has not hesitated to do many harmful and unreasonable things in order that he may get results. It is unfortunate that his so-called good administration is known far and wide. Don't you think that in a few years he will be promoted, and be still more harmful to society? If he presides over a prefecture, the prefecture would be injured. If he governs a province, the province would suffer, and if he rule the country, the country would be ruined. Therefore, I put to you this question, whether it would be better for the talented to become government officials, or the non-talented?' " (Liu Ê, *A Tramp Doctor's Travelogue*, trans. Lin Yi-chin and Ko Te-shun [Shanghai: Commerical Press, 1939], p. 78).

4. [The author seems to be referring to the situation in medieval Europe, neglecting the fact that the bases for the concept of law and of constitutional government in the West are to be found in the formularization of laws, which approached a written constitution in fifth-century Greece and which was later expanded and developed by the Romans. In traditional China the limitations on the power of the monarch, or of his representative, seem never to have been derived from a concept of justice defined by law, written or unwritten.]

And we may note that the American constitution, which was drafted before industrial development had taken place, had the point of view that the best government is the one which governs least. In China, men had recourse not to legal but to ideological restrictions upon the absolute power of the monarch. It was probably due to the influence of Confucian ideology that the abuse of political power was to some extent lessened.

THE POLITICAL TRACK FROM THE BOTTOM UP

In this section I do not wish to emphasize the first line of defense, however, but rather the second. In our traditional politics, on the one hand, we restricted political power by ideology and, on the other, restricted the sphere of the administrative system. We somehow managed to "hang up" the centralized power so that it did not reach to the ground, since the officials sent by the central government stopped at the district *yamen*. Ordinarily, students of Chinese administration have paid little attention to the connection between the *hsien* (district) government and the gate of each house. But, in fact, this connection was both extremely interesting and important in that it was the meeting point of the powerful central authorities and the local self-governing community. Only by understanding this meeting point can we know how the Chinese traditional system actually worked.

Let us start with the district *yamen*. I have said that the officials sent by the central government stopped at the district because, formerly, we did not recognize any political unit below the *hsien*. The head of the *hsien*, who represented the emperor, was called the "parent-official," or *fu-mu kuan*. He was supposed to maintain an intimate relationship with the people, but, in fact, the office of this *lao-yeh* was as high as the sky—so high, indeed, that no ordinary person could reach up to it. Nor was the *yamen* a place in which any common person could enter freely. But between the parent-officials and the children—common people existed intermediaries. Those who made the actual contact between the *yamen* and the people, the ruler and the ruled, were the servants of the officials. These official servants (*ya-i*) occupied one of the lowest positions in the Chinese social scale; they were deprived of most of their civil rights, and their sons were not allowed to take the examinations. It is a significant point in the Chinese power structure that these men who were in the position of most easily abused power should have been held so low. If society had not suppressed them by despising them and depriving them of a decent social position, they might have become as fearful as wolves. But with no hope of ascending in the social scale, even if they abused their power, they still would not be too formidable.[5]

Under a political system that upholds the do-nothing policy, the local officials will have very little work. So history shows us many officials spending much of their time in leisurely expeditions or in developing their literary talents. Their job was merely to collect taxes and to act as judges. So far as the latter occupation went, there was not much to do, because the ideal was to have no litigation. The duty of governmental servants was to keep order among the people, to collect money, and to conscript labor when needed. If the district ordinances had applied to each and every household, it would have

5. [The typical *ya-i* would be a man with a little education but not enough to enable him to get ahead. Being literate, he would not want to sink to manual labor.]

meant that the *hsien* was actually a basic unit of administration. But in fact this was not true. District orders did not come to the various households but to the local self-governing unit (called, in Yunnan, the "public family," or *kung-chia*). I speak of this type of organization as a "self-governing unit" because it was organized by local people to look out for the public affairs of the community. Public affairs included problems of irrigation, self-defense, mediation in personal disputes, mutual aid, recreation, and religious activities. In China such things are local community affairs, and, according to the tradition still preserved, they are not an affair of government but are managed by the local community under the leadership of the better-educated and wealthier family heads. Practical affairs such as might come up in dealing with irrigation, for example, might be dealt with by nonscholarly responsible individuals, but the more scholarly would generally have greater prestige in the making of decisions.[6]

But besides deciding local public affairs, another important function of the *kung-chia* was to represent the people in their dealings with the government. With good reason I have separated these two functions—the self-governing and the dealing with the central government.

6. [Lu Hsien, in a short story entitled "Divorce," satirized the role of the gentry in deciding village disputes. A girl wishes to leave her husabnd and refuses to accept the advice of her relatives. So a member of the local gentry, Squire Seventh, is brought in. The girl thinks, "Those who know the classics and are men of justice must always defend the oppressed." Squire Seventh's authority is urged upon her with the words, "Squire Seventh is a man of wisdom and learning, very different from us villagers, with a knowledge of what is right. . . . Here is a fact which will not escape Squire Seventh's notice, for those who know the classics and wisdom know everything. . . ." In the end the girl is forced to accept Squire Seventh's obviously biased decision.]

The responsible leaders of the *kung-chia* organization kept clear of any official dealings with the *yamen*. Instead, there were special individuals who represented the community in their dealings with the government. These people were called *shang-yao* (the term used locally in Yunnan). As I said before, in the *de jure* political system, there was no recognized track from the bottom up, the emperor being absolute. To reject an order of the emperor thus was a crime. Nevertheless, the fact that the emperor had ordered it was not in real life a guaranty that the people would accept it. Therefore, in actual practice, there had to be a means for communicating with the people and discovering their sentiments. The servant of the government brought the orders not to the *kung-chia* but to the *shang-yao*. The *shang-yao*, whose office was filled in turn by members of the community, was in a particuarly awkward spot because he had no real power or influence in the community but merely served as the terminus of the track from the top down. After he had received an order from the government, he in turn reported to the head of the *kung-chia*. The latter then talked the matter over with other leaders of the gentry in the teashop, and if he, along with the others, decided that the order was unacceptable, he rejected it and turned it back to the *shang-yao*. This unfortunate in turn must again communicate with the *yamen* and receive the brunt of official annoyance due to his lack of success. But in this way the "face" of the emperor would have been saved, since the refusal to comply was not direct but merely indicated in a roundabout fashion. Meanwhile, informal negotiations would be carried on. The leaders of the local community, whose status as gentry placed them on a footing of equality with officialdom, would make a friendly call upon the district official in the course of which they discussed the governmental order. If no agreement resulted from these negotiations of local gentry and local government officials, the local gentry would be inclined to get their friends and relatives in town to take the matter up with the higher levels of the bureaucracy, in time, perhaps, working up to the very top. Eventually, an agreement of some sort would be reached, the central government would change its order, and things would settle down again.

According to this system, the local leader did not come into contact with the despised governmental petty servants. If the self-governing unit had been an actual part of the *de jure* administration, however, the track from the bottom up would have been blocked. The official in charge of the *yamen* could not have a free discussion with subordinates in office but only with those outside the bureaucracy and his social equals. In the Ch'ing dynasty (1644–1911) a man who had passed the district examination could call on the local official, using his own card. Besides this privilege of a scholar, he was also protected from corporal punishment, unless his degree were first taken away. And this latter act was in the power not of the district official but only of the local education official. Such people who were able to deal with the governmental officials are those who were called gentry.

I hope I have made certain points clear in this somewhat simplified account. (1) In the traditional Chinese power structure there were two different layers: on the top, the central government; at the bottom, the local governing unit whose leaders were the gentry class. (2) There was a *de facto* limit to the authority of the central government. Local affairs, managed in the community by the gentry, were hardly interfered with by the central authorities. (3) Legally there was only one track—from the top down—along which passed imperial orders. But in actual practice, by the use of intermediaries such as the government servants and a locally chosen *shang-yao* or functionary of the same type, unreasonable orders might be turned back. This influence from the bottom up is not usually recognized in discussions of the formal governmental institutions of China, but it was effective nevertheless. (4) The mechanism of bringing influences to bear from the bottom upward was worked through the informal pressure of the gentry upon their relatives in office and out or upon friends who had taken the same examinations. By this means influence could be brought to bear sometimes even upon the emperor himself. (5) The self-governing organization so called arose from the practical needs of the community. The power of this group was not derived from the central imperial power but came from the local people themselves. When the central authority collected only a limited amount of taxes and of conscripts, the people would be likely to feel that "Heaven is high, the emperor is far away." But the necessity for maintaining some contact between centralized and local authorities meant that the local gentry always tended to have strategic and leading positions in the local organization.[7]

7. [Fei wrote of the village of Kai-hsien-kung, south of Lake Tai, in 1939: "The basis of the headmanship lies in public recognition and support in the leadership in community affairs, and in being the representative of the community against the outside world. Chen started his career as a school-master and Chou as an assistant in the silk factory. Their service and ability have given them authority and prestige. In the village there are few who are literate and

THE BREAKDOWN OF THE LOCAL SELF-GOVERNING GROUP

In describing the power structure above, the term "inefficiency" was not derogatory. Actually the need for efficiency did not arise, in that the affairs which directly concerned the people were carried on outside the formal government. The work of local self-governing groups followed local needs and conformed to local attitudes. Occasionally, the local organization attempted to regulate life in minute detail. For example, in a certain village in Yunnan, if a married couple did not produce children, they would be symbolically beaten and even fined a small amount. Traditional and religious actions were maintained by the local organization. Thus, a do-nothing emperor might enjoy high peace and order under the heavens during his reign because the local organizations throughout the country kept things going. Since the im-

---

still less who are at the same time willing to take up the responsibility without economic reward. Young men of ambition are not satisfied with the position: it is considered by the two middle-school graduates I met in the village as sterile and hopeless. Thus the range for the selection of village heads is not very large.

"Although they have no direct economic reward, they enjoy prestige and presents from the persons who have received services from them. For example, they are respected by the people, and can call the generation senior to them, except their own near kin, by their personal names without adding any relationship term. This cannot be done by an ordinary person.

"Village heads are always accessible, because they are known to every villager, and a stranger will be received by them immediately. The visitor will be impressed by their heavy burden of work. They help the people to read and to write letters and other documents, to make the calculations required in the local credit system, to manage marriage ceremonies, to arbitrate in social disputes, and to look after public property. They are responsible for the system of self-defence, for the management of public funds, and for the transmission and execution of administrative orders from the higher government. They take an active part in introducing beneficial measures such as industrial reform into the village" (*Peasant Life in China* [New York: E. P. Dutton & Co., 1939], pp. 108–9 and 106).]

perial power demanded only two things—taxes and conscripts from the people—the existence of inefficient,
poetry-writing officials was, in a sense, a blessing. But
such a system could work only in an economy which was
to a high degree self-sufficient. When intervillage affairs
developed, such as large-scale irrigation or other public
works projects, or warfare was initiated, an inefficient
centralized government was a bad thing. This point is
easy to see. The development of Chinese economy increased the work of the central government. Theoretically, no changes were needed in the government itself,
since we already had a highly developed centralized political system; we required only more efficiency in its
working. It is true that since, legally, the power of the
central government was unlimited, increasing its efficiency might break down the first line of defense against
a tyrannical authority. But since the do-nothing policy
was, after all, a very negative means of restricting power,
a means indeed which could hardly be maintained in a
modern society, its decline could hardly be regretted.
The damage which occurred to the second line of defense, the highly developed local self-government system, when the supposedly more efficient *pao-chia* system
was introduced (or, rather reintroduced) was another
matter, however.

The *pao-chia* system[8] has brought the political track

8. [The *pao-chia*, under which ten households, the members of which were
held to be mutually responsible for one another's behavior, were grouped in a
chia, ten *chia* forming a *pao*, was more or less in force in China from 1932 until
recently, when the Communists, on taking over the government, abolished it.
It had been first instituted in 1069 or 1070 by the famous statesman Wang
An-Shih. According to Fei's *Peasant Life in China*, the *pao-chia* system was introduced for military purposes, in order to register and organize the people more

from the top down to the gate of every household and, in fact, as a state system of policing, has even entered every house door. The introduction of the *pao-chia* system was for a reason. In the old traditional system governmental administration was handicapped by its lack of thoroughness, the fact that it only went halfway in carrying out orders. It seemed it would be much more efficient for the government to deal directly with the people instead of having to have everything pass through the local organization. Moreover, when the *pao-chia* system came into force in the 1930's, it was intended that it should, in time, take up the function of self-government, so that, as the recognized track from the bottom up, there might be built up a system of really democratic representation. But the latter result has never been realized. The *pao-chia* system has certain defects which make it unsuited to a democratic system of representation. According to *pao-chia*, the people were to be organized, with slight variations, in uniform numerical groups. But such units did not necessarily coincide with actual social

---

effectively against the Communists. Yang says: "Since the revival (a supposed revival of an older system of social control) of the *pao-chia* system, each family must post on the top of the front door, a card bearing the name, age, sex, kinship status, and occupation of the family members. . . . The government has recently initiated the *pao-chia* system but the villagers do not, except very rarely, comply with it. They would not report that a son of their neighbour was involved in anything wrong. This reluctance is largely due to the traditional relations between neighbours, which make it very hard for one villager to report another's bad behaviour to a government authority or an outsider. It is also due to the fact that the system was primarily adopted for eliminating politically undesirable persons, especially those who have been accused of being communists, and often a person in disfavour with the political authorities may be on good terms with his fellow villagers" (Martin Yang, *A Chinese Village, Taitov, Shangtung Province* [New York: Columbia University Press, 1945], pp. 9 and 150).]

groups. The size of a community is determined by historical and social forces; we cannot add members to a family or to a local community and have them fit in. By instituting the principle of uniformity in the *pao-chia* system—this was actually worked out only for convenience in administration and especially for dealing with conscription—the principle of local self-government has been weakened. Often a community will be divided into several *chia*, while several unrelated units may be combined in one *pao*, the result being much confusion. In fact, there now came into existence two overlapping systems: one, the *pao-chia*, imposed from the top; the other, the natural local organization, which had now become illegal, and these two systems tended to come into conflict.

TEARING UP THE DOUBLE TRACK

The first serious problem over which conflict developed was the selecting of the head of the *pao-chia*, the *pao-tsun*. The *pao-chia* was an administrative system which executed orders from above, but at the same time it was the legally recognized organization for directing local public affairs. Under the traditional system the carrying-out of this double function was shared by three different groups: the servants of the government; the *shang-yao*, or local representative and intermediary; and the leaders among the local gentry. Now that these three were all combined in one man, the *pao-tsun*, it was assumed that the orders of the central government would be accepted by the people, as always, and carried out by them. But practical difficulties arose at once as the result of the new system. First of all, those people of the community who possessed prestige have usually been unwilling to accept the job of *pao-tsun*. As local gentry, if they wished to preserve their equal status with officialdom, they could not accept a place in the system which would make them lower in status and unable to negotiate but only to accept orders from those above. As a mediator, in fact, the function of the *pao-tsun* was only equivalent to that of a *shang-yao*. Yet the *pao-tsun* and the *shang-yao* are actually not at all the same. The *shang-yao* has no power, while the *pao-tsun* is legally upon the same level as the local leaders, with the right to keep the public funds and to manage local affairs. The difficulty is that the functions of mediator and of administrator have become confused. An energetic *pao-tsun* is likely to come into conflict with the local gentry, and in this conflict there will be no longer any bridge between governmental and local interests. A local leader of the gentry who accepts the post of *pao-tsun* as being in his own interest and a position of authority will find that actually his situation has changed for the worse, in that he can no longer reject any order from above. Thus the local community has become a dead end in the political system. The people now have no way to express themselves against the central authority, and, when the situation becomes intolerable, the only way out is to rebel.

The *pao-chia* system, thus, not only has disrupted the traditional community organization but has also hampered the developing life of the people. It has destroyed the safety valve of the traditional political system. Nor has the new structure of the *pao-chia* effectively taken over the work of the traditional self-governing organization. The net result has simply been to outlaw the old system so that it can no longer work openly. Deadlock, inefficiency, and even the disruption of the basic administrative machinery have been the results.

The extension of the track from the top down was intended to facilitate the execution of governmental orders. Though it is true that through the *pao-chia* system a more centralized administration has been realized, greater efficiency has resulted in form only, since, when there is a deadlock at the bottom, orders tend not to be carried out actually. In the more efficient collection of taxes and of conscripts, the new system has achieved something, it is true. But in all projects of local reconstruction or increase of production, all that is accomplished is the placing of the orders in the files of the *pao-chia*. In fact, it has become generally accepted that this storing of documents is one of the main functions of the *pao-chia*. Under such conditions even a good man in the office of the *pao-tsun* has little chance of bringing about any practical measures of social reform.

v / *Village, Town, and City*

Having discussed the place of the gentry in the political structure of China, I now turn to their place in the economic order. But, in order to understand this, we must first make clear the difference in form between rural and urban communities and the nature of the economic and other relationships which hold them together. Five types of concentration of population may be recognized: the village, the walled or garrison town, the temporary market, the market town, and the treaty port.

POPULATION AND URBAN COMMUNITIES

What do we mean by "urban" as applied to a community? This question is difficult to answer. In the United States the Bureau of the Census calls a community of 2,500 people or more a city; and a community in which the incorporated area has a population of 50,000 and the outlying suburbs a population density of 150 per square mile is termed a metropolitan area. But not all sociologists agree to this standard. In fact, there exists no absolute generally accepted standard. Mark Jefferson, for example, calls a city an area with a population of 10,000 per square mile, while, for Walter F. Willcox, 1,000 individuals per square mile is enough to enable him to designate the area as a city.[1] Although these men disagree as to the numbers to be used, both use population density as the criterion for differentiating rural and urban areas. This is possible because in the United States a dense population is always organized into a city. But in China the situation is different. For instance, in my native province of Kiangsu the average population density is over 500 per square mile; in Shantung it is 615; in Chekiang, 657; and in some parts of these provinces it is more, even, than 6,000 persons per square mile.[2] If we applied Willcox's criterion, this whole area should be called a city. But to do so would be simply to abandon common sense. If we accept the notion that different standards must be adopted for the situation in China, which is so different from that in the United States, the question arises: What sort of standard, then, shall we use? It is clear that the density of population alone is insufficient for differentiating rural from urban communities.

In studying urban and rural communities from the point of view of population, the emphasis should be laid

1. [Walter F. Willcox, *Studies in American Demography* (Ithaca, N.Y.: Cornell University Press, 1940), chap. vi, "Density of Population: Urban and Rural," p. 117. The Mark Jefferson reference has not been found.]

2. [China has never had a real census. Rather, population has been computed for purposes of taxation and compulsory labor on the basis of not very accurate estimates. However, from 1932 to 1937, seven experimental censuses, confined to one *hsien* (district) each, in the case of six, and part of a *hsien* for the seventh, were taken. These *hsien* were scattered through five provinces, three in Kiangsu, and one each in Hopeh, Shantung, Chekiang, and Fukien (Tâ Chen, *Population in Modern China* [Chicago: University of Chicago Press, 1946]).]

not upon quantity or density but rather upon distribution. We see that, as economic life develops among human beings, the population begins to concentrate at certain points which seem like nuclei or cells. The nuclear concentration in an area may be called urban; the area surrounding it, rural. Inevitably, there will be a difference in population density related to the process of concentration in the nucleus and in the area surrounding it. But we cannot pick this or that number of persons per square mile as a basis for distinguishing communities at different stages of economic development. Assuming a high density of population, our main problem is to analyze why the population concentrates in a few spots.

In self-sufficient economies, whether nomadic or agricultural, each unit may live by itself, and its population may be dispersed over an area. There is no economic necessity for a nucleus, and, even if individuals come together, there is no economic differentiation. In cultivating the land, for practical reasons, if for no other, we should expect to find farmers settled on their own land so as to be near their work and to have their produce close at hand. This is what we call the dispersed type of agriculture, which is the usual thing in America.[3] But in China, except for a few places, such as the hilly areas of Szechwan, the situation is quite different. Chinese farmers live not in isolation but close together in villages. Two factors, the kinship organization and the need for mutual protection, are important in particular in bringing this about. Where, as in China, brothers inherit their father's land equally, all tend to remain together

3. [The dispersed farms of America are the exception, of course. Throughout the world old farming populations tend to cluster their houses into villages and go out to their fields.]

upon the land. If there is any free land near by, the family may spread out, and in the course of several generations a clan village may be developed. The fact of kinship keeps people living together in the same locality. Moreover, it is true that, although the lengthening of the distance between farms and living quarters is disadvantageous from an economic standpoint, living together in one place has great advantages from the point of view of security. Farming communities are easily invaded, and the best way to be safe is for the farmers to concentrate their families and produce in one place which is easier to protect and which may be inclosed with some sort of wall. A concentration of farm families of this sort we call a village.

The emphasis on defense appears from the very construction of the farmhouses themselves. In the mountains and hilly areas villages are smaller, and there may appear scattered homesteads with their own walled inclosures like primitive fortresses. Or, if structures of this sort are lacking, we will see that in the outer walls there are no windows, so that the house looks entirely inward. In larger villages we often find a central walled-in place to which the people can retire when necessary and where they can store their produce in case of an attack from outside. Even in more peaceful and orderly spots like Kiangsu, which we call Paradise, where river transport is more important than roads, the river will be blocked with a wooden gate every evening or in case of emergency. But here the form of the houses is modified, and windows are open to the street.

Whatever the variation in form and whatever the size, as an assemblage of self-sufficient units, without a differentiation of function or division of labor among its members, we may recognize it as a village or rural community rather than as a town or urban center. The village, then, may be seen as one type of organization. The towns of China, on the other hand, are not all of one type but vary according to their function.

THE WALLED OR GARRISON TOWN
A POLITICAL CENTER

An important type of urban center is the walled town or *ch'eng*. The original meaning of this word is "wall," "inclosure," or "defense work." Constructions for defense may vary in size and quality. Sometimes they are built for a single family; sometimes for a village. But, when the word *ch'eng* is used, it designates a wall or defensive construction on a larger scale, one built to protect a political center. To make a wall of this sort is a big enterprise which cannot be accomplished by private means alone; it must be a public work shared in by the people over a large area. Both political power and political purpose are needed to construct this kind of large wall.

A *ch'eng*, then, is an instrument of the ruling classes in a political system where power resides in force. The *ch'eng* is the symbol of power and also a necessary tool for the maintenance of power. As a result, the location of a *ch'eng* is usually chosen with its political and military uses in mind. In the places where the representative of the monarch was used to stay there had to be a wall to protect him. Every *hsien* had to have a *ch'eng* where the representative of the emperor resided. Sometimes, however, when a *hsien* could not afford to build a *ch'eng*, the representatives of several *hsien* would concentrate in one *ch'eng.* In other words, the *ch'eng* existed in order to protect the *yamen* (the bureaucracy). And the existence of the *ch'eng* clearly illustrates the theory expounded in previous chapters that, in China, monarchical power needed always to be vigilant and on the defensive.

In Yunnan we see that, in building a walled city, the custom is ordinarily to build the wall partly on a hilltop and partly on the plain because this type of construction is easier to defend. If built on flat ground, a moat, called a *ch'ih* ("pond") or *huang* ("ditch") was dug about it. (By extension, the guard who rules the district in the spirit world, who is a counterpart of the magistrate who rules this world, was called a *ch'eng huang.*) It is clear that the wall and the moat have symbolized a seat of authority far back in Chinese history. Within the walled inclosure, even in cities such as Peking and Nanking, there was usually a large amount of cultivable land which in case of siege even in these days has often been useful for providing perishable foodstuffs. The ideal city, from the traditional point of view, was a self-sufficient castle. And even now the government may, in emergencies, order the gates of a city to be closed. Recently, even before martial law was established in Peking, the city gates were closed every evening at seven o'clock.

Although the *ch'eng* symbolized security, the population within the walls might not necessarily be greater than in communities outside. In fact, in Yunnan it is common to find the walled towns smaller in size than the adjacent villages. Yet the well-protected area of the town had its attractions for certain people. To be a rich man, or even one just a little well-to-do, has never been safe in China, as we said before. Owing to the low cost of labor, landowners need not be very wealthy in order to be freed from the necessity for working their own lands, and in such a case they might feel moved to rent out their land and move to the walled town. Riches obtained from exploitation need to be protected by political power, and governmental authority might be used, when necessary, to collect rent for absentee owners. In Yunnan a troop of soldiers was, at one time, sent to collect rents.[4] As previously described, the landowners tend to maintain a close personal relationship with the bureaucracy. And it was this combination of officialdom and landed gentry which gave the walled or garrison town its special character.

For the use of the dwellers in the walled town there developed handicraft industries. The greater the concentration of landowners as well as of wealth, the greater the development of craftsmen and the more skilled and varied the types of things produced. The silver of Chengtu, the embroidery of Soochow, the silk of Hangchow, and the cloisonné of Peking are all examples of art handicrafts which attained a high degree of development. In centers of this sort a more far-reaching trade in the local specialty as well as in local country products, such as fur or herbs, might grow up. But the walled town was not typically a trading center, nor did it serve to

4. "Landlords of big estates establish their own rent-collecting bureaus, and petty landlords pool their claims with them. . . . At the end of October, the bureau will inform each tenant of the amount of rent that should be paid that year. The information is forwarded by special agents. These agents are employed by the bureau, and have been entrusted with police power by the district government" (Hsiao-tung Fei, *Peasant Life in China* [New York: E. P. Dutton & Co., 1939], p. 188).

supply the needs of the peasant population. Luxury goods of the sort mentioned above were not within the reach of the country people living on an economy of bare subsistence. The craftsmen who lived in the walled towns, such as the tailor (who occupied a place at the front gate of a big house and served as gateman as well), the carpenters, the dispensers of drugs and tonics, the silversmiths, and all the others did not serve the villagers but rather the landlords, somewhat as the artists and craftsmen in the Middle Ages served their lords. Economic activity in these fortified centers of administration, then, was based not on an exchange of goods between producers but on the purchasing power of consumers who gained their wealth largely from exploitative relationships with the country.[5]

Besides their money from rents, landowners derived income from investing their capital in pawnshops, in the loaning-out of money at high rates, and in rice shops. Once I asked a resident of a walled town about how much moneylending went on there and was told by him that *everyone* in town engaged in this activity. He probably merely meant that most of the townsfolk did so. And the poor country people who come to borrow money

5. [Compare with Pirenne's description of medieval towns of Europe during the period of closed domestic economy: "As can be easily seen, the burgs were, above all, military establishments. . . . In case of war, its inhabitants found there a refuge; in time of peace, there they repaired to take part in the assemblies of justice, or to pay off the prestations to which they were subject. Nevertheless, the burg did not show the slightest urban character. . . . Neither commerce nor industry was possible or even conceivable in such an environment. It produced nothing of itself, lived by revenues from the surrounding country, and had no other economic role than that of a simple consumer" (Henri Pirenne, *Mediaeval Cities* [Princeton: Princeton University Press, 1925], pp. 75 and 76).]

will usually be forced to sell their land eventually in order to pay their debts.[6] The investment of the rice-shop owner may be increased through speculation as well as through merely buying and selling rice. He will then buy rice when the price is low and keep it to sell when the price is higher.

In a number of places the rice shop had still another function—that of husking the rice, either, as in former times, by means of machinery run by water power or, as at present, by crude-oil or electric power. (But in the villages of the interior, in particular, we may still see the villagers husking their rice by pounding it.) In general, this type of town was not conducive to the development of either industry or commerce, and that which did exist, for the most part, served the wealthy classes who had taken up their residence there for political or security reasons.

6. [D. K. Lieu, in his recent *China's Economic Stabilisation and Reconstruction* [New Brunswick, N.J.: Rutgers University Press, 1948], does not quite agree with Fei's picture of the typical landlord. "While there are landlords who exploit tenants, the worst kind of exploiters, both of tenants and small farmers, are the professional money lenders. . . . In some sample studies made before the war, the rate of interest charged by these rural Shylocks was from 50 to 100 per cent per annum, or many times the rate on bank loans in the cities, which was from 10 to 15 per cent before the war. . . . While miserly landlords often lend money to their tenants on the same terms as the money lenders, they are comparatively few. It is to their interest to keep the tenants from being unduly burdened with debt, which would affect the latter's work on the farm, and thus also affect the rent to be collected, especially if it is on a share-cropping basis. Besides, the landlords, particularly the larger ones, have their social standing, and would not like to be regarded as belonging to the same class as the money lender. . . . In some cases, however, landlords may lend to independent farmers, with the object of obtaining possession of their land, since these farmers, when they are heavily burdened with debt, are usually compelled to sell their land for debt settlement; but such scheming landlords are not very common" (pp. 42–43).]

MARKETS AND TOWNS DEVELOPED FROM TRADE

Self-sufficiency was highly developed in the rural economy of China, but it was not complete. Some of the necessities of life of the villagers came from exchange with other villagers and some from the outside. So we do find trading activities in the rural areas, and this is another factor in the concentration of population. We may distinguish, as centers of trade, temporary markets from market towns.

In interior China temporary markets are still common. These have names which vary with the locality and which indicate that they are a local development rather than something imposed from the top and alike throughout the country as the *ch'eng*. The terms for temporary market refer to places where producers exchange goods among themselves.[7] Since the producers

---

7. "The intimate relation between the periodic market and local production, which is overwhelmingly agricultural, is shown in the monthly sales record for livestock for the year 1932 in central market Sun-chia-chen. Sales fluctuations correspond entirely to the local agricultural calendar. . . . During the sowing season, fertiliser, hoes, plows, and other market implements connected with the work of the season are sold widely on markets. In harvest seasons, the markets are abundantly supplied with sickles, ropes for bundling stalks, screens and mats for threshing grains. Immediately after harvest, when farm work is in a temporary lag, markets are alive with cardboards for making shoes, cotton yarns and shuttles and other weaving supplies, silk threads and other sewing articles. . . .

"Among the total traders of eleven markets, in one market day, 69.8 per cent of them came to sell their own service and products, both agricultural and handicraft. . . .

"Inquiry into thirty-seven farm families shows that thirty-three rely entirely upon the periodic markets for disposing of their agricultural products; and only four, whose farms are larger than the rest, sell about 25 per cent of their grains directly to merchants. . . . Products of home industry such as hand loomed cloth, home-made shoes and sewing materials, depend on the market as the sole outlet" (Ching-kun Yang, *A North China Local Market Economy: A Summary of a Study of Periodic Markets in Chowping Hsien, Shantung* [New York: Institute of Pacific Relations, 1945], pp. 10–11).

cannot engage in trade every day, this kind of market usually takes place only every few days (in Yunnan the common practice is to hold a market every six days). On market day the villagers bring to the market the things they wish to sell and bring back, at the end of the day, what they have bought in exchange. The size of the market varies according to the area which it covers, large markets having sometimes more than ten thousand people. On the Dragon Day, Sheep Day, or Dog Day markets in Yunnan, when one stands on the top of a hill and looks down, there appears to be a sea of human beings moving back and forth like waves. People are so crowded together that their shoulders touch, and it is hard to move. But the crowd does not last long. At sunset they will be leaving, and by evening the place will be empty.

Markets of this temporary nature do not represent a community. The term "market" refers merely to a location which has been selected for its convenience in communication. Usually it must be a large open space, often the open area near a temple, where people are apt to gather. Where trading is more developed, markets of this sort become more frequent. Gradually around the big open space will spring up small storehouses for the merchants who buy up local products and transport them to other places as well as teahouses for those who wish to sit and rest. As the demand grows for more supplies from outside, what is brought in by the peddlers will not be enough. In time a store may be established close to the market center, and eventually there will develop a permanent community which we call a market town, or *shih*.

In the Lake Tai area, where communication by water is much quicker than by land, this type of town has had more chance to develop. As described in *Peasant Life in China*, a so-called "agent boat" buys things for the villagers, each boat roughly serving about a hundred households. By using the morning to go to town and the afternoon to come back, a boat of this sort can cover quite an area. In town there are usually hundreds of these agent boats, supplying tens of thousands of rural families. The stores in town have special arrangements with one or more boats for their supplies, and thus, by having access to such a large number of consumers, a large commercial center may be maintained. But in the interior of China, where communication is difficult, towns of this sort are very few.

Market and garrison towns can be differentiated not only theoretically but also by mere inspection. In Yunnan their aspects are very different. Around Kunming, which is a big walled city, there are six or seven temporary markets. It is true that Kunming has recently also become a commercial center, but it has not developed through rural consumption. On the main street of Kunming there are department stores selling foreign goods and merchants selling gold. Those who buy here are mostly city dwellers or traders from various other towns. Very few villagers come to buy things directly from these shops. They buy the things they need from the markets which surround the city walls.

We may take another example of a small garrison town of Yunnan in which there is only one main street inside the town walls. On this street are several teashops, a barbershop, and a shop with miscellaneous drygoods and sweets. Outside the walls, a fifteen-minute walk away, is the Dragon Day market. Though within easy reach of the town, it is quite distinct from it. The town represents a political center in which, the chief interest being security, the location chosen was a hillside, which is easier to defend. The latter, developing through trade, selected a position at a crossroads, which makes it easily accessible to the villagers round about. In the Lake Tai area in my own native district, Wukiang, the garrison town is much smaller and less prosperous than the nearby market towns, such as Chen-tse. In the Ch'ing dynasty this garrison town contained two district governments, but, besides the governmental *yamens*, it had mainly private residences and only one main street. Here one sees clearly the difference in function between garrison and market town.

It is true that these two types of town do have certain similarities, since the market town is also the place where landowners gather. When they live in an economic center, they have more opportunity to make commercial use of the capital which they have accumulated from the land. But, according to traditional standards, the landlord who engaged in trade occupied a lower position than did the landlord who was an official in the *ch'eng*. However, as this tradition has been gradually breaking down, a high position in the market town is often a step toward a high position in a garrison town. In the market town, where the shops are the center of the community, there are also small industries and handicrafts developed to serve the community itself and for export to rural areas. In this way the two types of town also resemble each other.

But even though these two types of towns do tend to overlap and are sometimes even combined into one community, it seems worth while to try to differentiate them conceptually, the garrison town as the seat of traditional bureaucratic authority and the wealthy gentry, the market town as a link between the peasants' local industry and more highly developed commerce and manufacturing.

THE TREATY PORT

We come, then, to the last type of concentration of population—the treaty port. I should like to make clear here that the Chinese modern city which developed from the treaty port not only differs from the traditional town, either of the market-town or of the garrison-town type, but also differs notably from the modern metropolitan city in the West. Those who advocate urbanization in China usually take the position that a city such as Shanghai is similar to New York and London. Such a conclusion is most misleading, because there is a real and very essential difference between Chinese cities and Western metropolises. Metropolitan cities like New York and London may be viewed as nerve centers for a wide economic area. The development of the center indicates the development of the hinterland, since they are bound up together. Through this relationship the economic division of labor of the different areas is facilitated. But Shanghai is different. It is not the center of an economically independent area but rather is a treaty port which was forced open by political agreement. It is a gateway to an economically underdeveloped continent, opened toward the Occident, rather than a city which, like New York or London, grew up through the economic development of its own hinterland. Shanghai and other treaty ports are the result of the impact of economies at different levels. Thus Shanghai originally was only a small fishing village occupying an insignificant position in the traditional economy. Since it has become a gate to the interior, it has entirely changed and has prospered mightily.

But its prosperity does not mean the prosperity of the hinterland, because it represents not a mutual development but rather the establishment of a superior economic force working its way toward a dominance of a less-well-developed area. The fact that treaty ports like Shanghai had for a long period a special political position as foreign settlements where Chinese power could not reach was no accident, since economically they were also separate from Chinese economy. On the one hand, they were a gate by means of which foreign goods could come in; on the other, they served as ratholes for dribbling away Chinese wealth. When I call the treaty ports "economic ratholes," I mean that they were fundamentally similar to the garrison towns, a community of consumers and not of producers. I may be challenged on this point by those who point out that commerce is mutual benefit and that the importation of foreign goods must be balanced by the export of other goods or that otherwise trade will stop. This may apply to New York, but it does not apply to Shanghai. To be sure, there are exports from Shanghai, not only Chinese raw materials but also silver and gold, when other goods are not enough to make a balance of trade. But these goods are not produced in Shanghai or in the industrial areas near by. They are raw materials from the countryside. If Shanghai played the role of connecting foreign consumers with their own producers, it might claim a status similar to that of New York or London. But the fact is that the producers of goods for export do not get back an equal value in imports. The Shanghai people collect the raw materials and sell them to foreign countries and then themselves consume the foreign goods which come in as imports. This relationship is quite similar to the traditional system in the garrison town, which I described above.

But there is a difference between the treaty port and the traditional garrison town. In the latter, goods are consumed which are produced in the local area or at least near by, while, in the treaty port, the goods consumed are largely those imported from foreign countries. The treaty port itself, as a great center of foreign influence, is very effective in bringing about the substitution of foreign goods for those produced at home. So we find a new class of wealth and influence in China—the comprador.[8] Part of the foreign goods pass into the towns of the interior, but the main market remains the treaty port or the international settlements. Because of the relative political freedom in these places, they collect all those people who feel they cannot stay in the interior, and, in

8. "I possess no sufficient data on the family background of those who form the first line of contact with Western traders, but I strongly suspect that those 'secondhand foreigners,' were, at least for the early period, recruited from the outcasts of the traditional structure, who had lost their positions and sought their fortune by illegal means. Treaty ports are open to them. If they find regular employment in the community, such as servants or interpreters in a foreign concern, they gradually become compradors, or first-boys; if they fail, they form gangs. They live in, and take advantage of, the margin of cultural contact. They are half-caste in culture, bilingual in speech, and morally unstable. They are unscrupulous, pecuniary, individualistic, and agnostic, not only in religion, but in cultural values" (Hsiao-tung Fei, "Peasantry and Gentry," *American Journal of Sociology*, III [July, 1946], 14).

fact, they become "Grand Hotels" for refugees of all sorts. In calling them "Grand Hotels," I am referring to the fact that most of those who enter the settlements bring with them money to spend. The source of this money is not the treaty port itself but is in the rural areas round about. Straws of various sizes thrust into the rural areas suck out the wealth of China into these ports. It is quite obvious that such an industrially un-developed metropolis as Shanghai, with a huge popula-tion next in size to New York and London, cannot have a self-sufficient economy but depends for its income upon the countryside.[9] As such, it is a garrison town and a community of dependent consumers and parasites rather than a highly developed city of the modern type.

Modern metropolises are the products of industrializa-tion. A country which has not been industrialized can-not have urban centers like New York or London. The treaty port brought about the invasion of an industrial-ized economy into an economically inferior area, where a simple economy still prevailed. This created a peculiar community which should not be classed with modern urban centers. In order to understand the nature of such a com-munity, we need more research than has so far been done.

9. [Compare this with the imperialism of ancient Rome. "All this bril-liant expansion of urban civilisation had in it the seeds of its own decline. It was an external and superficial development, like that of Modern European civilisation in the East, or in the eighteenth century Russia. It was imposed from above, and was never completely assimilated by the subject populations. It was essentially the civilisation of a leisured class, the urban bourgeoisie and their dependents, and though the process of urbanisation promoted the ad-vance of civilisation, it also involved a vast increase of unproductive expendi-ture and a growing strain on the resources of the empire. As Professor Ros-tovtzeff has said, every new city meant the creation of a new hive of drones" (Christopher Dawson, *The Making of Europe* [London: Sheed & Ward, 1932], p. 12).]

VI / *Rural Livelihood:*
Agriculture and Handicraft

With regard to the relationship in China between rural and urban areas, there are two distinct points of view, the first holding that rural and urban areas complement each other and are mutually beneficial, the second maintaining quite the reverse—that they are antagonistic.

Theoretically, of course, rural and urban communities are necessarily related integral parts of the whole country. Villages are the places where the agricultural products necessary for the subsistence of the country are produced, while those who stay in the city are not engaged in agriculture and depend upon a food supply from the country. Thus the urban communities are markets for the village produce, and the more developed the market, the higher will be the value of the food consumed and the more profit will result for the villages. Urban centers are also industrial centers for which raw materials such as soybeans, tung oil, cotton, and tobacco may be produced in the rural areas. These raw materials for industry sometimes have an even higher value than the foodstuffs produced and are then a cash crop. When modern industry develops in the city, its hinterland has the opportunity to develop crops of this sort according to the nature of the soil and other conditions. On the other hand, industrial products, manufactured goods over and above those needed for supplying the urban dwellers, will for the most part go to the countryside. Thus, there will be a constant exchange of raw materials and food for manufactured goods, a type of rural-urban trade which raises the standard of living for both sides.

The theory of the complementary nature of country-side and city is one generally accepted. Thus, if the Chinese standard of living is to be raised, the strengthening of urban-rural economic relations is of paramount importance. Most Chinese are still living in rural areas and are engaged in agriculture. To increase the income of these people, it is important to expand their exports to the cities and also to develop Chinese industry in the cities so as to enlarge the market for rural products.

But, judging from recent Chinese history, the development of the Chinese city seems not to have promoted rural prosperity. On the contrary, the rise of modern Chinese cities has been paralleled by the decline in Chinese rural economy. In the first few years of the last war with the Japanese, when most of the modern coastal cities were occupied and economic relations between rural and urban areas were cut off by blockade, a period of recovery, if not of prosperity, appeared in the Chinese villages. This seems to prove that the relation between urban and rural areas in China is to the disadvantage of the latter. If this view is correct, then, for the sake of the Chinese rural population, the lighter the connection between country and city, the better for the country.

To me there is truth in both these points of view. The first theory applies to economic relationships in a normal situation; the latter, to the present situation in China. Let us analyze the rural economy on the basis of which the relationship which should have provided prosperity for both sides has failed and has even caused disaster in the villages.

DISTRIBUTION OF LAND AND THE WELFARE OF THE PEOPLE

When one comes to examine the economic decline of the country, what strikes one most forcefully is the system by which tenant farming is carried on. When a man has no land of his own and rents land from others, he generally has to give at least one-half of his main crop to the landlord as rent. Is such a rent high? Let us see what this amounts to in relation to total income. I shall take one village as an example. In Kiang-ts'un, a village near Lake Tai midway between Nanking and Shanghai, the average area cultivated by each peasant family is 8.5 *mow*, which is equivalent to 1.29 English acres. The average production of rice is forty bushels per acre, each bushel weighing 67 pounds, a rich harvest in China. Thus every peasant family in good times will produce on the average about 51.6 bushels of rice. The average size of a farm family is 4.1, which, referring to the consumption of food, is equivalent to 2.9 adult males (according to the

Atwater scale, which has been adjusted by us). On the average, every male adult eats 7 bushels of rice, or 470 pounds, while an average family will consume 20.3 bushels of rice. Subtracting the quantity consumed from the total amount produced gives us 31.3 bushels. Now in case the land is rented rather than owned, the normal rent will amount to one-half the total, or 25.8 bushels. After paying the rent and reserving the amount needed to feed the family, there will be no more than 5.5 bushels of rice left. We may presume the value of supplementary products, including handicrafts, to be equivalent to about 10 bushels of rice. Thus, after the rice is eaten and the rent paid, what the family can spend amounts to about the value of 15.5 bushels of rice. Is this enough to live on, assuming that the items of general expenditure for a Chinese farmer are proportionately as follows: 42.5 per cent for rice, 42.5 per cent for other expenses, and 15 per cent for agricultural reinvestment? According to this, a family probably needs the amount of money equivalent to the value of 20.5 bushels of rice for other expenditures besides that employed for basic subsistence. If a family has no other income besides that from the farm, it will probably lack the value of 12.9 bushels of rice.[1] In order for such a family to survive, it must either find other sources of income or go into debt.

It is true that, if the farm is somewhat larger, the surplus after the farmer has paid his rent will be some-

1. [See the comparative material on family budgets in three villages of Yunnan and the village of Kiang-ts'un in Hsiao-tung Fei and Chih-i Chang, *Earthbound China* (Chicago: University of Chicago Press, 1945), pp. 84–108 and 297–302. The explanation of the apparent discrepancy appearing in the figure "12.9" may lie in an assumption that part of the supplementary products are consumed by the family.]

what increased. But not only is the amount of land available for cultivation restricted but under present farming techniques the area of the farms is limited to that amount of land which the farm families themselves can cultivate. In an analysis made by us in some villages in Yunnan of the problem of farm labor in the busy seasons of the year, it was found that husband and wife by themselves could cultivate only 3 *mow* of land. In other words, if they wished to run a larger farm, they must either hire help or exchange their labor for extra help in the busy season. The amount of land cultivated thus depends not only on availability but also on the labor force. Generally speaking, the area which a family can cultivate by themselves cannot exceed by very much the amount cultivated by the average farmer of Kiang-ts'un.[2] Landlords who own comparatively large areas of land are not able to cultivate the land by themselves but usually split the land up into small pieces which they rent out to tenants. Thus, from the point of view of management, the problem is not so much one of redistribution of land as of improved techniques of cultivation and of organization.

Actually, even an equable distribution of land among all the inhabitants of a village would not in most cases increase the area of the average farm by very much. Compared to areas farmed in the West, even the amounts of land held by so-called "wealthy landlords" tend to be insignificant.[3] A redistribution of land would not relieve

2. *Ibid.*, chap. xiii, "Farm Labor," pp. 141–49.

3. [Li Tso-chow, in a paper on "The Big Landlords of Wei-Hsien, Shantung," republished in Institute of Pacific Relations, *Agrarian China* [Chicago: University of Chicago Press, 1938], reports one family as owning 8,000 *mow* of land (or about 4,000 acres) by local standards of measurement; 24,000 by the official standard *mow* of China (pp. 15–17). In this same volume, Wu Sho-peng,

the pressure of population upon the resources provided by agriculture. The need to decrease the population of the rural areas would remain in force.[4] Yet it would be a mistake to think that, because the redistribution of lands would not increase the area of the farms by very much, owning their own land would contribute nothing to the welfare of the people. According to my statement above, if the farmers of Kiang-ts'un did not need to pay rent, they probably could live fairly well on what they themselves produced. The value of the harvest and of handicrafts together being equivalent to 61.16 bushels of rice, this would allow 20.3 bushels of rice for food, 20.3 bushels for consumer's goods, and 8.4 bushels for agricultural reinvestment. And this would allow them the minimum standard of well-being described by the phrase, "not hungry, nor freezing."

RURAL LIVELIHOOD—HANDICRAFTS AND AGRICULTURE

If the foregoing analysis is correct, tenant farmers cannot rely upon the products of their land alone for maintaining even a minimum standard of living. But tenant farming has existed in China for a long time. Why did not the problems connected with it become really serious until about twenty or thirty years ago? I believe that

in "Land Concentration in Northern Kiansu," reports landowners holding 10,000–20,000 *mow* (pp. 11–14). Yet the "lord" or rich man of the Yunnan village described by Fei in *Earthbound China* (pp. 278 and 296) became a rich enough man to build a large temple and large house by having acquired 300 *mow* of land. Merchants who are reported to have acquired "huge amounts of land" have bought up 300–500 *mow*.]

4. "The fundamental fact, it is urged, is of a terrible simplicity. It is that the population of China is too large to be supported by existing resources" (R. H. Tawney, *Land and Labour in China* [London: George Allen & Unwin, 1932], p. 103).

difficulties in rural economy did exist from very early times but that, in the traditional rural livelihood, there was a factor which prevented serious conflict between landlord and tenant. This factor was the rural industry or handicrafts, mentioned before as a supplement to farm incomes. China has never been a purely agricultural nation. As far back as the time of Mencius, the peasants were being urged to plant mulberry bushes at their homesteads for the production of silk.[5] China's early lack of interest in commercial relations with the West rested partly upon her self-sufficiency in producing both raw materials and finished products for the necessities of life. These necessities were not produced in large-scale manufactories, to be sure, but were scattered throughout numerous villages. Besides the specialized products of certain regions, such as the raw silk known to the English as *tsatlee*, which came from a small district near Lake Tai, the tea of Lung Ching, and the china of Ching-te-chen, widespread rural industries,[6] such as cotton-spinning, were carried on by many farm families very largely within the home. In my youth I helped my grandmother spin cloth, and among my mother's marriage gifts there was a spinning wheel. The fact that these manufactures were scattered among the various families was probably an obstacle in the way of improving them

5. "Let mulberry trees be planted about the homesteads with their five *mau*, and persons of fifty years may be clothed with silk" (James Legge, *The Works of Mencius* in *The Chinese Classics* [2d ed.; Oxford: Clarendon Press, 1895], Vol. II, Part I, chap. iii, p. 13).

6. [*Peasant Life in China* discusses the importance of the silk industry in Kaihsienkung; *Earthbound China* gives an analysis of the economic role of the cottage industries of basketmaking and weaving and the larger-scale paper-making manufacture in villages of Yunnan.]

but an important fact in the traditional livelihood of China. The additional income from such family industries gave the farmers who had insufficient land to support them enough to live on.

Let us return to the problem of the small size of the average Chinese farm. We may say that the direct cause of this is that the rural population is too large. Why is this so? Some people may regard this as a foolish question in that they think that the growth of population is a biological rather than a social phenomenon. Or, again, they may see the basic cause of overpopulation in the value placed by traditional Confucianism on a large family. But from the point of view of labor requirements there is, as I indicated above, still another answer to this question. Rural activities are quite seasonal. The farmer's busy time, when more labor is needed to get the work done, alternates with the farmer's slack time. The difference between the amount of labor needed for the busy time and the slack time is great. Actually, the number of people in the village is just enough, with present techniques of cultivation, to enable the people to cultivate their farms at the periods of special activity. Thus, from the point of view of agricultural production, the population of the Chinese rural districts is not too large. In fact, during the latter part of the Sino-Japanese War there was a shortage of labor in a number of villages. Not only were many men conscripted but some fled their homes to avoid conscription. Unless there is an improvement in agricultural techniques, the population of the rural districts is not likely to increase. And yet there are certainly too many people to permit all to enjoy a good standard of living. Even though agriculture demands a large labor force for short periods, there remains about two-thirds of the year when there is no work for the extra laborers. As a result, there is periodic unemployment. We are "spreading out over a year all the labor which is needed for just the busy time."

In the past this extra labor occupied itself with handicrafts. Rural industry, co-operating with agriculture and sharing with agriculture its source of labor, was able to maintain the local economy in a healthy state. In this case, even though the landlord took his half of the produce of the land, there would still be no unrest among the people. Those who are critical of the part played by the landlord may regard the existence of the rural handicrafts as affording simply an opportunity for the landlord to squeeze more from his tenants. But, from the point of view of economics, there was a genuinely organic adjustment of agricultural techniques, the demand for labor, the size of the population, the area of the farms, the rural handicrafts, the amount of rent, and the rights of the landlords. So long as such an adjustment gave the people a standard of living which was "not starving, nor freezing," traditional Chinese society could be maintained. Any economic system which did not maintain such a minimum standard could not have endured.

THE TRADITIONAL MECHANISM OUT OF GEAR

During the last one hundred years the traditional mechanism or organic adjustment mentioned above has begun to break down. How did the breakup begin? I should say that the one important gear broken was that of the rural handicrafts. Other parts, such as agricultural technique, size of population, farm area, amount of rent collected, and the rights of the landlord, have remained relatively unchanged. Following the decline in rural industry, the traditional adjustment which had maintained a minimum standard of decent living for the peasants no longer functioned.

It is easy to see that the decline in rural industries was the result of competition with Western, highly mechanized industries, since with their large-scale production they were able to decrease costs and improve the quality of their products. "Local products" became the synonym for inferior. How could the homemade goods compete with the handsome, cheap, and often even more durable foreign goods? The fact that the market for handicrafts was taken over by foreign goods gave to those who could afford to buy them a higher standard of living while at the same time it created unemployment in numerous villages. The ruin and poverty which followed the decline in rural industries resulted from a purely impersonal force against which there was no way to rebel or to defend one's self. If a countrywoman who has spun some cloth cannot find anyone to buy from her, whom can she blame? She will simply sigh and cease to spin. She will have to put all her hopes on the harvest from the land. But when the earth must bear the expense for the whole family, the difficulties which result from the traditional system of landholding and rental come sharply to the fore. The landlord has not lost the right of collecting rents, and, moreover, the rents have not even been reduced. In the traditional society landlords are not producers; they are "fed by others." In a changed situation they do not lower their demands. On the contrary, stimulated by the influx of imported goods, they have raised their standard of living and consume more than ever before. They will not easily give up the income they derive from rents. But when they go to the country to collect these rents, they find that their tenants are no longer so docile. How can they be? If they pay their rent, they will be faced by famine. If they are to maintain their very lives, there must be conflict between them and the landlords. The landlords, on the other hand, do not understand why the attitude of their tenants has changed. The unwillingness of the tenants to pay the established rental seems to them quite unreasonable. But in the eyes of the tenants the landlord who comes to collect their last grain of rice becomes a sort of devil who bears folk away to death. The fact is that noiselessly and invisibly the invading foreign industries have dislocated the traditional mechanism by doing away with the rural handicrafts, which, unbeknown to the landlords, all this time enabled them to enjoy their special privilege.

The force dislodging the rural industries is both powerful and deeply penetrating. Behind it are big battleships and guns, the "imperialism" of well-organized industrialized countries. The traditional handicraft worker who is also a farmer lives in scattered villages, belongs to no organization, and has no power of modern science to help him. It is an ironic fact that the power and the influence of the landlords are very weak compared to those of foreign industrialism. But the landlord is near at hand, and, in order to live, the peasant must resist him. Thus the land problem of China becomes more difficult day by day.

THE REASONABLE WAY OUT FOR THE
LANDLORD CLASS

"Not starving, nor freezing" is, we must confess, a minimum standard of living for the people. Since the right of man to live is recognized, the right to struggle for such a living standard ought to be recognized as just and reasonable. This is the fundamental basis of the doctrine of "people's livelihood." But China is being constantly drained of her wealth. Her original industrial productivity, far from making the country people well-to-do, has made them "rather poor," and from rather poor the descent has been to "very poor," and from very poor to the lowest depths of poverty. Since the prosperity of the country has been eroded away in this way, it is not strange that the peasants are demanding their right to have back as high a standard of living as that which they had formerly.

Under such conditions, if we cannot revive our declining industries, those of the landlord class who have been depending upon income from rents must sooner or later be attacked and then eliminated. Landlords who cannot themselves cultivate the land can only rent their land out to others. Yet this piece of land will not feed both the landlord and his tenant at one and the same time. The landlord cannot find a way to eliminate the tenant and get income directly from the land, but the tenant can cultivate the land without the assistance of the landlord. Therefore, in a struggle between landlord and tenant, the tenant will probably win. Since the tenant system in China is not built up on the basis of a surplus of produce from the land but rather is supported by the surplus income derived from rural industries, rural industries really determine the basic rents for land and, in fact, the future of the landlord class. It is true that the use of oppressive measures may for a short time bring about "forced agreements." But to employ force means additional expense at the moment and, moreover, leads to bitter and unlimited resistance in the future. Rent seizures do not offer a permanent solution.

From the landlords' point of view the reasonable way out should not be to take action which will only hasten their own ruin but to try to adjust themselves to the changed circumstances and find some means of livelihood other than merely living on rents. If they had wished to continue in the old way, it would have been well to have struggled against the invasion of foreign industries in the very beginning. For their own protection, the landlord class, who are in such a critical situation, should give up the right of collecting rents from the peasants. Only in this way can the country as a whole gain the support of the peasants and their co-operation in overcoming the present economic crisis. The farsighted policy of Sun Yat-sen that "every cultivator should have his own piece of land" is the reasonable solution.

But the goal of Chinese rehabilitation should also be the reconstruction of her industries. And, in order to build up national industries, we must rebuild rural industries, so that our peasants, who make up 80 per cent of the population, can have a share in an improved standard of living. It is true that the destruction which is the result of civil war has made more difficult an increase in productivity. Yet the effort to rebuild industry must be made. The Chinese have endured and can continue to endure suffering, but simple endurance seems hardly to be a reasonable ideal.

We see now how the development of modern cities with their flow of imported foreign goods, on the one hand, and large-scale manufacture of articles of daily necessity, on the other, has deprived the countryside of an important source of income. It is true that, if the growth of these modern cities had stimulated prosperity for agriculture by creating a greater demand for rural products and thus raising their price, it might have compensated rural industries for the injuries done to them. But unfortunately things have not worked out this way. It is true that the increase in population in the large cities has increased the demand for foodstuffs, but the farmer does not get more for his produce, since, owing to the very poor system of communications, it has been found cheaper to import food from foreign countries than to buy it locally.[7] Modern transportation in China seems mainly to connect consuming centers. Railroads connecting large cities parallel ancient lines of communication along the rivers rather than supplementing them, while rather primitive means of transport for the most part tend to connect rural and urban areas. Moreover, there is no direct connection between the modern city

7. [In 1928 an American commercial attaché wrote: "China grows enough wheat to keep all the flour mills in the country running at full capacity throughout the year, but only a fraction of this wheat can be gotten to the flour mills sufficiently cheaply to make it profitable for the mills to buy it. . . .

"Even were the Shensi farmer to present his wheat to any of these Chinese flour mills, they could not afford to take it, so long as they would be obliged to pay the transportation costs in getting the wheat to their mills. They could, in all cases, better afford to go to the Dakota farmer and buy his wheat at the prevailing American market price and transport it a thousand miles across the Pacific, and several hundred miles up an interior waterway in China than to take the Shensi farmer's wheat as a gift" (Julean Arnold, *Some Bigger Issues in China's Problems* [Shanghai: Commercial Press, 1928], p. 1). This situation has hardly been improved in recent times, especially with the damage done to rolling stock by wartime destruction.]

and the village, since the traditional town serves as a middleman. Here live in idleness the unproductive landowners who formerly bought manufactured goods from the countryside but now prefer Western-made goods. Garnering in the rural products as payment for rent or interest on loans, they send them to the city in exchange for foreign goods of which the country people catch never a glimpse or, if they do see them, are unable to purchase. Instead of having an expanding economy, life for the countryside is deteriorating, and the common folk are forced to cut down on the bare necessities of life. Under the present system any profits to be made from farm products will accrue to the middleman or speculator rather than to the producer, and the countryside continues to support those who consume modern manufactured goods, the *rentier* class, without gaining any benefit from modern industrialism for itself. It is true that the villagers have little use for such things as toothbrushes and tooth paste, foreign coffee or preserves, or ready-made foreign-style clothing, but they could make use, for example, of better tools of all sorts, seeds, fertilizers, blankets, warm knitted underwear, and leather shoes.

From this analysis we can see that, to some extent always, but even more at present, urban centers and rural areas are antagonistic to each other. And, if there is no great change in the future, this antagonism will continue; that is, the rural areas will continue to be at an economic disadvantage. Under these circumstances the severing of rural and urban relations is good for the villages but very bad for the cities. Knowing this, we can understand why during the recent war with the Japanese the villages in the interior of China had a period of prosperity and why Chinese rural co-operatives developed so quickly. This also explains why the Communist-controlled areas have not worried about the severing of rural-urban relations and the dislocation of Chinese town economy during the civil war. Taking the last one hundred years, Chinese cities and large towns have not achieved a sound productive base. They have been largely distributing centers for foreign goods. Although foreign goods have not reached rural areas in any large quantity, this has drained the wealth of the country, since the foreign goods gained by exchange are consumed in the towns in place of local handicrafts. But when the relations between the townsfolk and villagers are cut off so that the townsfolk's sources of income are stopped, the importation of foreign goods must stop unless funds are obtained through relief or loans of various sorts. This cannot continue indefinitely.

THE GROWING GAP BETWEEN RURAL AND URBAN AREAS

Ever since the building of railways connecting the northern and southern parts of China, the separation of the three river basins as natural areas has gradually lessened. It is hard to believe that China will ever again be divided into north and south. But the separation between urban and rural areas which has developed during the last one hundred years has become a new source of cleavage. During the war with Japan, Chinese troops practiced guerrilla warfare, occupying the interior and leaving rail lines and key points in the enemy's hands. Guerrilla tactics of this sort have an economic basis, as we have shown above. But, as a result of these wartime tactics, economic relations between town and country have become more and more disrupted. From a short-term view of the situation, the countryside is not suffering, since once the rural people are cut off from the towns much of their produce will be kept from moving out, and, as a result, they will have enough food to live on. This does not seem a very good way out, however. Once the rural areas are detached from the urban centers, they must rely entirely upon themselves. Self-sufficiency leads to security of a sort, but the price paid is the lowering of the standard of living and a return to a more primitive way of life. This does not seem to be the right solution for Chinese economic problems. Although the decision of the villages to rely wholly upon themselves will not actually decrease very much their already extremely low standard of living, it creates for the towns and cities which have lost their hinterland a very critical situation indeed. We must recognize that Chinese villagers tend to prefer the alternative of lowering their standard of living by self-sufficiency to that of keeping up relations with the town in that this latter means that they will be exploited by the townspeople and still have little chance to raise their standard of living.

The industry and the commerce of the modern cities are not supported by the consuming power of the rural producers. The markets for modern manufactured goods are among city and town dwellers, and the purchasing power of these people depends largely on income derived from the countryside in the form of rent and interest. The separation of the country from the town directly threatens those city dwellers who live on their income from the country and affects the traditional organization of town economy. In order to continue to maintain the traditional relations of town and country, it becomes necessary, then, for the *rentier* class to break the blockade, even if by force. And this, I understand, is one of the real causes for the present civil war, a war in which the traditional privileged class is fighting against the people who refuse to carry on their traditional obligations. As the conflict goes on, the antagonism which has accumulated for centuries becomes fiercer, and it seems that, unless there is a real change in Chinese economic structure, the proper relation between town and city cannot be established.

Chinese economy cannot afford to stay in a situation which means bankruptcy of the town, the reduction of the village to more primitive conditions, and, taken as a whole, the decline of Chinese economy. The question is: How can urban-rural relations be restored? The direction which this restoration should take is quite clear: an effort should be made to realize the principle mentioned earlier—that rural and urban areas should mutually supplement each other in production and consumption. But to achieve this end is more difficult than to conceive it. Essentially the problem is how to change towns and cities into productive centers which can maintain themselves without continually exploiting the villages. From the point of view of the rural areas, the problem is how to increase their incomes either by developing rural industry or by developing specialized agricultural cash crops. City and village are equally important; they should work together. But the initiative in making changes must come from the city. It is most essential that the character of the traditional town be changed from a group of parasitic consumers into a productive community in which the people can find some other source of income than that derived from the high rents for land and exorbitant interest on loans. In other words, the main issue is land reform.

VII / *Social Erosion in the Rural Communities*

EROSION: OF LAND AND OF MAN

Lilienthal, in his book on the TVA in America (*Democracy on the March*), uses the term "mining" to describe the methods of growing cotton on the played-out farmlands of the South, methods by which for the sake of a single crop the wealth of the soil was taken out and its riches exhausted. Even the addition of chemical fertilizers could not combat the evil effects of soil erosion accelerated by floods—floods at least in part directly due to the decrease in cover crops, deforestation, and the resulting lack of organic matter in the soil to make it hold water. It was through this sort of erosion that the soil of the Tennessee Valley, originally quite fertile, became barren and unproductive. Lilienthal's project for the TVA was to restore the organic equilibrium of nature, so that man should no longer attempt to defy nature but to understand and co-operate with her, and should bring it about that the river, whose floods had been a yearly threat, should now be harnessed for the service of man.

If I mention the TVA here, it is not so much in order to make clear Lilienthal's ideas as to draw an analogy between physical erosion of land as described by Lilienthal and the social process which is going on in China today. In China today we are interested in promoting the principles of soil conservation. But we shall also do well to extend this concept to rural life in general, that is, to the conservation and encouragement of talents and human resources. In considering the TVA experiment, it has become clearer to me that Chinese agriculture is not only a matter of techniques but also a system of customs, institutions, morality, and leadership which, in the past at least, worked together to maintain the life of China. But in the last one hundred years it seems to me there has been at work a process of social erosion suggesting that which went on in the Tennessee Valley. As a result have come poverty, illness, oppression, and suffering. In the traditional organization of society it appears we had a system under which most of the people could manage to live. It is true that standards of living were very low and that life was not without its hazards and disturbances. Yet there was achieved a stable organization of society in which most people did not starve and did not suffer excessively. This traditional way of life was built upon an economy which carefully served the land and preserved the fertility of mother-earth so that people could continue to live upon the land without destroying its richness. The Chinese attitude was not one of the exploitation of resources but rather of companionship with and adaptation to nature. From what I understand of

Lilienthal's work, he seems to have been working toward a goal very close to the Chinese conception.

Any visitor who has had an opportunity to observe the life of a Chinese countryman cannot but perceive his close bonds with the soil. He carefully uses those things which grow from the land and then as carefully turns them back to the land. In this way human life is not a process of exploiting the earth but only a link in the organic circulation. And the fact that, when life has left a body, the corpse goes into the soil is a source of comfort. It seems there is a close bond between man and the land. This is doubtless one reason why it is so important for a man, when he comes to die, to go back to his own native spot, the place from whence he came. The stream of life of which everyone is a part flows parallel with the life of the earth, which has its own life.

In the folk society man and the land are linked by strong bonds of sentiment—an attachment called, in Chinese, the *sang* ("mulberry") and the *tzu* ("catalpa"), a name derived from the two varieties of trees (*sang* and *tzu*) traditionally in ancient China planted near the house.[1] Men, it is suggested, are like plants that take their nourishment from the land. But when the springtime of their growth is past and they come to the fall of life, they must return to the land, just as leaves of a plant fall and come in time to nourish its roots. Such a conception, in recognizing genuine ties between man and nature, emphasizes the fundamental unity of life. But

1. [According to the *Book of Poetry* one should revere the *sang* and the *tzu* because they symbolized parental and even ancestral ties. Since then the phrase has come to stand for a man's attachment to his own region and particularly to his own homestead.]

when carried to extremes an attachment of this sort may appear unreasonable and even absurd, as, for example, when overseas Chinese laborers work day and night to send back money, penny by penny, and leave as their dying command that their coffins be transported from afar back to their native spot. This kind of yearning to return even after death can hardly be appreciated by the West. But in Chinese traditional culture such a feeling is of supreme importance. Among my own forefathers there was one man who passed a high examination and was sent by the government to Yunnan to supervise the salt-mining industry. At that time Yunnan was a far frontier and, moreover, dangerous on account of the prevalence of malaria. In fact, my ancestor contracted malaria and died soon after his arrival. He had a younger brother who, when he heard the news, made up his mind to go to Yunnan and bring back the coffin of his brother. After working for several years to save up enough money for the trip, he set out, struggled through all kinds of difficulties in wild mountain country, and at last succeeded in having the coffin carried home. To accomplish this task, which to modern minds would appear quite unnecessary, he not only sacrificed his career, since he gave up his chance to take the government examinations, but even risked his life. In our family chronicle this exploit is written up as though it were the one really big thing which had been done in the family.

It seems to me that one does not understand what the underlying feeling here is if one does not see that this strong sense of the importance of kinship ties is extended to a symbolic kinship between man and the earth. Better not to leave one's own place, but, if one goes, one must come back. Coming back from Europe in the steerage during the war, I met Chinese peddlers who had been living for years in France selling a certain type of jade. They could speak nothing but Chinese and had taken no part in the life of this foreign land. Instead they had struggled to save every penny they could in order to send it home where their relatives put it into the building of fine houses. When the Nazis closed the borders, they risked their very lives to see that the money got out, and now, old and worn out, they were going home, not to enjoy life but merely to die.

From the peasant's first act of the morning in collecting manure from the streets to the putting of a coffin in the ground, all is part of the same big cycle of nature and of man's attachment to the soil. And it is the strength of this relationship which to my mind has maintained Chinese culture throughout the years. I hope, however, the reader will not misunderstand me as advocating this type of attitude. I wish merely to emphasize the existence of this spirit in Chinese life and particularly in relation to the changes now taking place—changes which I call the process of "social erosion."

Among country children in my native area one of the most common names is Ah-kên ("The Root"). Man has roots. Indviduals are like the branches of a tree which has grown up from its roots and which depends for its well-being on the strength of these same roots. For man the roots are the society from which he gets his material well-being and his education; they are the family, the village, the region, and the nation. These roots are something like what Lilienthal refers to in American life as "grass roots." From the point of view of society, whether human or plant, that which is taken away must eventually be returned. If basic elements are taken away by a "mining" process, then after a certain length of time the community will become bankrupt. The cycle of giving and taking away may become very complicated. The TVA represents the more complicated, the Chinese farm the simpler, form of the process. The greater and more highly developed the cycle, the higher the standards of living; but, simple or complex, it must still remain a cycle of reciprocal action. The mining process is suicidal, for, though it may give returns for a while, eventually it exhausts all available resources, and the mining town becomes a ghost town. Thus it is clear a healthy community can survive only when it can draw adequate nourishment from its environment.

THE DESERTERS—RURAL BOYS WHO DO NOT COME BACK HOME

In our traditional culture the men of talent were spread throughout the local communities. Recently I analyzed with Professor Quentin Pan the source of origin of nine hundred and fifteen scholars who passed the high-ranking imperial examinations (those above provincial rank). The distribution was as follows: 52.5 per cent came from the Chinese traditional town, 41.16 from rural areas, and 6.34 from intermediate small towns. If we divide the series according to provinces, the percentage from rural areas surpasses that from urban areas for four provinces in North China: Shantung, Anhwei, Shansi, and Honan. These statistics show that even in this field of activity, which requires long literary training, half of the students were at this time from rural areas. Still more significant is the question whether their fathers had literary degrees or not. This turns out to be about the same for rural as for urban areas, the ratio in the city being 68 to 33 and in the country 64 to 36 (the larger number applies to those whose fathers did have degrees).

This shows that, in China, men of ability and learning were not concentrated to a very large extent in the city as they are in the countries of the West. According to Sorokin's theory, in the West, unless a man becomes a city dweller, he will have no chance to rise.[2] But, in China, the tradition of "the leaves going back to the roots" seems to have helped to maintain the high quality of the rural population. People who attained high social honors still did not forget their place of origin and, when they were old at least, would come back and would do their best to make use of the prestige and advantages gained outside for the benefit of their home community. Thus, having one distinguished man in an area might lead to there being more, since this man would help others to get a start. Able men formerly did not leave their grass roots permanently. As a result not only did intellectual men share in the life of the countryside but they also helped to encourage others in the same region.

Now the situation is quite changed. At the present time those whom the community supported in their youth no longer return in order to become useful to it. Recently we said goodbye to a number of college graduates who were threatened with unemployment. One of their teachers was urging them to go back to their own

2. Pitirim A. Sorokin, *Social Mobility* (Microfilm Collection, University of Chicago Library, 1927).

birthplace. All agreed that in principle this would be a good thing to do but said that, speaking realistically, they could not go back. And actually I do not know of one case where a graduate has returned to his own community. Instead they either managed finally to squeeze into positions in the city or remained unemployed, living with the help of friends. They were unable to go back to their homes not only because they felt unwilling to do so but because it would have been impractical for them to try to live there. At the time that they had left their homes there seems to have been some force from outside which pushed them out. Their parents, brothers, and other relatives had done their best to help them realize their dream of going to the city. In order that they might do so, some families even sold land or borrowed money. Yet, when the young people came to graduate from college, they were apt to find that these several years of absence had severed their links with the home community. In the country there are no jobs for college graduates. It is not so much that in the modern college the student may have learned Western science or technology as that he has become accustomed to a new way of life and to a system of ideas quite different from that found in the country. The change is enough to make him conscious of the fact that he is different. So the college graduate of today feels that in the country there is no one to talk with, no one who understands him, and he often even feels alienated from his own kin. If he does go back, he will not find a suitable job where he can apply the knowledge he gained in college, since Chinese colleges are not preparing men to work in rural areas. What he will have learned in the university is usually knowledge imported from the West. It is true that knowledge should have no national boundaries and that the need in present-day China to modernize quickly must be met by the introduction of Western knowledge. Modern knowledge must provide the plan for the reform of the traditional system in the rural areas. But the point is that the students who have been trained in the universities have usually failed to find a bridge by means of which they might bring over and apply their knowledge to their own communities. Without such a bridge, modern knowledge is ineffectually hanging in the air. And as a result the countryside, which is constantly sending forth its children, is losing both money and men.

This holds true not only for most Chinese university students but also for the middle-school students. In Yunnan I studied a village near a walled town. A short distance from the village was an agricultural school. This village depended for its livelihood upon market gardening. The village gardeners used to point to the school farm and laugh, saying, "The teachers and students in that school plant their cabbages like flowers. That doesn't pay." On the other hand, the teachers, who had been trained in modern methods of agriculture, told us that the cabbages grown by the villagers could be improved, and they even demonstrated to us improved varieties. There was truth on both sides. Unfortunately the students when they left school would not be able to continue using modern techniques or experimental methods, since their families neither could afford nor did they wish to do so. There seems to be an unbridged gap between the school and the farmer. The farmer is not prepared to learn from the school. As a result the graduates of this agricultural school either became teachers in the primary grades or entered the military academy to become officers, or some of them did nothing at all and simply spent their time loafing around the district town. Parents who send their children to school believe, according to the traditional idea, that education will give promotion to a higher social level. But they are not rich enough to enable their children to complete the education which is necessary to permit a young man to take a job in the big cities. On the other hand, for young men who have passed a number of years in being educated, to go back to working in the fields would be a disgrace in which the family would share. So they are caught and are unable to go forward or back. It seems that during the last few decades the army and party (Kuomintang) organizations have attracted people of this sort; this explains to a certain extent, I believe, modern Chinese Fascistic tendencies. It reminds one of the situation in Japan before the war, where young men from rural areas frustrated in other careers became part of the political and military machine and developed extremist ideas which sometimes even led to irresponsible attempts to seize power. Formerly, the traditional educational system took care of such people by enabling them to come up for examinations, the passing of which gave some official status and enabled them to achieve satisfactory social positions in the community as petty gentry. Moreover, they might keep on working and hope to pass a higher examination. But changes in the present educational system and the gap between the modernized city and education in the interior now all combine to frustrate their ambitions.

College graduates have more chance for employment in the city than do the graduates of the middle schools, to be sure, but even for them the problem is essentially similar. In the first place, there is little opportunity for them to reform the traditional ways of doing things by using the modern methods in which they have been trained, and, second, since there is no way for them to earn a living through productive activities, they must do so by striving for power and influence in the political field. Thus in a poor community there is always the burden of maintaining a huge number of political appointees in administrative offices. This explains some of the inefficiency of our administration. Thus I am afraid that the present educational system has not successfully carried out its function of modernizing China but on the contrary has drained off the sons of the well-to-do farming class from the country and brought them to town without providing them with useful employment there. This I call the "process of social erosion."

THE PARASITIC LAYER

Some may think that modernization always implies urbanization. Modern civilization is the product of the city, and the city population must of necessity come from the country, since the city cannot replace itself. In the country the able man does not have a chance to develop his abilities, but, once he comes to the city, he finds opportunities for developing them. In this sense the city is the place where human capabilities may be realized. Potential talents of the countryside, we may say, can be developed only through the process of urbanization. But this principle does not hold entirely for China. I mentioned above Lilienthal's work. From what he says I suspect that this principle is not alway true for America either. Especially in the south of the United States there seems to have been going on a somewhat similar process of social erosion. As in China, the process of organic circulation has been disrupted, and men and wealth have been constantly drained away. The TVA, as I understand it, aims, by introducing modern knowledge, to restore this circulation and, by creating the bridge I spoke of above, to restore prosperity. To create a bridge, there is needed not only knowledge of modern techniques but a utilization of the human element in such a way that those who have received a modern education will be able to go back and serve their own communities. Without such a bridge, the development of the city will cause a dislocation of the social mechanism.

At present the growth of great urban centers is like a tumor from which China is suffering. The economic aspects of the unfavorable relations between city and country I explained in the foregoing chapter. Here I merely wish to add a cultural perspective to the picture. It is not correct to my mind to take the modern city as representing Western civilization and the rural areas as representing the traditional Chinese civilization. In my opinion the modern Chinese city is the product of the contact between East and West. Those individuals who, through contact with Western culture, have changed their way of life and their way of thinking will not find themselves able any longer to live in the country. Some portion of them will be taken in by newly developing urban enterprises. But, since such enterprises are limited in number, there will be sure to be some who are left out to roam about without being attached to anything. Thus there develops a new type of person, one who avoids productive work in either city or country but rather goes in for seizing political power. This new type of person is both directly and indirectly recruited from the country. Before the contact with the West, the examination system would have taken care of these people, and they would have continued to live in the country or small towns as gentry. Being versed in the classical Confucian philosophy, they performed the function of the "man who knows." It is true indeed that such men were parasitic in so far as they derived their support from the working people, living mainly as they did on their rent from land. But, since they continued to live in the country, there was at least no large outgo of wealth from the countryside.

If in Chinese modern cities industrial enterprises might be quickly developed, the elements that have been taken in from the countryside might find their proper place. Although the countryside would then still suffer from a certain measure of "erosion," this would be compensated for by the prosperity of the city. And, like TVA in America, China might be enabled to turn back benefits from the city to the country. If this were so, the situation in China would be very different. Unfortunately China is still in the status of a semicolony. Large-scale industrial development is not feasible. The essence of Western civilization, industrialism, has not been really introduced as yet. What has been brought in is the superstructure of the more superficial elements of this civilization, including the desire for material comforts and satisfactions. But there has not been constructed as yet the material foundation on the basis of which these things would make sense. This lack of foundation creates a special class of people who live superficially in Western culture but without a traditional base from either the West or the East. These are both the victims and the directors of China's tragedy.

BENEATH THE FLOOD

Erosion of land takes place when the land is bare of grass and tree cover and thus not able to hold water. Then floods follow and bring disaster to the people. Social erosion has a similar effect, causing an exodus of the population. In the process of social erosion, at first only the top layers are carried away, those economically well-to-do and better educated who no longer choose to remain. But, as both wealthy and able men are washed away in this fashion, the pressure of city industry continues with this fact to press the country people still further down into poverty. Well-to-do people who remain become poorer. And the really poor can no longer remain but must desert the land. Movement away thus comes from both upper and lower levels, leaving behind only the middle class of peasants.

As for the elements mentioned above who are left outside of productive work, they tend to form a new class of organized parasites. Since villagers are both naïve and not very well organized, they may easily become the prey of such people. When I was in a village one time a roving individual came and tried to blackmail my landlord, because, he said, my landlord's son, who had left military school, was a deserter. Actually the boy had done nothing wrong, and the man was simply trying to work a racket. I said to this man, "You come from the country yourself. How would you like it if someone like you came to your village and tried to bully and blackmail the people there?" He could not find an answer. I felt that the man himself was rather pathetic, a dislocated drifting individual. But it is people such as this who have aroused the hatred of the peasants. The lot of the conscript is a hard one also. The government takes all the able-bodied men from the country and enlists them. But, when these men are discharged, no one pays any attention to them. Country people say that those who have gone as soldiers will never return to farming. Once enlisted, they become disorganized and are no longer accustomed to obedience but rather to looting and other wild behavior. Thus conscription accelerates the processes of social erosion. The banks are broken and a flood results: in this case, peasant revolt. The disorganization of life, economic, political, and moral, has confronted China with needs for new leadership and reform.

EDITOR'S NOTE

To most thoughtful and dispassionate Chinese it seemed, especially in the postwar years 1946–49, that the new leadership and reform for which they had been looking for so many years could not come from the repressive and discredited right but (because there was no effective "vital center") from the left. Yet, though it is obvious that Fei was looking forward to Communist "liberation," the leadership and the doctrine were to be Chinese in origin rather than either Russian or Western. The following sentences from a lecture delivered by Fei in 1947 at the London School of Economics present the point of view of the Chinese patriot who hoped for co-operation rather than domination by any outsiders in the solving of China's problems.

"If, in advancing to the present stage of technological development, the West had achieved a new order—that is, an integrated social system—the problem in the East would be simpler. All we would need to do is to learn to transplant the new form across the ocean. There would be difficulties, but if the new order offered greater material advancement as well as social satisfaction and happiness, reluctance would be only a matter of unfamiliarity, which could be overcome by better instruction. . . . The defect of Confucianism in denying the importance of man and nature relationship is apparent in our inability to cope with modern Western civilization. But the one-sided emphasis [of the West] on material advancement without due consideration of a corresponding development in social relations is equally dangerous. It is therefore clear that the process of social change in China should not be a mere transplantation of Western culture but should imply a reorganization of social structure in conformity with the inherited spirit of harmony and integration. The question of how these two developments can be made to keep pace with one another is essential for the solution of the present chaotic state of affairs in China, which is manifested in grave economic and political disturbances. These disturbances are primarily symptoms of a process of change without a definite aim. Unless China is to perish, we have to find our own solution from our inheritance of experience over thousands of years. . . ."

Life-Histories

A Note on the Life-Histories

Westerners interested in China have known China largely through the few sophisticated and Western-educated Chinese or, if Sinologists, through classical Chinese learning. In recent years descriptions of peasant life in the villages have begun to add an understanding of the problems and values of the common man. But of the provincial landlord and petty gentry, to whose history and function in traditional China Fei refers in his writing, there has been little direct documentation. Fei, in surveying the role of the gentry in the local community as well as in the imperial system as he does here for the benefit of his fellow-countrymen, does not find it necessary to add those realistic details which his readers would already know from their own experiences.[1] The six life-

1. In writing for Westerners, as in *Earthbound China*, Fei does give more detailed descriptions of the life and problems of upper and lower gentry. These are largely from an economic standpoint, however.

histories which follow, selected from a much larger number collected by Mr. Yung-teh Chow during 1943–46 in the *hsien*, or district, of Kunyang, the province of Yunnan,[2] as a part of his study of social mobility, do represent individuals of this sort. Since they were collected as a quite separate enterprise, they cannot be related point by point to Fei's analysis, but the careful reader will find much here which fills out the picture and corroborates his hints as to fundamental assumptions of Chinese life.

In remote Yunnan, Western influences have penetrated far less than on the coast; Fei's "social erosion" has been less active here than in other parts of China. Social mobility for the most part appears to follow old patterns. "Land breeds no land." The upward start toward rising in the world comes typically not through hard work and thrift in farming but through branching out into commerce, gaining advancement in the army, or employing other and less legitimate means for accumulating capital. A financial basis for the family once established, the gentry position is consolidated, socially through higher education for the sons, economically through the accumulation of land which will provide rents to live upon. But the breakdown of the traditional system in which moral authority as well as material power resided in the gentry seems evident here as elsewhere in China, and a local government "under the leadership of the better-educated and wealthier family heads," creating

2. Each *hsien* consists of hundreds of villages, themselves locally organized, but forming together an integrated community and possessing a political, economic, and cultural center. The *hsien* of Kunyang is located in a mountainous area about 60 kilometers south of Kunming, bordering Kunming Lake and connected with Kunming by steamboat and motor road.

a situation in which "the more scholarly would generally have great prestige in the making of decisions,"[3] seems largely to have given way to domination by the less educated and more unscrupulous. It is true that power derived from ill-gotten wealth and sustained by force receives some check not only from the traditional respect for learning but also from a social tradition supporting good human relationships, willingness to help others, and lack of arrogance. Although the desire for "respect from the people" influences the behavior of the elders, it appears to have little effect upon the restless and uprooted younger men.

It is difficult to determine from the materials we have here and those available for historical comparison just how disorganized life in Kunyang, Yunnan, during the years covered by the life-histories was in comparison with life in other parts and times of China. In China it has doubtless always been true that "in a closed economy the striving for material gain is a disturbance to the existing order, since it means the plunder of wealth from others,"[4] and that the traditional saying, "To be promoted in political rank is to become richer and richer," has long been accepted as part of the natural order of life. The ideal of the official who did not profit from office at all has rarely been realized, and it seems a "reasonable squeeze" has been generally accepted as a proper way for providing for one's family. But the rampancy and extensiveness of the corruption pictured here, if not in the careers of all the men at least in those of their sons,

3. See above, chap. iv, "Basic Power Structure in Rural China," p. 81.

4. Hsiao-tung Fei and Chih-i Chang, *Earthbound China* (Chicago: University of Chicago Press, 1945), p. 84.

indicates that the situation has worsened to the point at which a "change of dynasty" was usually called for. Of the sweeping changes, thorough disruption of the old order, fresh human suffering, and probable further corruption which have come through Communist "liberation," there is no indication in these pages, however. The six life-histories which follow all to some degree or other throw light on life as it was lived in a remote corner of China before Communist domination. How much or little remains of this old life in these days cannot be determined.

All personal names in these life-stories are fictitious.

The Scholar / Chairman Wang

*Chairman Wang, who comes from a genuine "scholar's family,"
represents the traditionally idealized gentry official and landlord. He is a Confucian scholar, without self-seeking or pride,
his ideal that of honesty, of serving the people, and of leaving
a good name to his children. "The most important thing for a
family is not money but that the offspring may do something
worth while." It seems also important to have had enough
money so that the traditions of culture could be maintained.
Wang's great-grandfather laid the foundations of the family
prosperity by exploiting iron mines and lumber, and the subse-
quent generations did not waste their inheritance. But Wang
has trouble in "serving the people" following the traditional
pattern of "neutralizing" or conciliation of opposing forces (as
described by Fei, p. 77). At fifty-four he would rather retire,
feeling too old for positions of responsibility, and would like to
have avoided the office in which later his lack of drastic action
against corruption loses him some of his former prestige. He appears even more helpless in regard to the behavior of his sons,*

whose relatively high degree of education seems not to have strengthened their morals. Of the four, one, an official of the Kuomintang, is so scandalously corrupt in office that he is dismissed; another becomes degenerate through opium addiction; the third, though not actually badly behaved, seems lacking in mental and moral fiber; and only the fourth escapes to a scholar's life in America.—EDITOR.

"Chu I-Chiang," or Chairman Wang—the chairman of the People's Political Council of the county—was a leading man among the gentry in Kunyang. At that time principal of the junior middle school and the two-year-system normal school of the county, he was the first one of the gentry whom I met. After my arrival in Kunyang, he came to my residence and asked me to be a part-time teacher at his school. I was deeply impressed by his earnestness. Although I was busy and had little time, I found it impossible to refuse his request. Through him I became acquainted with many of the gentry. We knew that he lived a simple life, was very popular, and, in general, had a very good reputation in the county. His family was well known as a *shu hsian chih chia*, or a "scholar's family." According to census data taken in 1942 by the Institute for Census Research of National Tsinghua University, among the population of 69,231, there were only six persons who were college students, four persons who had graduated from college, and three persons who had returned from Japan, France, and the United States, respectively. Chairman Wang had four sons—two of them had returned from abroad, one of them was a college student, and the other had graduated from a four-year-system normal school. Since I had been a guest at his home several times and knew him very well, I told him frankly that we wished to interview him and to write his life-history. Though he said humbly that he was not important enough to be written up, he asked us to talk with his youngest son, Wen-hua, first. He said that, if we had any questions, we might come to him with them at any time. After several days my assistant reported to me that Wen-hua would like to write a life-history of his father for us. Wen-hua was a student of the Southwest Associated University in Kunming, of which Tsinghua was a part at this time. Moreover, Wen-hua was a good friend of my assistant. As a result this life-history was the easiest to obtain of all those we collected. After two months Wen-hua handed us a life-history of his father. Since it gave few details, I asked him to rewrite it according to my suggestions. The final manuscript was satisfactory. My assistant told me that it was dictated by Chairman Wang in the first person and written down by Wen-hua. So it may be called an auto-biography. Much supplemental material was added by my assistants and myself.

Chairman Wang was born in a village which is about forty miles west of the walled city of Kunyang. One of my assistants had visited there twice. He describes it in this way: "The village is on a mountain, and communications are very difficult. Also the climate is very bad. The main occupations of the 585 villagers are blacksmithing, acting as merchants for the selling and buying of iron, mining iron, hiring out as day laborers, and farming. Every day at daybreak we could hear the sound of the hammers pounding iron. The village seemed full of activity."

The following passages are taken from Wen-hua's manuscript:

"The native province of my ancestors was Kiangsi Province. However, in the Ming dynasty, they came to Yunnan Province. In the beginning several generations were army officers. But my great-great-grandfather began to operate a big shop. Probably because of a decline in the business, my great-grandfather, Wang Kai-hsin, moved to Kunyang when he was thirty years old. He operated a shop there.

"My great-grandfather had studied six years in a private school. He was good at writing and in figuring with the abacus. He was very strong and was much interested in the study of military arts. After arriving in Kunyang, he was informed that there was an iron mine in the vicinity west of Kunyang. The area was mainly mountainous and inhabited by Lolos[1] and filled with bandits. My great-grandfather risked his life several times in going there to make a survey. At last, he decided to move into a village named Liu-ho-ts'un in order to try to mine the iron.

"He moved in, bringing with him several workers, some money, and simple household goods. But, because he could not understand the Lolo language, he was suspected by them of being a spy. He felt himself in a ticklish situation. He knew that, if he could not improve his relations with the Lolos, he not only could do nothing but also would be in great danger. So he invited the leaders of Lolos to have dinner at his home and talked with them frankly and pleasantly. He tried to tell

1. The Lolos are native peoples who live in the mountainous regions of southwestern China and have hardly been acculturated or Sinicized.

them of his ambitions and plans and lent them money when they were in need. At last, many Lolos became his good friends.

"Since he now felt quite safe living there, he moved his family to the village. At first, he engaged simply in buying and selling wood. He bought several hundred *mow* of thickly wooded mountainside and hired Lolos to work for him. If they were in need of money, he paid them their wages in advance. Since the Lolos got such favors from him, they were grateful and obedient to him. He, then, bought more mountains which were not only covered with forest but also rich in iron. Since the Lolos were backward in knowledge and were always in need of money, he was able to buy their mountains and forests very cheaply.

"After buying the forests, he associated himself with some merchants who bought and sold wood in the city and began to have the trees chopped down in order to sell them to the merchants at market prices. In a year's time he made a lot of money. He used part of the money to buy 20 *kung* of farmland which he rented to tenants. The rice collected from the tenants was quite enough for the family's consumption.

"Then he planned to mine the iron and hired many workers to dig it. He failed again and again but never lost his confidence. He hired more workers and continued to look for ore. At last, he discovered a rich vein. He was very happy and organized the mining of the ore, the melting of it into blocks, and its transportation for sale to the city. But, because of the isolated location of the village, the limited demand for iron in the market, the high cost of production and transportation, and the backwardness of the techniques employed in mining, he did not expand this enterprise. Nevertheless, he laid a foundation for prosperity in iron-mining for his family. Now the village was becoming the center of iron-mining in the district. This enterprise prospered particularly during the years of the War of Resistance against Japan.

"As a person, my great-grandfather was very strong and shrewd; he was benevolent to his friends and persistent in his undertakings; he had a sense of humor and a spirit of adventure. He passed away at seventy-three years of age.

"My great-grandmother was diligent and thrifty. She was good at tailoring, so many of the Lolo women came to ask her to cut out clothes patterns for them. She was clever, beautiful, and kindly. She bore her husband two sons and one daughter and died at sixty-nine years of age.

"My grandfather, Wang Chu-tung, was the elder of the two brothers. From boyhood on he had a very strong character. Once, when his father reproved him, he not only refused to eat anything at home but also stripped off all his clothes and threw them at his parents and left home without any property. He began to study when he was eight but left school at eleven.

"After leaving school, he did nothing but hunt and practice weight-lifting. He was tall and strong and with his strength beat everybody in his native place. He passed the military examination of the county when he was twenty-four and received the degree of *Wu Hsiu Ts'ai*, or Bachelor of Military Arts.

"He wanted to become an officer very badly. He felt that there was no future in living at home and decided to serve as a private in the army. He studied military science diligently and worked very skilfully, was honest and obedient to his superiors, and, after three years, was promoted to the rank of second lieutenant.

"During these years he found, however, that the officers were unfair to their junior staff members and that life in the army was corrupt. Sometimes one who had no 'pull' with the high officers worked faithfully, yet was reprimanded for no good reason. On the other hand, one who had a 'special' background had an easy time and was promoted quite rapidly. Moreover, my grandfather was upright in attending to public duties and therefore could not get along with his colleagues, who liked to gamble or to visit the houses of prostitution. He became disillusioned and left the army.

"After leaving the army he went back home and en-engaged in farming and mining. Because he was respected by the villagers, he was elected to be a manager of the public affairs of the village. He often settled or mediated quarrels for the people and helped to avenge the wrongs of others. Thus the strong dared not bully the weak, and the village was peaceful. If there were any lawsuits or calamities of any sort, or any illness, he was always the first to try to help solve these difficulties. He promoted improvements in the village, such as paving roads, constructing bridges, or building temples. Anything he undertook to do, he would fight it through. The people said after his death: 'He ate the rice of only one family; yet he wisely governed the affairs of one thousand families.' Since he did not care much for amassing property, he did not increase the wealth of his family. He was sixty-seven when he died.

"My grandmother was kind, hospitable, and industrious. She often gave charity to the poor and was a good wife to my grandfather. She gave birth to three sons and two daughters, all of whom lived except the third son.

"My father, Wang Hai-liang, was the oldest one among the brothers. He began his education when he was seven and worked diligently in school, making a good record.

"When he was around fifteen years old, the economic condition of our family became much improved. Both businesses, that of iron-mining and that of selling wood, prospered. My father had no need to worry about his family and devoted himself completely to studies. When he was twenty-three years old, he became a literary graduate, receiving a grant from the government through competitive examination. After three years, however, he was compelled to stop his studies on account of his father's death.

"Since he could not continue studying, he returned home and taught in a private school. Because of his devotion to this job, he gained a very high reputation. He died at the age of sixty-four.

"My mother came from a noted family. She was gracious, benevolent, and well disposed. She worked all day and set a good example of industry for us. She would never let us just eat and do nothing. She often told us that one who knew nothing about bitterness did not know anything of sweetness. She said: 'If one does not know the meaning of pain before thirty and does not become rich at forty, he can only look forward to the grave.' She also said: 'Every person respects the rich; every dog bites the people who wear shabby clothes.' She often said: 'Li tu jen pu kuai,' which means that no one is offended by too much politeness. She died at the age of sixty-eight.

"I am the oldest of three brothers and two sisters. The brother next to me in age, Chun-hui, studied in a private school for eight years. He passed the civil service examination and received the degree of *Hsiu Ts'ai*, or Bachelor of Arts. He has served in my native place for thirteen years as a special representative to encourage self-government. He is honest and righteous. [My assistant told me that Wang Chun-hui is a noted *lao hao jen*, or a "very good fellow." His business is in iron-mining and wood-selling, but he does not make too much money.]

"My second brother, Chun-chi, studied in a private school for five years. Later he graduated from the provincial normal school. He started to be a teacher in a private school when he was twenty-two years old and has stuck to this job throughout his life. He is enthusiastic and satisfied with his occupation. [Once he told my assistant: "Since teaching is a spiritual life, we should be contented with our poverty."]

"I was born in 1881. As the eldest son, my parents loved me very much. The proverb says: 'To have a son early in life is more important than to become rich.' When I was a month old, my father gave a dinner party to about a hundred and sixty persons. The guests included grandparents-in-law, relatives, friends, and villagers. The entertainment lasted for three days.

"I started to study in a private school at the age of eight. [One of his friends told me that, even when Chairman Wang was a boy, he studied very hard. Because of the reputation of his family, the teacher paid special attention to him. This enabled him to progress faster.] I liked to study because of my father's encouragement. My father arranged a special room for me and my brothers, so that we could continue our studies at home. He liked to recite poems and tell stories about the people who had become famous scholars. This inspired me.

"My father sometimes brought me to Kunyang and to Kunming, the provincial capital. This stirred me to study harder and gave me some knowledge of other ways of life which my schoolmates did not have. I came to the city of Kunyang to study at the age of fifteen. Since I was brought up in the country, I felt proud of studying at the same school with city students.

"I married at the age of nineteen. This gave me a new experience of life and further inspiration to study. My wife was a great help to me. Unfortunately, she died fifteen years ago, when she was fifty-five. [My assistant told me: "Chairman Wang's wife was tall and thin. She wore clothes just like a poor woman and was kind and warmhearted. Chairman Wang married a second wife and took on a concubine. His first wife gave birth to four sons, and his second wife gave birth to one daughter. The concubine is an opium-smoker."]

"At twenty-two I passed the civil service examination and received the degree of *Hsiu Ts'ai*. After receiving the degree, I taught at a private school in my native place. Because of additional income contributed by me, the economic condition of my family improved, but I felt that there was no future in a career there at home. My father served as a good warning to me. He had labored as a teacher all his life and had never got rich. Moreover, the political situation was in a transitional stage. The old system of education had been abolished. I thought that

I should continue to study. So I went to Kunming and entered the provincial normal school. The new system of schooling was quite different from that of the private school I had attended. In the latter only Confucian classics were taught; but in the former there were various courses, such as foreign languages, national and foriegn histories, geographies, mathematics, chemistry, physics, and physical education. All these aroused my curiosity. Moreover, I had had to struggle and worry, and it had been very hard for me to get this opportunity. Therefore, in the four years I was there, I applied myself diligently.

"After graduating from school, I was appointed as a teacher to the primary school of Kunming. The salary in Kunming was ten times higher than in my native place. My life was certainly much improved. I was most conscientious in my work. [One of his colleagues told me that he was praised for his modesty, his consideration for others, and his strong sense of responsibility. The students liked him for his teaching methods. He was asked by a number of schools to be their teacher, but he declined all invitations, because he did not want to change his school.]

"In 1913 the gentry of Kunyang suggested to the magistrate that he invite me to return and serve as the principal of the primary school of the county. If I were to refuse their request, they would think I was too proud, so I had to accept. [The colleague of Chairman Wang told me: "At that time everybody admired his ability. The school improved day after day under his direction."] In the next year I was also appointed as the chairman of the Office of Compulsory Education and as the general inspector of education of the county."

The colleague told me: "During these years he traversed the villages of the county and gave speeches to urge the peasants to send their children to school. Up to that time all the schools had been private. Teachers had taught only the Four Books[2] and other ancient classics. Nobody wanted to enter school under the new system, and the teachers could not use the new books as textbooks. So Chairman Wang invited them to the city to reeducate them. By degrees the new system of education became established. Wang's reputation in Kunyang rose a thousand fold."

The colleague also said: "Chairman Wang is a man with high morals. He felt that a good reputation was difficult to get but easy to lose; personality and reputation are the second life of man. He behaved carefully at all times. He often said that only good character could make others admire you forever; authority could not force others to be obedient to you in heart. If a person played tricks in order to cheat other people, it would be discovered in the long run; so the most important thing for us was honesty, persistence, and ability."

This same individual added: "In 1917 an educational inspector of the provincial government came to Kunyang and found that Chairman Wang's enthusiasm and constructiveness in local education had borne very good results. After going back to Kunming, the inspector sent a petition to the governor asking for a citation for Chairman Wang."

Wen-hua's manuscript continued:

"In 1918 I was elected by the gentry of Kunyang as a

2. The Four Books are the "Great Learning," the "Doctrine of the Mean," the "Confucian *Analects*," and the "Works of Mencius."

commander of the county guard. During the year I directed the soldiers of the county guard in paving roads, in constructing bridges, and in building a public house. [My assistant told me that graft was easy in this position but that Chairman Wang was honest. Chairman Wang often said: "The first rule in serving the people is honesty; and only after this rule is carried out can one possibly be praised by the people. Moreover, only long-standing virtue can bring benefit to one's posterity. The most important thing for a family is not money but that the offspring may do something worth while."]

"In 1919, 1920, and 1921 I was elected three times as a member of the provincial People's Political Council and appointed as inspector of opium suppression of I-mên District. [My assistant told me: "During these years, though Chairman Wang had a very high social position, yet he was as humble as ever. He treated everybody as an equal and liked to associate with any kind of people. He dressed in a common gown made of rough cloth. Several of his teeth, however, were inlaid with gold, which was then coming into fashion in the county."]

"For convenience in my work, my family and I moved to Kunyang. I rented my farms to tenants and went back only once a year to collect the rents. [My assistant told me: "Chairman Wang had then about 70 *kung* of farmland. His income could only provide for the tuition of his children. Though not rich, he was very happy. His daily life was reading his official correspondence and newspapers at home. If there were a meeting of the provincial People's Political Council, he would go to Kunming to attend the meeting. But he sponsored no bill. After the meeting, he came back home again. In 1921 he was also appointed as governor's counselor in bandit suppression. During these years his prestige reached its height. If he suggested any resolutions to the magistrate, they would be accepted without question. The gentry of Kunyang had faith in him. When he had any suggestion for the magistrate or gentry, he would not care whether it were adopted or not, though his suggestion was usually very important. He said: 'Is he not a superior man who manifests no indignation even though no one takes note of him?' He did not force his influence on anyone. He neither blackmailed any common people, nor flattered any high officials, nor boasted of himself."] In 1924 I was appointed as the head of the Bureau of Education and the inspector of education of the county government of Kunyang."

My assistant told me: "When he was in this position, he carried out a number of worth-while activities, such as discouraging traditional private schools, increasing support for public education, selecting good teachers, and encouraging the establishment of new schools. He was invited to attend all public meetings and to offer his opinion on most of the administrative activities of the county government. Because of his brilliant service, he was, at the recommendation of the governor, honored with a decoration by the central government. He felt very happy, because his services had been properly rewarded."

One of his colleagues informed me: "In 1929 the provincial government was reorganized. Chairman Wang was at home without any position. During these days he returned to his native place very often. He just stayed at home and encouraged his children to study hard in school. He never paddled them and scarcely even scolded them, because he hoped that the children would work hard of their own accord. He liked to hunt game of all sorts and appreciated country life very much. Sometimes he busied himself in buying and selling iron, but he never made much money. He often said: 'I do not seek to amass wealth; my sole desire is to have my posterity be wise.' "

The colleague continued: "In 1936 he was fifty-four years old. He was again elected chairman of the People's Political Council and appointed a member of the Committee for Opium Suppression. He felt that he was too old to take the responsibility of these positions. Nor as a good fellow did he want to offend anyone. He did not take situations as seriously as others, but he did everything according to the principles of 'clearing up misunderstandings and settling difficulties for others' and 'smoothing down matters instead of taking drastic action and pacifying people.' So he accomplished nothing important for the People's Political Council and the committee."

I asked my informant why, since Chairman Wang did nothing important for the people, did the gentry elect him, the government appoint him, and the people support him? He explained the reasons to me as follows:

"Why has Chairman Wang had the highest prestige among the gentry for more than twenty years? There are several reasons: In the first place, he has very good qualifications. Since he is a *Hsiu Ts'ai* of the Ch'ing dynasty, he is able to compose various classical literary pieces, such as couplets, birthday scrolls, elegiac prayers, and so on, which are still necessary for social intercourse.

But he is not only a Confucian scholar; he also graduated from the provincial normal school. Among the older generation of gentry, nobody is better qualified than he. His age and virtuous behavior are also reckoned in. Second, his children have added to his prestige. Thus, his first son is a returned student from Japan and is working in the provincial government; his second son is in the United States; his third son is the principal of a primary school of his native district and the head of the *hsiang*, although he is an opium-smoker; his fourth son is studying at the National Southwest Associated University in Kunming. Since scholars are traditionally respected by the people, his family is regarded as most promising. Third, when he was thirty-four years old, his prestige was increased by the following incident. Many of the gentry were jealous of him and anxious to involve him in some crime. It happened that a merchant was killed by bandits in his native district. Chairman Wang's enemies accused him of associating secretly with the bandits and even of being the main criminal in this affair. Moreover, he was accused of being a dictator in local affairs and of being corrupt. As a result, he was put in jail. Though his friends knew that he was innocent, no one tried to help him. But he himself was very calm and tough. He insisted that 'when the water is shallow, the stones will appear.' At last, the real facts came to light. 'Pure gold stands one more test.' Though he was not actually involved in this crime, he was impressed so deeply by what had happened to him that ever since he has acted even more carefully than before. He felt the ways of the world were difficult and dangerous. He is honest and righteous. He is neither proud nor mean before his superiors nor contemptuous and insulting to his inferiors. He is now sixty-four years old and has served the government for about thirty years, yet he is still *liang hsiu ch'ing feng*, or has 'two sleeves full of wind.' Fourth, since he is old and lacks energy to do heavy work, he is not averse to inviting the able and strong youths to help him. When he invites someone to help him, he is very earnest. He always goes personally to a man's residence to make the request. The one requested cannot refuse him through respect for his age. He trusts his junior staff members and allows them to take responsibility for their acts. For example, in 1940 he was appointed to be the head of the Department of Education of the county government. [My assistant told me that the People's Political Council has been canceled.] In 1942 he was also appointed as the principal of the normal school and junior middle school of the county. At the same time he was appointed as the chairman of the Mobilizing Committee of the War Resistance. It seemed impossible for one person to run these three jobs. But he did them easily. He chose Mr. Ch'en as his right-hand man in the Department of Education, asked Mr. Yuan to be dean in charge of the school, and requested Mr. Li to be general secretary of the committee. He himself only acted as their adviser and attended important meetings. When there were decisions to be made, the men in charge went to his home to ask advice. The county magistrate liked him because he did not like to create trouble."

My assistant told me further, however: "In 1943, owing to the emergency of war, the People's Political Council was reorganized. Wang was elected chairman. During these years the administration was inefficient, the magistrate of the county was very corrupt, the officials—especially the officials charged with conscription and collecting the land tax—were greedy, and the heads of *hsiang* or *ch'en*, and *pao* exploited the people by every means possible. The people naturally all hoped that Chairman Wang would come out strongly for the impeachment of these corrupt officials. Unfortunately, he was blind to all this. Moreover, some of the members of the People's Political Council co-operated with the magistrate in 'squeezing' money. Chairman Wang not only refused to join the people in accusing the magistrate to the provincial government but, when the magistrate was dismissed, wrote a eulogistic scroll to present the magistrate and saw him off at the bus station. As a consequence, his prestige was lowered to a large extent. If he had retired earlier, it would have been better for his reputation; in this case, the people would not have rebelled against his authority. Certainly, he himself recognized the situation. He often said: 'I am too old to do anything important. I have become a useless man.' Nevertheless, since he is not rich, he cannot retire to enjoy his old age. This is quite regrettable.

"Chairman Wang was accustomed to live a simple life. He generally wore a long gown of a dark color, a pair of homemade cloth shoes, and a cap. When he was invited to join a party or attend a formal meeting, he would put on a jacket. He smoked tobacco in a long thin bamboo pipe. When he rented a house in the city, all the furniture was made of wood of the old fashion. Hanging on the walls were several couplets written by noted scholars of the province. In the court were a couple of pots of orchids which symbolize the scholarly character. We often saw in his hall one or two pretty birds which he had caught in his native place and which he kept in a cage."

Another of his colleagues told me: "Chairman Wang's meals are very simple. His favorite pastime is playing mah-jongg. He plays it with several intimate friends almost every night. He goes to bed very late. He feels happy that all his sons can live independently. He often says: 'Some people leave their sons a full chest of gold; I leave my sons only the ancient classics.'"

We have already said that one of the sources of Chairman Wang's prestige is the social position of his four sons. So it is necessary to introduce them. My assistant gave me the following information:

"Chairman Wang's oldest son, Wen-hung, studied in a primary school in the city, the capital of the county of Kunyang. After graduating from primary school, he went to Kunming and entered a middle school, and from here he entered the Central Political Academy of the Kuomintang in Nanking. Graduating from the academy at the age of twenty-eight, he returned to Yunnan and served as the head of a division in the Department of Finance of the provincial government of Yunnan. After one year he went to Japan and entered Waseda University in Tokyo, where he received the degree of Master of Arts. He was the first to go abroad from Kunyang. After returning to China, he served as a secretary in the provincial government of Shansi. After six years he returned to Yunnan and served as a head of a division in the Department of Education of the provincial government. After four years he was recommended by the director of the Department of Education to the governor as a candidate for magistrate. For the purpose of approaching the governor he spent $500,000[3] to send some top officials to the governor, for entertainment, and for gifts to officials. The governor asked him many questions about his qualifications and the careers of both himself and his father. After visiting the governor, he spent a million dollars to buy gifts for the high officials of various departments and to invite them to have Western-style dinners. Then his appointment as magistrate was announced by the provincial government. Finally, he spent more than $100,000 on the petty officials of the government. Then he received his certificate of appointment. After succeeding in his campaign for the position of magistrate, he rushed back home to ask his father to get together two million dollars for his expenses in taking over the position of magistrate and to pay the salaries of faithful helpers. His father sold 200,000 *chin*, or catties,[4] of iron to meet this need."

My assistant continued: "One who wants to be a magistrate must have at least three million dollars for capital. Otherwise he cannot obtain this position. Though Wang Wen-hung spent such a large sum of money in advance, he got back this sum after half a year. 'The wool comes from the body of the sheep.' If he had spent more money for the position of magistrate, the people would certainly suffer the more, because he would then 'squeeze' more money from the people to compensate for his previous expenditures."

3. At that time this sum was equivalent to about 1,900 silver dollars, or about U.S. $1,000.

4. The *chin*, or catty, is a term of weight. One *chin* is equivalent to 16 *liang*, or exactly 1⅓ lb. (604.8 gm.).

One of Wang Wen-hung's helpers in his term as magistrate told me: "Wang Wen-hung is a man who is slow in his actions. He smokes a large quantity of opium. When he was a magistrate, he was very greedy. It seemed to him that this term of magistrate was his only opportunity for making money. If his junior staff member could not help him to get money, the junior member would be despised by him as having no ability. He considered himself so important that even his wife, also a college graduate, could not get along with him. He often quarreled with her. We saw that many attendants of the magistrate who came to our county made a lot of money in Kunyang. But we who followed him to the county under his regime were so poor that we did not even have enough money for traveling home with. After having been in the position of magistrate for two and a half years, he was reported to the governor for corruption and was dismissed. After being dismissed he was forcefully detained in the county by the action of the local gentry. After half a year he was released on condition that he return part of the money which he received illegally during his term of office."

One of the former schoolmates of Chairman Wang's second son, Wang Wen-ta, told me: "Wen-ta was clever and gentle. He studied very hard in school. In the middle school he obtained a scholarship twice. When he was twenty-three years old, he entered the National Tsinghua University in Peiping through competitive examinations. After studying there for two years, he left the university to serve as a member of the Provincial Headquarters Committee of the Nationalist party of Yunnan. In a year he gained a scholarship to study abroad from the Central

Headquarters of the Nationalist party through a competitive examination among the members of the party. He went to the United States in 1931."

One of Wang Wen-ta's friends in the United States told me: "Wang Wen-ta received the degrees of Master of Arts and Doctor of Philosophy at midwestern universities. Now he is working in the United States. He is married to an American girl, and they have two children."

Once Chairman Wang showed the pictures of Wen-ta's family to me and said: "I receive one letter a month on the average from my second son, Wen-ta. He usually reports to me about what he has been doing in the United States."

"Do you expect him to come back to China?" I asked.

"I can only let him do as he wishes," he answered, smiling.

My assistant told me: "Chairman Wang's third son, Wang Wen-chang, studied in Kunming when he was a boy. He was lively and handsome. But he seemed to be spoiled by his father. He liked to play and eat and did not like to study in school. His father let him come back to Kunyang and enter the county normal school. After graduating from the normal school, he taught in the primary school of his native place and managed his home and farm simultaneously. During these years he became an opium-smoker. He would smoke opium the whole night. He went to bed in the early morning and got up around two o'clock in the afternoon. He was lazy and in low spirits. Nevertheless, because of the prestige of his father and brothers, he was respected by the local people and elected to be a *hsiang chang*, or the head of a district government, and the principal of the central primary school of his native district."

My assistant continued: "The youngest son of Chairman Wang, Wang Wen-hua commenced his studies in the capital of the county. After graduating from the normal school of Kunyang, he went to Kunming and entered the provincial normal school. He entered the teacher's college of Southwest Associated University in Kunming when he was twenty-six. He is shy, gentle, and reserved. When he was still studying in college, he was invited by the magistrate to go back to Kunyang to serve as the principal of the normal school and the junior middle school of the county. After graduating from college, he went back to Kunyang. He said that it was out of the question for him to be appointed principal of the normal school and the junior middle school of the county. The magistrate appointed another man, Mr. Liu, as the principal of the school and asked Wen-hua to serve as a head of a division in the Tax Department of the county government. He was disappointed and thought of going to Kunming to find a job. However, his father was so old and the other boys in the family could not live with him, so he decided he had better stay home to keep his father company. Thus he agreed to assume the position."

My assistant also informed me: "In 1946 many of the gentry of Kunyang reported the corruption of the magistrate of the county to the governor. Wen-hua took this golden opportunity to attack the principal, Mr. Liu, for his inefficiency and dictatorialness. The magistrate was changed, and Mr. Liu was also dismissed by the new magistrate. Wen-hua took over the position of the principal but found that the salary was not enough to live on and that he was not paid regularly. The teachers could not support themselves by their salaries and, therefore, did not take their jobs seriously. He was disappointed and showed no more interest in this new position. He did not care much for the affairs of the school. Many of the students were encouraged to create disturbances by some gentry who were against him. Though he said, 'Disturbances can make a strong school,'[5] he did nothing to improve the situation. In reality, the difficulties were beyond his ability to solve. He was indecisive in everything and could not control his junior staff members. In a word, he lacked experience.''

My assistant added: ''Before he would not smoke, drink, and gamble. After he became the principal of the school, he felt that it was necessary to be social. Now he could smoke cigarettes, drink wine, and play mah-jongg. He would go to bed late and get up late, just like an old man.''

5. This refers to the Chinese proverb, "Disturbances can make the country prosperous," which itself is derived from Mencius: "When Heaven is about to confer a great office on any man, it first exercizes his mind with suffering, and his sinews and bones with toil" (James Legge, *The Works of Mencius*, in *The Chinese Classics* [2d ed.; Oxford: Clarendon Press, 1895], II, 929).

The Military Man / Commander Chu

The history of Commander Chu, not quite a warlord but a well-known local military figure of the old style, may throw some light on the social status of the military man in traditional China. Although he does not rank so high as one descended from a line of scholars, we still find him proud of his descent from outstanding military people as well as of his ability to lead and promote the welfare of his troops. This pride does not, however, prevent him from accumulating in service a "reasonable" amount of wealth, nor does his criticism of corruption in government enable him to keep his own family from scandalously corrupt behavior. More than Head Wang, whose prestige, rooted in scholarly attainment, is firmer, does his position in the community suffer from family misbehavior. On the whole, however, he is recognized as a leading member of the gentry, so important, in fact, that a newly elected competitor representative to the National Assembly of the Democratic Socialist party is asked by higher-ups to vacate his place in Chu's favor. Nor does

*he expect to pay taxes ("officials, with their relatives, formed
. . . a special class . . . exempted from taxation," as described
by Fei, p. 27), and he is insulted when someone tactlessly suggests that he might do so. According to his own conscience, he
is evidently a good man who has served his country and is free
to criticize the actions of others.*—EDITOR.

Before interviewing "Chu Sau-ling-kuan," or Commander Chu, I had heard much about his family, career,
and character. My assistants were local people and knew
their native place very well.

One afternoon one of my assistants and I visited Commander Chu's younger brother Chu Hsin. He was sitting
on a chair in the hall and smoking a pipe. When we
walked into his hall, he stood up. My assistant introduced me. Chu Hsin asked us to sit down.

"Is there anything I can do for you?" he asked my
assistant.

"I have wanted to call on you for a long time but
have always been prevented by business," I answered.

"Are you busy today?" my assistant then asked.

"Oh, no. Head Chow is busy and hardly ever has time
to pay calls. Certainly I welcome his coming."

Then I explained the significance and purpose of my
work and asked him if he would like to tell us something
about his ancestors and family. He said that he would be
very glad to tell us what he knew. He asked me many
questions about the work of the Institute for Census Research. After talking at length about the war and the
government, I fixed another time for my assistant to
come to talk to him and left his home. The following is
the record of my assistant's interview:

"Our great-grandfather, Chu Yuan, resided originally at a village named Wang Sien[1]—as you know. He was a farmer. Though illiterate, he was intelligent and upright. Our family was well-to-do at that time. But the village was filled with ne'er-do-wells, gamblers, and loafers who created many disturbances in the village. My great-grandfather often overzealously urged them to be industrious. As a result he was bitterly hated by the rascals and was shunned by the villagers. The location of the village was also unfortunate; since it was close to the lake, there was a flood every two or three years. When there was no flood, there would be drought instead. He felt that there was no future for him in the village.

"Because of the difficulty of living and his isolation in in the village, he decided to move into the city with his family. Before he left he sold 5 *kung*[2] of land and mortgaged 10 *kung* and rented the remaining 25 to others. Once in the city he rented a room facing the street and opened a grocery store for selling items such as salt, wine, tobacco, bean oil, sugar, and soap. The first two years in this venture were dull, for he lacked experience in business. During these years the whole family still depended for their living on the rent from their farm. My greatgrandfather wished to return to the village but feared the ridicule of the people. He found it very difficult to find a solution.

1. The village is situated at the edge of Kunming Lake and is 5 kilometers east of the city of Kunming.

2. In Kunyang the size of a farm is expressed in terms of *kung*, which is described as the amount of land which can be worked by one laborer in one day. The standard *mow* of 666 square meters is roughly the equivalent of 2.6 *kung*. For further discussion on this see Hsiao-tung Fei and Chin-i Chang, *Earthbound China* (Chicago: University of Chicago Press, 1945), pp. 28–30.

"One day an old woman came to my great-grand-father's shop to buy some bean oil with an earthen pot which held a little more than 1 *chin*, or 1 catty. Usually 1 *chin* from other shops did not fill the container, but this time the container was filled to the brim. The woman was so happy that not only did she become a regular customer at my great-grandfather's shop but she also told of this generosity to others. As a result, his business improved gradually. He learned from the old woman that a person is always glad to get a little more than the amount he has bargained for. Furthermore, my great-grandfather noticed that it is wise to have a pleasant disposition and to acknowledge the fact that the customer is always right. If the customer has received a good impression, he will come again. Thereafter, his business prospered by leaps and bounds.

"Since he was now admirably successful, he continued to enlarge the business. When he needed capital, he would go to his village to sell farmland. He rented two more rooms at the back of his shop for purposes of residence and after ten years was able to buy them. My great-grandfather thus became quite a rich merchant in the city. He felt satisfied with his successful change from a farmer to a merchant. Many people who despised him before had changed their attitude and now admired him. He continued in his business until his death at the age of seventy-five.

"My great-grandmother was a good helper at home. When she was still in the village, she was industrious and willing. She not only managed her house and garden well but also worked on the farm. She was kind to others, with a quiet speech and amiable disposition.

After moving into town, all her neighbors admired her for her ability and kindliness. She talked to all customers with a ready smile, even though they did not buy her goods. She passed away at seventy-one years of age.

"My grandfather, Chu Hun, was an only son. He entered a private school at the age of nine but stopped schooling after five years to assist his parents as a salesman at their shop. He recorded the accounts during the day and in the evening reported them to my great-grandfather.

"My grandfather married when he was eighteen years old. My grandmother was a well-bred girl. The young couple loved each other and led a happy life. My grandfather stayed at home and kept my grandmother company all day. But my grandmother encouraged him to pursue his studies and to take the civil service examination. He came to feel, too, that, although his family was wealthy, he still had no real prestige. A wealthy man without other attainments was not respected by the people. At twenty-one he began to study military science and arts. He also got up very early and practiced weightlifting. Everyone admired his great strength in feats of this sort. After three years he passed the county civil service examination and received the degree of *Wu Hsiu Ts'ai*. In another three years he passed the provincial civil service examination and received the degree of *Wu Chü Jen*.[3]

3. The ancient Chinese civil service examination was divided along two parallel lines: (1) The *wen*, or literary examination, was established for the purpose of selecting officials; (2) the *wu*, or military examination, was established for choosing officers. Examinations were of three different grades: (1) That of first grade took place once every three years in the prefecture or county. Those who passed the examination received the degree of *Hsiu Ts'ai*, or Bachelor of

"After receiving his degree of *Wu Chü Jen*, he was respected by the local people everywhere. Those who met him would bow to him. If there were an important military affair, he would be consulted by the magistrate of the county before any action was taken.

"When my grandfather was thirty-six years old, he sold all his farmland and his house in the village and bought 30 *kung* of farmland near the city and added a room to his city home. The rent in terms of rice collected from the tenants was more than enough for the maintenance of the whole family. He enjoyed both his wealth and his reputation. The only thing he had to do was to give daily orders to his family and servants about what should be done. The villagers envied his leisurely life in the city.

"My grandfather was tall and strong, a man of marked individuality. He was deliberate in his decisions and would never change his mind. My father told me again and again that my grandfather's orders had to be obeyed and his every word taken note of, otherwise my grandfather would scold and beat them. My father and uncle feared him very much. On hearing his commanding voice, they would quiver. My grandfather died at the age of seventy-three.

"My grandmother was a kind, gentle, pretty, and virtuous woman. When my grandfather lost his temper,

---

Arts. (2) That of the second grade took place once every three years in the province. Those who passed the examination received the degree of *Chü Jen*, or Master of Arts. (3) That of the third grade took place once every three years in the capital. Those who passed the examination received the degree of *Chin Shih*, or Doctor. Those who passed the examination or examinations not only received special honors but also became the candidates for high or low official positions.

she was so patient that she would never get angry with him. Because of her affableness, the business at the shop was wholly dependent upon her. She managed the housework, served her family, and entertained guests. My grandmother felt that, since my grandfather was a man of reputation, she had to uphold his honor. Throughout her busy life she never complained. She paid special attention to the education of my father and my uncle at home, because she understood that the future reputation of our family depended on the next generation. If young people were ill-bred, she herself would be responsible for the criticism which would come to them. She died at seventy-six years of age.

"My father, Chu Kan, studied in a private school for three years. Though he was intelligent, he had no interest in the academic field. During his years in school he often played truant. One day he told my grandfather that he was going to school. In reality, he gathered a group of children and led them to a hill to play war games. He told them that everyone should bring his own weapons, such as clubs and stones, and he divided them into two groups of equal strength and ordered them to fight each other. Consequently, many of them were injured and cried. This incident was told to his parents. My grandfather punished him by having him kneel on the ground and beat him until he promised not to play truant any more and to study harder in school. Hereafter, my father applied himself to his school work, but no marked progress was evident.

"My grandfather thought that, since my father was tall and strong and had no wish of becoming a man of learning, he would probably do better in studying the military arts. So my grandfather allowed him to stay at home and look after the business at the shop and often told my father about his enthusiasm and experience in the field of military arts. My grandmother also told my father about her experience in handling the business, but he showed no interest in anything except military arts. My father married at seventeen. Three years later he began to practice military arts.

"My father had a great deal of strength and beat everyone in boxing and fencing. He could raise a square stone of 60 *chin* with one hand. He passed the civil service examination of the county at twenty-six and again passed the examination of the province and received the degree of *Wu Chü Jen* at twenty-nine. [My assistants told me that their family was well known to be *i men wu jen*, or an "outstanding military family."] Then he was chosen by the gentry and appointed by the magistrate to be captain of the county guard. He collected a group of volunteers and trained them daily in the use of the sword and spear. He was adventurous and brave.

"During the period of 1847–72 an uprising of Lolos spread widely throughout Yunnan. Kunyang did not escape. My father led his group of volunteers to resist the enemy at Kunming Lake. He was unfortunately wounded in the left leg by a bullet of the enemy and fell from his boat into the lake. He was rescued at once and escorted back home, where the local people showed him great respect and he was visited by the magistrate personally. After two months his wound healed. The medical costs were, of course, paid by the local government.

"After this incident my father stopped serving in the county guard. He was asked to be an agent of the salt transportation station between Kunming and Yuchi by a salt company in Kunming. The salt was transported by horse. He collected fifty cents per horse as a service fee. At the end of every year he would also get some bonus. The salt which dropped on the ground also belonged to him. [My assistants told me that this was a job which paid well and that it was not easy to get such an occupation at that time. They said that the manager of the company trusted him because he was an honest man of good repute.] After five years he had accumulated $120,000[4] from this work.

"My father had the same personality traits as my grandfather. He was very temperamental. In any argument he would never yield to others. He easily lost his temper and knocked others down. Once when he quarreled with a man, he got angry and hit the fellow with his hand so hard that he died from hemorrhage. The families, relatives, and members of the clan of the deceased were furious and rushed into our home in a body. They destroyed everything in sight and butchered our livestock for dinner. At the funeral everyone who walked by was invited in for a good meal and given a big piece of white cloth.[5] Monks and Taoists were invited to chant the canon of Buddhism and to go through rituals to keep off spirits or to recite dirges. The cost for us was incalculable. After this incident the manager of the salt company had no more confidence in my father and fired

4. This was the provincial note of Yunnan, the official rate of which to a Mexican dollar was ten to one. The Mexican dollar was worth about U.S. $0.5 at the normal rate of exchange. The province had its own note, because it was then in reality independent from the central government until the beginning of the Sino-Japanese War in 1937.

5. The white cloth is used to symbolize mourning for the dead.

him as an agent of the salt transportation station. More-over, my grandparents passed away in quick succession. Their funerals cost our home a great deal of money. At this time our home became a mere shell of four walls. My father sold 6 *kung* of farmland to meet expenses. He re-gretted that the fight had caused us to lose half of our property. [My assistants told me that later, though Chu Kan became more controlled than before, after this his prestige decreased day by day until the third of his four sons became an officer.]

"My father treated us very severely. If we did not obey his orders, we could not escape his heavy punishment. My father went to bed early and got up early; he was in good spirits every day. He liked to putter around. He could not rest in leisure; he was clever in mind and quick in action. He died at the age of sixty-eight.

"My mother treated us very severely too. She trained us to be brave and adventurous. If any of us showed signs of cowardice, she would scold him fiercely."

My assistants told me that Chu Kan's wife was proud and haughty. She was conceited and complacent, tend-ed to show off and look down on common folk, liked to gossip and nag at others, and hated persons who did not flatter her. The local people said: " 'If the wife is virtuous, the disaster of her husband will be less.' She is equally responsible for the calamity of her husband." Though adversity had fallen upon her home, she did not change her attitude.

An old man who is a clan member and former school-mate of Commander Chu told me: " 'Chu Ssu Ling Kuan' was born in the walled city. [The city is the capital of the *hsien* of Kunyang.] He has two older brothers and one younger brother. When he was a young boy, he looked handsome and imposing. He was quiet, reserved, and stubborn. If there was something which did not suit his fancy, he would cry unceasingly. He often bullied other boys, and no one could retaliate because Commander Chu was too strong for them. Since he had marked individuality and unrivaled courage, his father let him serve in the army.

"Commander Chu entered a private school when he was eight. He was very interested in school work and made rapid progress in it. His teacher praised him highly, and his schoolmates respected him verymuch. This made him study harder.

"After four years in the private school, he was recommended to enter a military primary school in Kunming by a friend of his father. He felt most fortunate in being able to study here, as few persons in his position had this opportunity. This inspired him to work very hand. On account of his good record, he was sent to the military middle school in Nanking on the recommendation of the military primary school. He was very happy at having this golden opportunity. He felt that his native place was comparatively backward and that Nanking would give him a fine chance to widen his knowledge.

"After three years he graduated from the military middle school and entered the military academy at Pao-ting, then capital of Hopei Province, through competitive examination. This was the turning point of his future career, because the academy was then the center for Chinese military training. He studied there for another three years. After graduating he returned to Yunnan Province and served in the army as a low-ranking officer.

"Commander Chu's financée was engaged to be married to him by his parents ten years ago. At this time his family was in fair condition. Therefore, after his return, his parents thought that it would be wise for the marriage to take place, since this would be a good opportunity to 'show off' their well-educated son. They gave a dinner party to about four hundred persons. The guests included relatives, friends, members of the clan, local gentry, officials, and the schoolmates of the groom. The entertainment lasted for three days."

As to his career, Commander Chu himself delivered a speech at the inaugural meeting of the Association of Veteran Officers in Kunyang. This was his campaign speech for representative of the National Assembly. One of my assistants reported to me that Commander Chu spoke for two hours and that it was said that his speech was very frank and honest. My assistant was also one of the members of the association, because he had served in the army as civilian personnel during the early years of the Sino-Japanese War. My assistant was elected secretary of the association and took down a complete record of the speech. Commander Chu said:

"I began my career as a soldier as a first lieutenant in the army. After serving one year I was promoted to the rank of captain and became commander of a company. I shared the money given me among my company.[6] I cared for my soldiers and respected the people. My troop was then stationed at the border of Kwangsi and Yunnan.

6. Commanders of any sizable company usually are given a sum of money to be given to the soldiers. However, commanders, as a rule, keep most of the money and distribute only a small portion to the soldiers. Commander Chu, therefore, was doing something unusual.

My mission was to suppress the bandits—this I carried out with complete success. From attacking the bandits I captured a good deal of money and goods. When I captured these things, I used them to improve the living of the soldiers and to supplement the expenses of the junior officers to encourage them to serve loyally. This satisfied my troops, and I accomplished my mission very easily. After three years I was promoted to the rank of a major and the commander of a battalion."

One of Commander Chu's colleagues told me that "he did not want money, but would rather get ahead." But this was only one factor in Commander Chu's success. Another important factor was his quality of leadership. He knew how to lead his men. Once when we were sitting side by side and talking about war news and the Chinese Nationalist army at the magistrate's dinner party, his face became scornful. I immediately took this chance to ask: "How did you lead your troops?"

He explained to me: "The most important thing in soldiering is morale. Leadership, good living conditions, training, and the relations between the officers and soldiers, between the commander and the junior officers, are the fundamental basis of good morale. We should not let the junior officers feel that they are only fighting for the commander. The whole group is a team, and every member should be working toward the same goal. During peacetime we should pay special attention to discipline, but it should be self-respecting and self-governing. Moreover, the troops should co-operate with the local people. The seizure of private property should be eliminated."

The colleague of Commander Chu also told me: "Following his promotion to the post of commander of a battalion, Commander Chu bscame most ambitious. He had a very strong sense of duty, and he was most successful in suppressing the bandits. The rich people, the merchants, and especially the local civil officials were grateful to him and presented him with various gifts.''

A clan member of Commander Chu informed me: ''During these years Commander Chu's family was in difficult economic straits on account of a bad drought. Moreover, the family was large, including seventeen members, and this meant that everyday expenditures were high. Although they ate very poorly, had few new clothes, and reduced unnecessary expenditures to a minimum, they could not make ends meet. At this time all the brothers were struggling very hard for a living. The oldest brother, Chu Fu, had borrowed a large sum of money and gone into the rice export-import business between Kunyang and Kunming. Chu Fu was intelligent and careful, for he had studied nine years in a private school. He made a great deal of money, and the family depended on him for a living. Commander Chu's second older brother, Chu Lo, also borrowed a sum of money to go into the rice-noodle business in a village. On account of his lack of experience, he lost money. Later he rationalized: 'Failure is the beginning of success.' So he borrowed another sum amounting to 100 *tael*[7] of silver to start a wine factory. Because of the small amount, he lost money again. Owing to these failures, he felt too discouraged to try again. But the debt must be repaid. He liquidated all his assets in the wine factory but still owed 175 *tael*. When

7. This was a Chinese unit of money roughly equivalent to one and a half silver dollars.

he returned home in disappointment, his creditors were still pursuing him."

The clan member of Commander Chu continued: "But when the news of Commander Chu's promotion became known in our native place, the condition of his family changed completely. His parents and brothers showed their sense of their new high position. At once the local people one and all began to speak of his father as 'Lao Tai Yeh,' or 'Grand Old Gentleman.' When Chu Kan stepped into a teashop or a restaurant, he would immediately be greeted with enthusiasm. Commander Chu's mother was especially proud. When she went to the market to buy something, she purposely asked the price of this or that. If the salesman knew her and lowered the price, she might buy it; otherwise, she would ask: 'Are your stupid eyes blind? Don't you know who I am?' Commander Chu's second older brother was no longer in great debt because the creditors dared not ask him to repay the money any more. Commander Chu's younger brother, Chu Hsin, had become an opium-smoker and a gambler and had long been despised by the local people, but now he was called 'Sze Lao Yeh,' or 'The Fourth Old Gentleman,' and flattered with flowery remarks."

The clan member added: "After residing at the border of Kwangsi and Yunnan for five years, Commander Chu returned to Yunnan with his troop and visited his home, bringing with him ten boxes of precious goods including 5,000 *tael* of silver. The boxes were carried by five horses. He bought 50 *kung* of farmland with his money, and all his family got new clothes."

Commander Chu himself said in his speech: "After

being stationed at Yuchi two years [my assistant told me that Commander Chu had taken a concubine there, because his wife had borne him no child], my troop was ordered to move to the border of the provinces of Szechwan and Yunnan to suppress more bandits, the notorious leader of whom was named San-new Lee. After fighting several times, I defeated them and killed Lee. I was immediately promoted to be commander of a regiment."

The clan member said: "After being promoted, he returned to Yunnan with his troops and visited his home again with thirty boxes of captured silver and other precious articles. These boxes were carried by fifteen horses. He bought more than 100 *kung* of farmland. He was talked about by the people everywhere in Kunyang and was praised to the skies."

The clan member also informed me: "When Commander Chu returned home the second time, he rebuilt the tomb of his great-grandfather with granite and set up columns and sculptured lions and horses of stone on the ground in front of the tomb." This made clear not only that some of the descendants of the dead in this tomb had prospered but also the filial piety of the descendants. Commander Chu did it because he considered his promotion to his high office as a result of *hao feng-shui*,[8] or "good wind and water," of the tomb of Chu Yuan.

Once a schoolteacher talked with me about Com-

---

8. *Feng-shui*, or geomancy, is based on the assumptions that the *Wu-Hsing*, or Five Plants, the *Pah-Kwa*, or Eight Diagrams, the direction of surrounding objects, and the physical configuration of the landscape have influence on a grave and in turn on the prosperity or misfortune of the descendants of the deceased.

mander Chu's family. He said: "When Commander Chu was promoted to be a commander of a regiment, his brothers and nephews were feared by the local people for their unreasonableness. Chu Hsin, twenty-nine years old, was formerly despised by the people, and he thought that now would come his chance for revenge. The active local gentry felt oppressed by the power of the Chu family. They feared that they would be foremost among those to be hated and attacked by the members of Commander Chu's family. So it would be better for them to give 'Sze Lao Yeh' a position. Thus the gentry elected him the head of the Bureau of Finance of the county government. The magistrate also praised him openly for his ability. At that time financial matters of the county government were controlled by a committee organized by the magistrate and twelve members of the gentry and were independent of the provincial government. After Chu Hsin assumed this position, he became the most powerful individual among the gentry of the county. He controlled not only finance but also education and construction and other public affairs. If he did not agree to a plan, it would not be carried out. The people who had lawsuits with others would necessarily ask him for help. If the lawsuit was not so serious, he would settle it by himself. If it were difficult to solve, he would discuss it with the magistrate and indicate the side he favored. The magistrate had to agree to his opinion. Then the other side would lose the lawsuit, even though it had an airtight case. Before he promised to settle a lawsuit, both sides must promise to accept his decision. Unless the case involved his relatives or friends, he would settle it justly.

It was said, therefore, that he was *tou tao yamen*.[9] As to his income, nobody knows how much he profited; but after four years he resigned his position and later built a big house and bought 30 *kung* of farmland."

Commander Chu said in his speech: "During the Revolution of 1911 I was in Shanghai and Canton. When I was in Canton, I served as commander of a guard battalion for Dr. Sun Yat-sen for almost two months. After returning to Yunnan, I continued to serve in the army and fought against the Manchurian army in Szechwan and Kweichow. [A junior colleague in the army of Commander Chu told me: "During his stay in Kweichow, Commander Chu recommended his oldest brother, Chu Fu, to the governor of Kweichow Province for the position of magistrate of a county.] Later I was appointed to be vice-commander of a division in Kwangsi Province."

Commander Chu continued: "After taking over this command, I noticed that the soldiers of the division were not well trained and that the commander was unable to lead his troops efficiently. The enemy before us was very strong. Nevertheless, I had to stay there and do my best. At last we were attacked by the enemy. After fighting one day and one night, my division collapsed. The commander was dismissed, and I was promoted to succeed him."

A junior colleague of Commander Chu informed me: "Commander Chu tried to withdraw his troops to the bank of a river in order to improve his position. He hoped to hold the enemy there until the arrival of reinforcements. But the enemy kept on his heels. He re-

9. *Tou tao* means "number one." Since both lawsuits and public affairs were first settled and approved by him, his office was the "first door" of resort.

treated, taking with him his personal property, but when he was only at the middle of the bridge across the river, the enemy rushed up and reached the bank of the river from which Commander Chu was escaping. The soldiers became disorganized, and everybody struggled to get across the river first. As a result, the pontoon bridge collapsed. Many soldiers and Commander Chu fell into the river. Fortunately, he was not far from the bank and was able to swim this short distance. He very narrowly escaped being captured or killed. All his money, silver, and precious articles accumulated through the years were lost. He went to Kweichow to meet his oldest brother and requested him to return home with him. Chu Fu refused, because he had accumulated a mass of money which could not be transported on such short notice. Chu Fu was afterward killed by the enemy coming from Kwangsi.''

A clan member of Commander Chu told me: ''Commander Chu regretted deeply his defeat and the death of his oldest brother. The local people criticized him behind his back and said that the reason for his failure was the evil-doing of his family. When he became an officer, his brothers and nephews in his native place had done many wicked deeds, such as beating the common people and blackmailing them. Commander Chu felt that the criticisms of the people were reasonable and blamed most of his failure on his family. He was too discouraged to serve as an officer again.''

The clan member continued: ''After retiring from the army, he bought a house of four rooms as his residence in Kunming. Henceforth, he did not send any more money back home. To avoid being subject to the bad opinion of the people of his native place was one of the reasons for his residing in Kunming. Though at times he stayed in Kunyang, most of his time was spent in Kunming."

In fact, Commander Chu was still one of the most influential gentry in Kunyang. I asked the clan member if Commander Chu might lose his position as a member of the gentry in Kunyang. He replied: "Commander Chu felt that the only way to correct the bad impression made by his family on the local people was to be of service to the people. That was why he tried to do something for his native place when the opportunity came to him. The political situation in Yunnan was then in chaos. A number of warlords occupied each a part of the province and there carried on warlike preparations. During the civil war which followed there was a group of soldiers who came one day to Kunyang. After arriving in Kunyang, they plundered the people The officer of the troop demanded of the magistrate and the gentry 50,000 *tael* of silver. Commander Chu bravely argued with the officer. He told him about the poor economic condition of the country and said emphatically: 'If you can find 50,000 *tael* within this city, I will be glad to have all of my property confiscated.' The officer was convinced, so he dropped his claim and after two days moved his troops to another place."

This was not the only good act Commander Chu had done. The clan member said: "At another time there was a company of soldiers coming to Kunyang as vanguard of an army. They were stationed outside the east gate of the city, being sent to investigate the condition of Kunyang to see if it could support their whole army. After several days Commander Chu led a group of volunteers to inquire their business. He warned them not to stay at Kunyang.

The soldiers refused to listen to him. He then ordered the militia to encircle them. Consequently, the company of troops fled away that very night. All of these public services, however, did not decrease the hostility of the people to his family."

He also said: "After several years without any position, Commander Chu was appointed in 1925 as a director in charge of munitions in Kunming. He became a man to be respected again. During his time of office in this position he made a large amount of money by graft. Commander Chu lost his position in 1929 when the governor was overthrown. He took part of his money to buy a machine for husking rice and to build a factory. The machine husked rice in the daytime and supplied electricity for the city at night. In 1930 he was again offered a position as superintendent of opium suppression in another county, but he rejected the job and recommended his younger brother, Chu Hsin, for the place. He and several hired technical workers managed his factory, which began to operate in 1931. Though he encouraged the people to use electric light, many people feared having anything to do with him and dared not use it. At the same time not enough electricity was produced to give much light. So the business was suspended and in 1935 was terminated."

The funeral of Commander Chu's mother was an exciting event in Kunyang. The same clan member told me: "In 1933 his mother died. Commander Chu suggested to his two brothers that they should jointly arrange an expensive funeral for their late mother, as the reputation of their family depended on what they did at this time. They invited more than twenty Buddhist monks and

Taoist practitioners to make up many idols, spirit banners, lions, elephants, and pavilions of colored papers. Besides these things, couplets and condolence banners were obtained from their relatives, friends, and officials. A big picture of the deceased was displayed, and the coffin was decorated with a silk cover and flowers. They hired an army band from Kunming, and Buddhist and Taoist monks also played various musical instruments. There were about sixteen hundred guests for meals, which were served continuously for two days. The funeral procession stretched out a mile long and attracted people from the four corners of the country.[10] [It was said that this kind of funeral had never before been seen and probably would never happen again.] Half a year after the mother's death, the large family was divided."

After his factory closed down, Commander Chu obtained another position. The clan member told me:"In 1937 Commander Chu was appointed superintendent of militia training in the district of northeastern Yunnan. He was enthusiastic and conscientious in this job. He brought along, however, two nephews with him: one he appointed as captain of the militia; the other, as the head of the police bureau. Both of them were opium-smokers and gamblers and very corrupt. The local people resented his nephews and reported them to the provincial government. Since Commander Chu was involved, he was dismissed. He spoke sadly about this matter, saying: 'I

10. The number of condolence banners and of guests as well as the social standing of those who participate are important to the living and the dead, as a matter of pride. The more the guests and the higher the social position of the condolers, the greater will be the prestige of the recipient family. For further discussion on this see Francis L. K. Hsu, *Under the Ancestors' Shadow* (New York: Columbia University Press, 1948), pp. 160–61.

was in a dilemma. If I did bring them, I would be involved unavoidably in scandal; if I did not bring them, I would be criticized by my relatives.' "

The clan member continued: "After this he returned to his native place and built two boats to ferry people and goods to and from Kunming and Kunyang on Kunming Lake. Simultaneously, he built two tile kilns in Kunyang. He transported the manufactured tiles and bricks by his own boats to Kunming to be sold. Though he was elected chairman of the boatmen's union in Kunyang, he had his residence in Kunming. He made a great deal of money from this ferrying business, although his two tile kilns closed, as they lost money. During these years he built a two-story house." The house was built in both foreign and Chinese architectural styles. Around the house was a large flower garden and orchard encircled by a wall. Furnishings consisted of such things as a sofa, foreign beds, and phonograph, things seldom seen in the community.

When I was in Kunyang, the title of respect of "Chu Ssu Ling Kuan" was still used by the people, though this had been his position of more than thirty years ago. When a new magistrate or other top official came to Kunyang, they would still visit him. He was still invited to all official functions in the county, and, if there was any important meeting, the magistrate would also ask him to be present.

Because of his high prestige, many people came to ask him for his help. For example, a person who wanted to be made head of a *hsiang*[11] would ask Commander Chu to

11. The county is divided into eight districts: seven *hsiang* (in rural areas) and one *chen* (in urban area).

use his influence with the top officials of the county. Magistrate Wang, who was reported to the governor by other gentry on account of his corruption, asked him to speak in his defense.

My assistant reported to me: "In 1947 Commander Chu was asked to become a member of the Democratic Socialist party. He said: 'Though I am too old to devote myself to political activities, the present situation in China is so critical that I feel I must join the party as a means of helping my country.' After he joined the party, his oldest son, Chu Lung, was appointed as general secretary of the Kunyang branch of the party."

My assistant continued: "Commander Chu was candidate for representative in the National Assembly for his party in Kunyang. He was anxious to be elected. Before the election day, he sent many agents to the country to campaign for him. But he was defeated by a magistrate who had been put up as a candidate for representative by the Nationalist party. Commander Chu was very unhappy at his failure and went to Kunming to ask his friends to arrange for him to have the seat. Because he was so very well known headquarters of the Nationalist party in Nanking telegraphed the Nationalist party of Kunyang to ask the newly elected man to vacate his position in favor of Commander Chu, who flew to Nanking to attend the Assembly."

During the eight years of the Sino-Japanese War, taxes including the land tax were very heavy. But Commander Chu did not pay anything. It was said that he believed that the county government would not dare to ask for his taxes. Once a staff member of the Tax Department of the county government stated openly in a financial meeting which I was attending that Commander Chu had never paid any taxes. After several days, my assistant told me: "After the meeting, the staff member was reproved for his *faux pas* and warned that Commander Chu would make things difficult for him. In explaining the reason for his father's not paying taxes, Chu Lung said: 'My father has served the government for so many years that he should not be asked to pay any taxes.' "

Commander Chu had built a public privy at the corner of the main street in the city. A farmer paid 240 catties of rice to him every year for the privilege of using the contents as fertilizer. The head of the Bureau of Public Sanitation was a comparatively well-trained administrator. (He came from Shanghai and later became a friend of mine.) He petitioned the magistrate to move Commander Chu's privy because it was bad for public sanitation. But Commander Chu protested vigorously, saying: "I have a right to build a privy on my own ground. No one can interfere with my property rights." (The petition was put aside without question. The head of the Bureau of Public Sanitation told me about this matter and often complained about the rottenness, selfishness, and conservatism of the local gentry.)

My assistant was informed by one of Commander Chu's nephews: "My uncle was fifty-nine years old in 1946. [He was still very strong.] He smokes opium but does not drink wine. He often urges us to accomplish noble deeds."

Commander Chu had an emotional temperament. His speech was sincere, frank, and direct. He often criticized the hostility and lack of co-operation among people. He said in his speech delivered at the inaugural meeting of the Association of Veteran Officers in Kunyang: "One person always takes advantage of another person instead of having an equal exchange. Everyone does everything for his own interest. The people have no idea of ethics."

He criticized society as unfair: "Everyone who has money and power can be independent, even though he got these things by illegal means. On the other hand, one who has no money and power not only must earn his living by his own blood and sweat, but also he has to bear the pain of being oppressed and insulted. This is a society of devils."

He criticized politics as too corrupt and too inefficient: "The officials speak with high-sounding voices but do nothing worth while for the public. So the administration is inefficient. Both the important officials and the lowly clerks are corrupt. There is no bright future in politics."

Nowadays he gave few public speeches and did not like to interfere in public affairs. He seemed very depressed and passive. Yet he hoped that each of his sons would become a man of distinction.

My assistant told me: "Commander Chu's wife bore no child. But his concubine bore him three sons and two daughters. All the children were very intelligent. The two daughters, Chu Mei and Chu Lan, twenty-nine and twenty-six, married many years ago. The oldest son, Chu Lung, twenty-four, was graduated from a middle school which was especially built by the governor for educating the children of the officials in Kunming. After his graduation, he could not pass the entrance examination into any college, however. His father sent him to a military academy. But after one month in the academy he ran away, because he could not bear the regimentation. He lived in Kunming and Kunyang according to his fancy. When he was in Kunming, he did nothing but go to see movies and Chinese operas, gamble, and smoke opium. The second son, Chu Hu, twenty years old, is studying in a middle school in Kunming. The youngest son, Chu Lin, fourteen years old, is studying in a primary school.''

He continued: ''Chu Lung married in 1940 when he was eighteen. His marriage was arranged by his parents. Several days before the wedding, he went to Kunming to buy something for the occasion. However, once there he was involved in a fight with the fourth son of the governor and was arrested by the military police. When he was released on bail given by his father, the wedding ceremony was already several days old.[12] Because his father-in-law was an opium-seller in Yuchi, Chu Lung often went there to get opium from him.''

He added: ''After one year of marriage, Chu Lung received through the recommendation of a friend of his father the position of secretary of a county government, but he was quite incompetent. After half a year the magistrate gave him $50,000[13] and sent him back home.''

In 1943 complaint was made by the local gentry to the provincial government of the corruption of the magistrate of Kunyang. Chu Lung felt that this was his opportunity to exercise his influence. He had printed the testimony of a number of people as to the honesty of the magistrate in the Kunming newspaper and presented a

12. In China marriages are a family rather than an individual matter, so the wedding ceremony does not necessarily have to take place with both contracting parties present, as long as the bride is present.

13. In 1941 this sum was equivalent to 4,066 silver dollars, or about U.S. $2,000.

petition to the provincial government to hold off judgment on him. Chu Lung was appointed by the magistrate as head of the Department of Military Affairs of the county government. Since the magistrate was, like himself, an opium-smoker, they became fast friends.

After Chu Lung became the head of the Department of Military Affairs, the temporary taxes of every family were suddenly increased. If a farmer of some means did not send his conscript son exactly at the appointed time, he would be arrested and put in jail. But, if the farmer bribed him, his son would be free from conscription. Sometimes Chu Lung led many policemen to the village at night to "shanghai" able-bodied men for the army. He often snatched the only son of rich people for purposes of blackmail.

My assistant told me: "Once the guards of the governor sent an officer to Kunyang to catch an escaped soldier. This officer was Chu Lung's schoolmate. Chu Lung, therefore, acted as go-between for the officer and the family of the soldier. This time he received $30,000. Soon after he was reappointed to the position of *chin chang*, or the head of a district government, because his grafting as the head of the Department of Military Affairs was found out. But this position gave him a good opportunity for grafting also. When the New Eighteenth Division sent officers to Kunyang to conscript soldiers in August, 1943, the number of able-bodied men of Nei Tien Hsiang was not up to the quota. Chu Lung led a group of militia in the seizure of two men in Pao Shan Hsiang instead and got $500,000[14] from the *hsiang* for this venture. Local

14. Owing to inflation this sum was equivalent to only 1,770.5 silver dollars, or about U.S. $880.

citizens reported to him that Mr. Lee, who had three brothers, should be conscripted, but Mr. Lee evaded this by giving Chu Lung two cartons of American cigarettes and $50,000.''

At the end of 1943 a new magistrate came into office in Kunyang. The new magistrate wished to dismiss Chu Lung but feared that this would hurt the feelings of Commander Chu. So no action was taken.

A junior staff member of Chu Lung informed me: ''For the convenience in smoking opium and taking bribes Chu Lung moved his office to his home. The servants of the *ching kung sao*, or the government offices of the district, worked every day in the Chu Lung's home. He smoked opium during the night and slept during the daytime. Every few weeks he would invite either the *pao-chang*[15] or some of the gentry to have dinner with him. This was in order that he might be presented to the people in a favorable light. The expense of these dinners was paid by a tax levied on the families of the district. When conscription was being carried on, if the man selected fled away, Chu Lung would put his family in jail and make them build a wall around the garden of his home.''

In 1944 the magistrate discovered his corruption. But the magistrate did not want to hurt his feelings and appointed him as head of the Department of Education of the county. Since Chu Lung knew that he would not get much money out of this position, he resigned.

15. According to the law each *hsiang* or *chen* includes a number of *pao*, ranging from six to fifteen, and each *pao* has a head named *pao-chang*. Each *pao* includes a number of *chia*, ranging from six to fifteen, and each *chia* has a head named *chia chang*. Each *chia* includes a number of families, ranging from six to fifteen, and each family has a head.

During the time he held two positions it was estimated that he accumulated at least five million dollars. Though the people saw clearly his corrupt behavior, no one dared to raise any complaints against him.

When the Japanese army attacked Kweichow, the county was ordered to organize a volunteer group. Commander Chu was appointed as commander of the group and Chu Lung as the vice-commander of a company. After the surrender of Japan the group was dissolved, and Chu Lung again had nothing to do. But my assistant reported to me: "When the Democratic Socialist party established a branch at Kunyang, he was appointed as the general secretary of the branch office through his father's association and influence."

Chu Lung was satisfied. He had three children in 1948.

The Bureaucrat / Head Chang

Head Chang represents the "new gentry" among whom the moral sanctions of the old order as to the gaining and exploitation of power seem very largely to have vanished. Coming from a family undistinguished for learning and whose economic base of prosperity has been dissipated by the extravagances of previous generations, he has all his own way to make. Success comes not only from hard work in studying and home practice in the arts of calligraphy and of letter-writing but also from flattery, "push," and extensive and ingenious grafting. Because he lacks full acceptance among the older gentry, he is said by the commentator to "have an inferiority complex." It appears from the commentary that his rudeness and arrogance are as much held against him as is his dishonesty.—EDITOR.

"Chang Ko-chiang," or Head Chang—chief of the Administrative section of the county—was the youngest among the gentry of Kunyang. Because the magistrate had once asked me to help the county government to do some work on the statistics of vital registration, I had the opportunity to associate with him for several months. In the strict sense, Head Chang was not a member of the traditional gentry class. He was an upstart, an opportunist; as a result, many of the gentry had no faith in him, though he was in power. He, however, represents a type of individual who has struggled to become a member of the gentry class and has succeeded. He put on an air of great pride to cover up his inferiority complex. I asked my assistant to call on him and talk over the matter of an interview. When my assistant visited him, he said to him haughtily: "What do you want to come to my home for?"

My assistant said: "I came to see you especially, because you are a virtuous and noble gentleman of our country." Head Chang turned his back and walked away. A little later his mother came over and asked my assistant whether he had something to ask Head Chang and conversed politely with him for a while. But, when my assistant visited him a second time, Head Chang's attitude to my assistant had changed greatly. This was primarily due to two reasons: (1) my assistant had asked Mr. Lu, who was a cousin of Head Chang, to go with him and (2) Head Chang was going to campaign for the position of the chairman of the People's Political Council of the county, and my assistant was an acting member of the Association of School Teachers of Kunyang. At this time he received my assistant warmly. Here is his story as my assistant noted it:

"My ancestors were the residents of a village named Miao Lin Tsun, which is situated 15 miles north of the city of Kunyang. They were engaged in agriculture and had about 60 *kung* of farmland. My great-great-grand-father, Chang Fu-tung, rented out his land to tenants and moved into the city to escape disturbances from bandit raids. After he had settled down in the city, he bought a small house and 15 *kung* of farmland near the city. He left off farming entirely and turned to business and returned to the village only once a year to collect his rents.

"My great-grandfather, Chang Su-sen, was born in the city. Because he was an only son, he inherited all the property of the family and from boyhood had an easy life. He married at the age of fifteen.

"When he was around twenty-four years old, Chang Su-sen began to make friends with gamblers and wine-drinkers. When my great-great-grandfather, Chang Fu-tung, discovered these bad habits, it was too late to correct him. Once my great-great-grandparents told him: 'Ever since you were young, we have been kind to you; we have never let you do any heavy work and never have spoken harshly to hurt you. But now you not only do not work but also squander your money with bad friends every day. Though you think that our property can provide for you, if you squander your money like this, you will only enjoy a small part of your life.' He answered: 'Please be generous! A man works only to live. Since our living is comfortable without working, why should we work?' He left home the next morning as a protest against his parents' remarks.

"My great-great-grandparents asked Chang Su-sen's wife to advise her husband; she also felt that her husband was spending his money unwisely and tried to urge him to mend his ways.

"Chang Su-sen returned home on the fourth day. At

dead of night his wife talked to him and said: 'Though we are married, we have never talked seriously. Tonight I want to talk with you about something about which your parents have talked with you often. Your parents have been very kind to you. Because you are an only son, they have let you do what you wish. Now all the people speak of you as a "bum." Do you know that? It is still not too late for you to change your conduct. If you do not, your future will be very dark.' He answered: 'You have no right to interfere with me.'

"Every year he spent the rent which he collected from the village within a few days. When he was broke, he would sell land he owned in the village. When he was forty years old, he had only 10 *kung* of farmland left. After five more years he sold 5 *kung* of this land for his father's funeral, and in another three years he sold the remaining 5 *kung* of farmland in the village for his mother's funeral.

"When my great-great-grandfather died, my grand-father, Chang Chia-lin, was twenty-two. Before his death, my great-great-grandfather called his grandson, Chia-Lin, to the front of his bed and secretly handed him the written bills of sale of the house and 15 *kung* of farm. My grandfather kept the bills in the home of his grand-parents-in-law. That meant my great-grandfather had no way to sell the farm and house.

"My grandfather was also an only son. Ever since he was a boy, he had seen how his father had sold off most of the family property. It served as a warning to him, and he tried very hard to recover the lost property for his family.

"Chang Chia-lin married at the age of nineteen. His

marriage was arranged by his grandfather and his mother. Su Sen [the father] cared little about it. Since he knew clearly the reasons for his family's decline, Chia-lin tried his utmost to save his family from disaster. He and his wife devoted a great deal of time to their farm and to their business of buying and selling rice. Chia-lin was filial to his mother and always kept his father contented, which made him squander his money less. At the same time he asked his father's friends not to lend money to him or buy anything from him. This lessened the harm which might have been done by his father.

"My grandfather worked very hard all year around. He went to the fields to work at daybreak and ate his breakfast at noon; he ate only two meals a day. After having dinner at five o'clock, he worked on until midnight. He worked hard not only at farming but also at buying and selling rice. Because of his skill in bargaining and his pleasant manners, he often bought rice cheaper than others.

"When Chia-lin was forty-four years old, the economic condition of his family had greatly improved. He not only had bought 15 *kung* of farmland, but had also increased the capital of his business. Since he had saved some money, he planned to go into the business of pressing soybeans into oil instead of buying and selling rice. Unfortunately, Chang Su-sen died at this time. During the next year Chia-lin's mother also passed away. So he used up all his savings for his parents' funerals. In order to get capital for his business, he sold his house in the village; from this sale he got 500 *liang*, or *tael*, of silver.

"Though Chia-lin was illiterate, he was strong, clever,

and expressed himself with great force and fluency. But since he was very miserly, he made very few friends. He died at the age of sixty-five.

"My grandmother was a generous and well-disposed person. She co-operated with my grandfather to support our family. She was married at the age of eighteen and gave birth to two sons and one daughter. Unfortunately, the second son died at eighteen.

"My father, Chang Wei-lung, was the elder one of the two brothers. Since the time of my great-great-grandfather every generation has had only one son. My father originally had a brother four years younger than himself. Unfortunately, this younger brother died when he was only eighteen. So my father became an only son again. Because of the scarcity in children in the family, he was especially loved by his parents from the moment he was born. He began to study in a private school at five. After nine years, he finished the study of the Four Books. He then entered a four-year provincial normal school in Kunming. He studied hard in school but showed special talent only in arithmetic.

"After graduating from the normal school he came back to Kunyang and taught arithmetic in the primary school of the county. After two years all his colleagues and students had come to feel that he was a good teacher. He felt very happy but resigned the job in the third year. [One of Head Chang's clan members told me: "Chang Wei-lung resigned his job, because of an awkward situation. Once, when he was solving an arithmetic problem on the blackboard, he made a mistake. The students clapped their hands and shouted loudly, 'It is wrong! It is wrong!' He blushed with shame and became rigid. Later one of his colleagues came over and helped him out of his difficulty. Though the students kept silent about it, he was made so ashamed by this that he resigned his job at once and swore off teaching forever. After resigning his job, he could not find another job for almost a year. He was disappointed and depressed."]

"Later, he felt that being a doctor was a noble occupation, because this profession would benefit his family as well as others; it not only would make money but also would win him a reputation. Moreover, it was an occupation free from the interference of others. He bought some Chinese medical books, such as *The Medical Herbs of Southern Yunnan* and *The Medical Dictionary*, and studied very hard. If he encountered problems, he would ask the advice of noted doctors in the city. He often invited these men to dinner, asked them to tell him about their experiences, and borrowed medical books from them. He paid special attention to typhus. After studying five years, he began to practice. Owing to his lack of experience, he still felt unsure, so he often consulted with other doctors about the prescriptions which he gave his patients. He studied the cause of his patients' illness. After another four years, he became a well-known physician in Kunyang."

One of Head Chang's clan told me: "Chang Wei-lung had a very strong character; he was violent and very temperamental. When someone came to ask him to cure an illness, he would go at once if he was feeling happy, and he would ask little money for his treatment. Otherwise, he would make an excuse about having some business and refuse to go. Sometimes, however, he was very kind. For example, when a poor man consulted him, he would not ask for any fee. He paid special attention to exemplary behavior, as he thought that, though his family was weak in that it had had only one son each generation in the last three generations, his kindness might accumulate some virtue for his posterity. He had had three sons and two daughters, but only one son was living, all the others having died when they were still very young. He regretted their deaths deeply. He passed away at the age of forty-four.

"When Chang Wei-lung died, Head Chang was only twelve. He was too young to be responsible for the welfare of the family. Wei-lung's wife was by nature very happy and willing to do any kind of work. However, after the death of her children and her husband, she became so moody that she was forced to look for distraction in order to forget her troubles. In her depression she took no more interest in the farm, business, or household. After several years her grief lessened, but by this time the economic condition of her family was very bad.

"Head Chang was Wei-lung's last son. By the time Head Chang came along, all his brothers and sisters had died. That was why Head Chang was especially loved by his parents. In our community one who has no son is pitied. According to the custom, one who has no son cannot be buried at the cemetery of his ancestors' tomb. Moreover, he will be despised by the people, because to have no son is considered to be most shameful. On the other hand, *er sun man tang*, or 'to have the hall full of children and grandchildren,' is rated most highly by the people."

Head Chang began to study at the age of six. Before six, he had had no opportunity to play with other children, as his parents overprotected him and would not let him out of their sight. If he wanted something, his parents would always give it to him. Perhaps this is the main cause of Head Chang's headstrong character. When he began to go to school, he liked it not only because of his parents' encouragement but also because of the companionship of the other children. He was clever and had a very good memory from boyhood on.

Wei-lung's early death made more difficult his family's ascent to the position of gentry. The last few generations of Chang Wei-lung's family had all been illiterate. But Wei-lung as a graduate of a middle school and as a schoolteacher was qualified to be gentry. His methods in the treatment of diseases made him well known in Kunyang, and gradually this raised his position to gentry. Moreover, he had made friends with members in every walk of life, such as educators, officials, officers, and rich merchants. He was generous and ambitious. He intended to let his son have the best education possible in order to contribute to the glory of his family. But, since he died early, his son had to start pushing himself ahead while still young.

Head Chang got to his present position by a long period of struggle. His success depended not on his family background but on his ability. Since I knew that Head Chang was a self-made man, I praised him highly on this score. My admiration for him gave him further encouragement to talk freely with me about his life-story as follows:

"When my father died, I was twelve years old. My mother wept every day, and I stayed home to look after things. The situation made me suspect that I might be taken out of school entirely. But I thought that, if I could not continue my studies, what could I do then? On whom could my mother and I depend? Unexpectedly three months after my father's death, my mother told me I might go back to school again. How happy I was! When I went to school with mingled feelings of sorrow and joy, my teacher and fellow-schoolmates came to console me. But their sympathy just made me cry more. However, many other schoolmates, who were jealous of my good record, could only talk about my dark future. The alternate coldness and warmth of men's feelings impressed me so deeply that I could never forget it. My mother was still in deep sorrow, but, when I came home from school, she would dry her tears at once and smile at me. I was deeply inspired by her. I studied very hard, because I wanted to draw some consolation from reading.

"I left the private school when I was thirteen and entered a primary school which followed the new system of education. After three years I graduated. At that time the question of my future arose again. I was anxious to continue my studies, but the financial condition of my family did not permit me to do so. I could only study by myself at home during my free time from farm and household.

"I married at the age of seventeen. My wife was a daughter of my mother's brother. Though making ends meet was difficult, we had very deep affection for each other. She became my able helper and encouraged me to improve myself.

"During these years I tried my best to find a job, but I failed again and again. Fortunately, when I was twenty-one years old, I was sent by the county government to the 'Short-Term Training School of the Bureau of Industry of the Provincial Government' through the recommendation of my father-in-law. [His father-in-law was one of the leading gentry of Kunyang.] After three months I was graduated from school and waited for an appointment to a job by the county officials, but I did not receive one. Then I taught in a primary school. After half a year, I was appointed a technician in the County Bureau of Reconstruction through the recommendation of my father-in-law.

"At that time my mother's brother encouraged me to write characters every day. I used a board which was painted with red lacquer instead of paper. After filling the face of the board with written characters, I washed them out, so that I could use it again. Even when I was very busy, I continued to write fifty large characters and one hundred small characters daily. After two years I was often asked by many people to write couplets and scrolls. A year later I left the Bureau. [One of his former colleagues told me: "When Head Chang was in the Bureau, he was enthusiastic about everything at the beginning and was polite to his colleagues, because he knew that both knowledge and experience were lacking to him. After a year, however, he became conceited and self-satisfied. He showed that he despised his colleagues and even the director of the Bureau. As a consequence, he was dismissed by the director."]

"After leaving there I was appointed as a clerk under Commander Chu, again through the recommendation of my father-in-law. I was then twenty-four years old. After two years I returned to Kunyang. [His colleague told me: "Though he was an only son, he had to join the army, because he could find no job in Kunyang. After two years he came home, because he could not bear the hardships of a soldier's life."]

"Since I had nothing to do at home, I devoted myself to the study of how to write public letters and characters and to the reading of many practical books, such as *A Manual of Social Intercourse*, *Daily Practical Literature*, and *Essentials for Writing Good Letters*. After one year, I was appointed as clerk in the county guard. Because of the low salary, I resigned after serving there one year.

"After resigning this job, I went into the business of trading in rice. Because I had no capital, I had to borrow money at high interest from others. I did not make any money.

"Since I had suffered a great deal and taken enough beatings, I had learned a great deal about how to act toward others in order to get on in the world. I saw clearly that, if a man wanted to ascend in the social scale, he should be an opportunist and do everything possible to gain the approval of society. His words and actions should conform to the psychology of the gentry aand educated younger generation of the community. Besides this he should be generally sociable and make friends with various kinds of people. I myself followed these principles and gradually won the confidence of the public."

My assistant commented on this: "The people—especially the young educated people—thought that Head Chang was an able youth. When the system of voting for people's political representative of the county was first established and the election for representative was held, Head Chang was elected. [At that time there was only one representative for each county.] His name was posted on the gate wall of the county, and he suddenly became well known in Kunyang. Then he was only twenty-nine years old.''

After he was elected as the people's political representative of the county, we could hear people talking about the reasons for his success in the teashops and restaurants. Some said that he had struggled hard; some said that it was because of his fine handwriting; some others said that he was supported by his father-in-law. Many of the peasants, who had had no chance to see him, even fancied that he was a man of extraordinary talent. During this period he was in high spirits and elated with his success. He played tricks to cheat others. If he had to ask a favor of someone, Head Chang would flatter and show great respect to him. Otherwise, he would show him no more consideration than if he were an ant. He became very much conceited and cared solely for profit. It was really abominable.

When Chang was thirty-four, Magistrate Chen came to Kunyang. Head Chang visited him very often as people's political representative. He described the general situation at Kunyang to the magistrate and told him how greatly drought harmed the crops of the county. He suggested to the magistrate that a dam be built at the foot of Sung Shan, or Mount Sung, to collect the water for irrigating the farms west of the city and that the owners of the farms south and east of the city be taxed so that a twenty-horsepower water pump could be bought. Thus the problem of drought in the area near the city would be solved completely. In this way he won the confidence of the magistrate and was appointed director of the Bureau of Reconstruction of the county government.

At that time he was happy in his success and promotion. Promotion means prosperity. He felt that, if his plans were to be carried out, it would be possible both to add to his reputation and to "squeeze" money. Though his suggestions had not been put into action in 1930, he was ordered to build two lines of highway from Kunyang to Yuchi and from Kunyang to Chinning. (The distances are twenty miles for the former and ten miles for the latter.) He selected the workers and designed the construction of the highways and sent a petition to the provincial government to ask for an appropriation of money. The provincial government promised to give ten cents per day for each person. He, however, withheld the appropriation money from the workers, keeping about 4,000 silver dollars[1] himself.

The highways were to be paved with basalt. This kind of stone should have been mined by stonecutters from a region ten miles away. Expenses were to be paid by the Department of Reconstruction of the provincial government. But he told the workers to pave the highways with stones which could be gathered from the mountains near by and to mix in only a little basalt. At last he received a sum of 6,000 silver dollars[2] from the provincial government for further expenses. He "squeezed" all this amount of money and built his own house with what remained.

The Chinese proverb says: "Everyone respects the rich; every dog bites people who wear shabby clothes." Since

1. This sum of money was equivalent to about U.S. $2,000.
2. This sum of money was equivalent to about U.S. $3,000.

he had grafted a great deal of money, the rich and great came running to pay respect to him just as flies hurry to sticky flypaper. People who flattered him or sent him gifts came to his home incessantly. The economic condition of his family changed suddenly. He dressed well every day and wanted to have wine and meat at every meal.

The next year he asked a stonecutter to cut five tombstones and twenty feet of big stone to be placed at his ancestors' tombs. While the work was going on he invited twenty monks and Taoists to chant the canon of Buddhism and to recite dirges. At the same time he built a house of six rooms in both foreign and Chinese styles. The design of the house was the most modern in the community. For example, there were water troughs to drain off rain water—a thing not seen before. On the day the beams of the house were to be set up, the guests, about two hundred and forty of them, came in an unbroken line. Two-thirds were officials or gentry of the county. Since the host had high prestige, the congratulatory presents were ten times the usual number. Unfortunately, the elder of the two sons of the house died the same day. So the righteous people whispered that Head Chang had been *pao ying*, or received retribution.

In 1939 Head Chang was thirty-seven years old. (The magistrate was now Mr. Ho.) The Bureau of Reconstruction was changed to the Department of Reconstruction, and he was appointed as the head of the department. After half a year, the county government was ordered to construct a highway from Kunyang to Anning. The route of the highway cut across many farms. Many of the farmers who wished to save their farms

〚 217 〛

bribed Chang to change the route. Thus he got a great deal of money. At the same time, he sold the basalt to the stonecutters who built the stone bridges. It was estimated that he got about $200,000.[3]

In 1940 he was reappointed as the head of the Department of Civil Affairs. Though he had no chance for graft in this job, he took advantage of his position to run a business. He borrowed a large sum of money from the Society of Farm Loans of the Farmer's Bank of China. He borrowed the money at a very low rate of interest, but the interest accumulated rapidly due to inflation. He used the money to buy iron and hoarded it until prices went up. He bought iron at five dollars a *ching*, or catty, but after three months was able to sell it for twenty-five dollars a catty. Then he bought salt at eight dollars a *ching* and sold it after four months at sixteen dollars. He again bought iron and sold it when the price went up. It was estimated he made about $1,500,000[4] on this type of speculation. The profit was equally divided between the head of the society and himself.

He cultivated a close friendship with Magistrate Ho. For the magistrate's birthday he suggested to the gentry they present him a eulogistic scroll along with gifts in honor of his virtuous administration. As a result Magistrate Ho liked him very much and often invited him to his bedroom to teach him the music to various verses. When Magistrate Ho was dismissed by the provincial

3. The value of money at the end of 1939 was estimated on the basis of January, 1937, to have decreased 2.5 times due to inflation. So this sum was equivalent to eighty thousand silver dollars, or about U.S. $40,000.

4. The value of money in December, 1940, had decreased nine times on the base of January, 1937. So the sum of $1,500,000 was equivalent to about 180,000 silver dollars, or U.S. $90,000.

government, Head Chang also suggested that the gentry build a pavilion in his honor.

Since Head Chang was a good friend to the magistrate and the magistrate agreed with his opinions and respected his requests, he took advantage of his position to obtain bribes of various sorts.

In 1943 the people complained about Magistrate Chao's corruption and inefficiency. Head Chang felt that to back the people's complaints to the government was his golden opportunity. He solicited the aid of "Wu Li-shih," or President Wu (of the Chamber of Commerce of Kunyang), "Liao Ko-chiang," or Head Liao (the head of the Department of Conscription), "Lee Ching-chiang," or Head Lee (the head of a district government), and others to suggest that the People's Political Council hold a meeting. In the meeting a special committee to accuse the magistrate was organized. Acting Chairman Wu, Head Ho, Head Lee, and himself were elected by the committee as the representatives. They went to Kunming for this purpose.

This task was not easy, because Mrs. Chao, the wife of the magistrate, and the governor's wife were sworn sisters. Mrs. Chao went to Kunming for help. At this time the gentry of Kunyang were divided into three groups: one was against Magistrate Chao, the leader of which was Head Chang; the second group was pro-Magistrate Chao, the leader of which was the eldest son of Commander Chu; the third group was neutral, the leader of which was the third son of Chairman Wang. Therefore, it was difficult to judge which side would win in the struggle to overthrow Magistrate Chao.

In this crisis Head Chang used desperate measures. He

was advised by his nephew, who was the aide-de-camp of the commander, to offer a bribe of half a million dollars to the eldest son of the governor, who was then the commander of a division. Since he was a very good friend of ex-Magistrate Ho, who was then the general secretary of the Provincial Administrators Training School, he asked Mr. Ho to help him write the petitions. He also published the facts of Magistrate Chao's corruption in the newspapers in Kunming and distributed handbills in Kunming and Kunyang to enlist favorable public opinion. After four months he attained his goal, and Magistrate Chao was dismissed.

During Head Chang's stay in Kunming for the purpose of accusing Magistrate Chao, his position in the county became insecure. He did not dare go home for fear of reprisals from the magistrate until Magistrate Chao was dismissed and a new magistrate appointed. When the newly appointed magistrate came to the county to take over the position, Head Chang and the other representatives of the Committee To Accuse Magistrate Chao followed him back to Kunyang.

After their return to Kunyang, two events occurred. One was street fighting between two groups of pro- and con-Magistrate Chao; the other was that the Committee To Accuse Magistrate Chao was renamed the Committee To Liquidate Magistrate Chao. Magistrate Chao was detained in Kunyang by the new magistrate and the committee.

Total expense for this task of bringing charges against Magistrate Chao was $1,002,000.[5] The money was ad-

5. The value of money in July, 1943, had decreased 263 times on the base of January, 1937. So this sum was equivalent to about 4,600 silver dollars, or U.S. $2,300.

vanced by Acting Chairman Wu, Head Liao, and Head Chang himself.

After several joint meetings of the Committee To Liquidate Magistrate Chao and the People's Political Council, a preliminary report was published. It said that Magistrate Chao had taken more than 400 piculs of government rice for himself. Other items of Magistrate Chao's corruption were still under discussion.

When the new magistrate arrived at Kunyang, a big dinner party was given by the county government in his honor. I was sitting at the same table with the two magistrates, Commander Chu, and others.

During the dinner time Commander Chu said: "After having served the government for a long period, I could only build a small house like this. But he [Head Chang] served the government only a few years, and has built a house much bigger and better than mine." (He shook his head with a deep sigh.)

Once when I talked with the new magistrate, who later became a friend of mine, about the local administration I asked him why the gentry often complained of the magistrate to the governor and why they did not cooperate with him.

The magistrate explained the reasons to me as follows: "Since most of the people are illiterate and are not organized, the magistrate and his few staff members cannot go directly to the people. There is a wide gap between the government and the public. The gentry are generally educated people. They are the leaders of the mass and control public opinion. This group of people includes the rich merchants, landlords, scholar-literati, retired officials, and the families of the active high officials. So they are most keen in their interest and are politically minded. Thus, even though the magistrate does not want any contact with them, they insist upon having contacts with the magistrate. One cannot get rid of them. In fact, if a magistrate does not co-operate with them completely, he cannot do anything and will be in danger of losing his secure place. However, some institutions, such as the Committee To Finance the County, must legally be a joint organization of the county government and the representatives of the people. If a magistrate wants to do something, he has to have money. Thus, he still has to co-operate with the leaders of the people, that is to say, the gentry.

"Since the magistrate cannot get rid of the gentry, he must try to co-operate with them. And since the magistrate has to co-operate with them, the gentry get to know most of the secrets of the magistrate. So, if they want to report any corruption to the provincial government, it is relatively easy to gather the evidence. Furthermore, since most of them belong to the propertied class, they can advance the money for the expenses involved in such an action. Since some of the gentry are retired officials or belong to families of active high officials, they have much influence in the provincial government.

"As the gentry are most keen in their interest and are politically minded and often divided into different groups, they readily take advantage of their opportunity of bringing charges against the magistrate as part of their struggle for prestige and power.

"The gentry co-operate with the magistrate for their own interest, because the status of the gentry depends on their association with the government. But, when the situation runs counter to their personal interest, they will be against the magistrate under the guise of protecting the interests of the people and their native place." (The magistrate was a university graduate and a student of political science.)

My assistant told me: "At the beginning the new magistrate did not appoint Head Chang to any position because he was the main instigator in the action against Magistrate Chao. After three months, however, the new magistrate appointed him as the head of the Department of Civil Affairs of the county government. At that time he considered himself a bringer of progress to his native place. He made a show of his conceit. When common people bowed to him in the street, he raised his head and did not pay any attention to them. However, when he met a superior, Head Chang would beam on him politely and earnestly.

"The following year he was reappointed as the head of the Department of Conscription of the county government. He knew that martial law was much stricter than ordinary civil law and acted very carefully. If corruption were reported to him and the investigation proved to be true, he would petition the magistrate to file his charges. He seemed very just.

"In 1944 Colonel Liang, once an army officer, came to Kunyang to carry on conscription. Head Chang sent $50,000[6] to him. The officer was honest and refused to accept the money. With urging, however, he finally accepted $20,000 for his daily expenses. Because of the officer's leniency, the conscription was not carried out satisfactorily. The officer was recalled. As a consequence, another officer, Colonel Su, came to Kunyang in his place.

6. The value of money in July, 1944, had decreased 776 times on the base of January, 1937. So this sum was equivalent to about 640 silver dollars, or U.S. $320.

Colonel Liang told the story of the bribe to Colonel Su. Colonel Su pretended to be incorruptible and sent his helpers to the county government to investigate the tale. The magistrate was asked to send Head Chang to Colonel Su. Head Chang knew that the officer just wanted to extort money and presented $100,000 to the Colonel immediately. Later Head Chang told others that 'with money you can make the devil turn your mill.'

"In January, 1945, Head Chang was invited by Magistrate Ho, who was then the magistrate of Yiming, to be his general secretary. After half a year he returned to Kunyang and was appointed as the head of the Department of Civil Affairs of the county government.

"The main reason for Head Chang's success was his shrewdness. He saw how local affairs stood and guided himself accordingly. That was why he did not get into trouble by his grafting. A self-made man without much schooling, he is proud, cold, and snobbish as well as able and realistic. In 1946 at forty-three he was prominent among the gentry of middle age. Many people were afraid of him because of his malicious ways. If one were not on good terms with him, he might make trouble. On the other hand, one could never count on his remaining friendly.

"Head Chang's wife is very pretty, but she is haughty. One scarcely ever sees her smile. She is industrious in her household and business and dresses plainly. Since the death of her first son, she has looked sad. She was thirty-nine years old in 1946 and had one daughter and one son. The daughter was then studying in the primary school. Her mother often went to the temple to pray for the health of her children and for more children."

The Merchant / Head Ting

*Head Ting comes from a family of leading gentry whose economic prosperity was founded on trade. But Ting's father died young, and his uncle squandered most of the family property, and he received only a small amount of education and little training for a career. His distinguished family line stands him in good stead, however, since it is this rather than any efforts of his own which enabled him to marry into another leading gentry family. Following the marriage, his father-in-law's influence and money start him up the ladder of success in trade. He shows himself unscrupulous in getting ahead, sacrificing his helpful father-in-law and allowing a brother-in-law to be shot without interference. But, having at length reached the top of the ladder, he becomes virtuous and kindly and criticizes corruption in government.—*EDITOR.

The *hsien cheng*, or the city of Kunyang, is a political, educational, cultural, handicraft, and commercial center with market days on the fifth and ninth of every moon.

The residential population of the city, according to our census taken on March 1, 1942, was 3,547 persons, the majority of whom engaged in business of some sort. The richest families in the county lived here, and the chamber of commerce was the most powerful organization. Hence, to be a merchant was important to social standing. Head Ting, whose life is given here, was one of the richest merchants of Kunyang, and, when we came there, he was already a *chin chiang*, or head of the urban district. I had talked with him several times at one of the county government parties where his gigantic stature and nervous manner marked him out. When he returned home to Kunyang, my assistant not only visited him very often but also had meals at his home from time to time. Because of Head Ting's suspiciousness, my assistant spent much more time in collecting the data on this case than on any of the others.

Head Ting's father told my assistant:

"My remote ancestors came from Lan Chi,[1] Chekiang Province, in Yuan dynasty. Our family were the descendants of Ting Huai-yin.[2] They were either high officers or scholars. The first to come to Kunyang came as commander of the army and brought with him prosperity for succeeding generations. My grandfather, Ting Nai-huan, was the richest man in Kunyang. His business was the transportation of salt from where it was produced to Kunyang. At least thirty horses were employed each time, and all the retail merchants of Kunyang bought

1. This county is famous as the commercial center of eastern Chekiang.

2. It was said that Ting Huai-yin had been a magistrate of Chu Fu of Shangtung Province in Ming dynasty, nationally famous for his honesty and justice and called "Ting Ta Sheng Jen," or "Great Saint Ting."

salt from him. In fact, he monopolized the salt supply in the county.

"My grandfather built a large, well-constructed house. There were three connected courts. The first court was the shop; the second was the residence; the third the warehouse. This residence was a well-known *ta fang-tzu*, or 'big house.'

"Unfortunately, because of the revolt of the governor of Yunnan against the Manchu government, there was a great battle in Kunyang during which our house was used as headquarters for one of the commanders. At this time my younger great-uncle was killed and our house looted and badly damaged by the soldiers.

"Fortunately, Nai-huan had buried his silver dollars in time. After the rebellion was suppressed, he used the money which remained to repair the house and resume his business. After five years our family became prosperous again.

"Nai-huan was one of the leading gentry of Kunyang. He was tall, dignified, eloquent, and earnest and was both intelligent and possessed of a strong sense of responsibility. He could write poems and compose couplets and 'eight-legged' essays and was noted for his calligraphy. He passed away at the age of sixty-one.

"My grandmother was a farmer's daughter but was able and clever. Almost all the domestic affairs of the large family depended on her. She was always busy in entertaining guests, preparing meals, and taking care of the farm and business. She gave birth to two daughters and one son and died at the age of sixty-four.

"My father, Ting Mu-tseng, inherited a great fortune from his father. After the death of his father, Mu-tseng devoted himself to trading in rice. He went often to the teashop to make inquiries as to the current price of rice and besides this managed 30 *kung* of farmland with the help of two long-term laborers. Though he had only four years' schooling, he could keep accounts and was good at calculating on the abacus. He was tall and strong and died at sixty-eight.

"My mother was clever and industrious, and most of our family affairs were planned by her. She was a good helper to my father. She gave birth to two sons and one daughter. We three children were much more influenced by her than by our father. Though she loved us very much, she was stern with us, while my father was very lenient. She passed away at sixty-two."

Head Ting's father continued: "When my father died, I was fifteen. When he was dying, my father called my elder brother and me to his bed and gave us a last message: 'Our family is a family that has cultivated the polite arts, loyalty, filial piety, etiquette, etc. The fortunes of our family have never declined. This may be attributed to our care for our ancestors. You should preserve this prosperity for those to come. All of them kept on the proper way. I hope that both of you may follow their virtues and cherish your estate. Then I shall be happy after my death.' This statement I still remember very well. But my elder brother put it out of his mind."

Head Ting's mother told my assistant: "After the death of my father-in-law, our home was wholly under the management of my brother-in-law. Though my brother-in-law was also an educated man (he studied in a private school for five years), he was not following the right path. Drinking and gambling, he squandered most of the property of our family. My husband had no right to interfere with what my brother-in-law did. Several years after the death of my father-in-law, my brother-in-law squandered a great part of the fortune of our large household. We could get only 10 *kung* of farmland and six rooms when we divided our household."

One of Head Ting's clan members told my assistant: "Head Ting's mother was very bright and capable. After her marriage, she knew that the property of their household would be quickly squandered by her brother-in-law and insisted that her husband divide the household with his elder brother. Before reaching her thirty-fifth birthday, though very saving, she was so poor that she had to support her family by selling doughnuts. Though all her neighbors laughed at her in secret, she was confident that she would excel most persons in the future. She often said that she was 'Pin kuo ming, lao lai hung' ('Her fate will be just like an apple which becomes red when it ripens').[3] She also said: 'Suffering while young is unimportant, but suffering while old should be avoided.' She was fifty-two in 1946 but was still very strong and got up early every morning. After arising she would sweep the floor and help her granddaughter prepare for school."

The clan member of Head Ting also said: "Head Ting's father, Ting Hsiao-chih, was a mild and honest fellow. Though sometimes he went to a teashop to drink tea or went to a restaurant to drink wine, he sat in a corner and did not gossip with others. When he was young, he was a handsome boy. He studied in a private school for more than ten years, finished the Four Books and the

3. This means that she would be prosperous when she became old. The red color symbolizes prosperity.

Five Classics[4] when he was fifteen, and got *Hsui Ts'ai*, or the degree of Bachelor of Arts, at seventeen. After getting his degree, he devoted himself to teaching. But he cared nothing about his family, even when there was no more rice or salt at home, and let his wife take the whole responsibility for the family. Only once, when his wife was about to have a child and could not support the family, he leased five out of his six rooms to others to obtain money to support them. Since he was always in debt, he was always discouraged.''

Another clan member of Head Ting told my assistant: "Because of the poverty of his family, when he was still a child, Head Ting had to work to help his mother. When he was six years old, his father let him go to school to study, but he often played truant. He studied in a private school for four years. After leaving school, he could find nothing to do. He just wandered here and there.

"When he was eighteen, Head Ting's mother tried to find a girl for him. Though the go-between had asked many girls, no one was interested. When the go-between suggested an engagement with Head Ting, he was immediately refused. After half a year, however, one of the leading gentry promised to marry his daughter to Head Ting. This gentleman, named Su Po-lan, was the commander of the Corps of People's Self-defense of Kunyang. He had a high regard for morality and thought that the success or failure of a person depended wholly on his virtue. If the ancestors of a family were able and virtu-

4. The Five Classics are *I, Shih, Shu, Chun Chui*, and *Li*, or the "Canon of Changes," the "Book of Poetry," the "Canon of History," the "Spring and Autumn Animals," and the "Book of Rites."

ous, even though the decendants were in adversity at the present time, the family would still be a *fa chia*, or 'rising family,' in the future. When he traced the genealogy of Head Ting back and found that Head Ting was the descendant of Ting Huai-yin, he decided to marry his daughter to Head Ting. Since Head Ting's family was poor, the engagement gifts which Head Ting's parents sent to Su Po-lan's family were insignificant. Su Po-lan knew in advance that he would have to help his son-in-law.''

Head Ting married at twenty. The wedding ceremony was arranged as simply as possible. On the other hand, because the girl was Su Po-lan's only daughter and also because Su was wealthy and had high status, Su Po-lan invited more than four hundred guests. According to custom, half of the dowry is paid by the bridegroom's side and the other half by the bride's family. But Head Ting's family paid nothing at all toward the dowry.

After marriage the young couple loved each other very much. Head Ting's wife was virtuous and capable. She would console him when Head Ting worried about his economic condition and encourage him when he was disappointed. She told him that she would persuade her father to advance some capital for some sort of enterprise. Hence, Head Ting loved his wife and complied with whatever she said. At the same time Head Ting's father-in-law also thought that it was not good for Head Ting not to have a permanent occupation. Then Su Po-lan requested his friend, Chien Tsai-wan, who was also one of the richest merchants and opium-dealers, to accept Head Ting as an apprentice in his shop. Chien Tsai-wan thought, however, that it was improper to accept Commander Su's son-in-law as an apprentice and declined his request. At last Commander Su invested 300 Mexican dollars in Chien Tsai-wan's shop on the condition that Chien would accept his son-in-law as an apprentice. Chien Tsai-wan felt that, since Commander Su was nominally a partner, Head Ting should be employed.

Henceforth, not only had Head Ting a place to earn his living but he also began his career. Though his reputation with the local people was bad, he became careful and industrious. He decided to try to get ahead. He was the last one to go to bed and the first one to get up in Chien's shop. After getting up, he would do every kind of work, such as sweeping the floor, moving out the goods, clearing the counter, and serving the customers. He was honest and faithful.

Since he felt that Head Ting was trustworthy, Chien Tsai-wan taught him all his secrets and passed on experience in business dealing, sharp practices in buying and selling, and the proper speech and manner to be used to various persons. Being successful in carrying out what Chien Tsai-wan had said, Head Ting felt very much interested in his career.

After four years of working in Chien Tsai-wan's shop, Head Ting decided to try to trade independently in opium and told this plan to his father-in-law. Head Ting's father-in-law agreed immediately and advanced money for that purpose on the condition that if there was any profit it should be shared equally. Su Po-lan was then the greatest opium-dealer in Kunyang. Head Ting collected the opium from producers in the country and transported it to Kunming to sell. Each time he transported more than a million *liang*, or ounces. At this time

Head Ting bought as much opium as possible under the name of his father-in-law. If he did not have enough money, he bought on credit. Because of the lack of information in the country, he could often buy the opium at a much lower price and make a high profit, but, when he reported the transactions to his father-in-law, he quoted the sale prices current in the city.

After two years Head Ting redeemed the five rooms which his father had leased out and had saved a lot of money. But, unexpectedly, all his creditors came for the payment of old debts. This was a real setback, and he was greatly discouraged. He had no more money left for his business. Then Head Ting's wife went to her father for help. Head Ting's father-in-law was compelled to lend him 300 Mexican dollars and organize a credit society[5] of 400 Mexican dollars for him. Head Ting continued in the opium trade and, after one year, was able to repay the 300 Mexican dollars he owed his father-in-

---

5. This society is a sort of savings system, into which each member pays a certain amount at certain intervals and from which he is paid a certain sum on a specified date. The size of the payment to be made by each participant and the time at which he was to be paid are prearranged. Anyone in need of money may organize a society by enlisting ten other members. Each will pay a predetermined proportion of the $400 which the organizer receives. Thereafter the society meets every six months, usually in March and September, at which time one member receives $400 and the rest make their payments. Members other than the organizer pay sums directly proportionate to the order in which they are paid, so that in effect, the first five are paying interest for loans they have received, while the last five are receiving interest for money they have deposited. The organizer, on the other hand, repays just $400 during the five-year life of the society and has thus secured a loan without interest. But he is obliged to offer a feast at each meeting and has the responsibility of collecting the money. Furthermore, in cases of default by any of the subscribers, he is held accountable. The functioning of this system depends on the invariable discharge of their obligations by the subscribers, and this is secured only by existing ties of friendship and kinship.

law; and the economic condition of his family was greatly improved. Unfortunately at this time, he caught such
a severe case of typhoid fever that he fainted many times.
His father-in-law came to his home and personally took
care of him for more than one month.

Under constant medical care his health gradually re-
covered, but his debts steadily increased. His father-in-
law made a deal for him with the county officials to take
over the collection of taxes. The sum paid by his father-
in-law was 800 Mexican dollars. As a result Head Ting
got the job of collecting the opium tax and in a single
year accumulated for himself more than $2,000. Later
the government began to control opium-smokers under
the Bureau for the Prevention of Opium-smoking. The
Bureau sold a kind of opium named *kung kao*, or "public
opium," which was mixed with morphia. According to
the regulations, every opium-smoker had to go to the
Bureau to register his name and to report the quantity
of opium smoked in a definite period. After registering,
the opium-smoker must periodically buy *kung kao* from
the Bureau or its agent and could not smoke his own
opium any more. If an opium-smoker still had some
opium, he was to sell his opium to the Bureau. After a
certain period, the opium-smokers should refrain from
smoking entirely. Head Ting bought the right of selling
kung kao from the Bureau for a certain sum of money.
From this business he accumulated for himself about
$3,000.

One of Head Ting's old friends told my assistant:
"When he sold *kung kao*, Head Ting ordered every
opium-smoker to buy a definite quantity of *kung kao*. If
an opium-smoker did not buy it and secretly smoked his

own opium, he would be arrested and punished severely by Head Ting. If Head Ting had a chance for blackmail, he would not show any mercy. Since he knew that his father-in-law was an opium-smoker and would not smoke *kung kao* instead of his own opium, the quality of which was much better than *kung kao*, he sometimes brought his men to the home of his father-in-law to investigate in the daytime; sometimes he went alone at night to the outside of the home of his father-in-law to listen for the sound of smoking. Once he heard the sound of smoking and discovered the opium which his father-in-law was using was not *kung kao*. Head Ting arrested him immediately. He did not remember his father-in-law's help in the past. Though many of his relatives and friends made an appeal to him with regard to his father-in-law, he refused. As a consequence, his father-in-law was fined 50 Mexican dollars for breaking the law.''

Head Ting's brother-in-law told my assistant: "In 1944 Head Ting's father-in-law thought of becoming a wholesaler in salt, buying salt from the government and transporting it to Kunyang, whence it would be distributed to different stores for retail sale. This was a profitable business. After getting this information, Head Ting immediately went to Kunming to try to take over this business. He presented some *tung-tiao* rice[6] and four salted ducks to the authority of the District Directorate of Salt Administration. As a result, he became a wholesale dealer in salt in Kunyang.''

In November, 1945, Head Ting's third brother-in-law

6. This is a kind of large-grained rice of very good quality, especially white and with a peculiar flavor. It is a product of Kunyang and well known in Yunnan.

was arrested (he was a private in the provincial army of Yunnan), because he was absent without leave. His commanding officer sent two soldiers to Kunyang to arrest him. When Head Ting's brother-in-law was arrested, Head Ting's father-in-law came to ask Head Ting to make an appeal to the soldiers. Since Head Ting was then the head of the Department of Conscription of the county, it would have been possible for him to secure the release of his brother-in-law. But Head Ting refused. Consequently, his brother-in-law was sent to Kunming and shot.

One of Head Ting's former partners told my assistant: "Once when he went to Nei Tien Hsiang and Chiu Tu Hsiang to sell *kung kao*, Head Ting, under the guise of suppressing opium, threatened the people with arrest and punishment. Many opium-smokers and opium-dealers came to bribe him. One day he led his men to a crossroad and searched the passers-by. As a result, he obtained more than 1,000 *liang*, or *tael*, of opium. Since this action was beyond his power, he was afraid of being reported to the magistrate. To avoid a possible accusation, he offered 400 *liang* of opium to the magistrate. This event gave him a hint that one who had no connection with officialdom would have no security even if he had money."

My assistant told me: "After taking graft money, Head Ting became very rich. He associated with rich and influential men and despised the common people. Above all, though his father-in-law had helped him many times, he not only made no repayment for his kindness but also talked about him behind his back. Therefore, some people said of Head Ting, 'One who makes a great fortune will be a cruel man.' Some other people quoted the ancient saying, 'The benevolent will not be rich; the rich will not be benevolent.' "

A colleague of Head Ting told me: "Ever since he became a *kung kao* seller, Head Ting had no other occupation. He had been anxious to get a position in the local government for a long time. In 1939 Mr. Hsu was first appointed to be head of the first *chu* government of the county. Head Ting thought that it was wise to approach Mr. Hsu. Consequently, Head Ting was appointed by Mr. Hsu to be a clerk of the district government. Because of his lack of training, this job was pretty difficult for him. His handwriting was bad. When he was assigned to write a public letter, he held the brush-pen in his hand and did not know what should be written. He was then hard pressed and uneasy, with his back covered with sweat. At that time he often sighed deeply and recited the popular couplet: 'When books are being diligently used, there is self-reproach for having read little / If an affair is not passed through, you do not know the difficulty of it.' "

Since he felt his lack of training, Head Ting tried to make up for his deficiency by being diligent and enthusiastic in doing every kind of work. If any question occurred to him, he would immediately ask Mr. Hsu to advise him. After half a year, Head Ting was promoted to be an assistant. During this time he learned about many things, such as entertainment of superior officers, social etiquette, and the technique of grafting. At the same time he associated intimately with Head Chang and other influential gentry. After two years, when he was then twenty-nine years old, the *chu* system was changed to the *hsiang-chin* system, and he was appointed to be *chin chang*, or head of the urban district. He was extremely delighted by his success.

After becoming *chin chang*, Head Ting was respectful to his superiors, such as Magistrate Ho, Head Chang, and Head Liao. He took advantage of every opportunity to send presents to them. He went to the county government offices at least once a day to report everything that had happened in the community to the magistrate. If Head Chang and Head Liao wanted him to do something, he would do it unhesitatingly. At the same time, Head Ting was harsh to his subordinates. When they asked him something, he would make a show of pride and talked with them reluctantly. Because of his fawning on his superior officials, he was nicknamed "Ha-Pa Kou," or "Pug Dog."

Since he found that Magistrate Ho, Head Chang, and Head Liao trusted him, Head Ting felt that he had someone to back him up, so he had nothing to fear. Then he plucked up courage to graft money by various means. He often used the public funds of the district to buy planking and salt and hoarded them until prices went up. Since during wartime prices kept on going up because of inflation, he made a great deal of profit very easily. It was said that he saved more than $500,000[7] from this business. Then he was ordered to build up several barns to store the tax rice of the government. Since he did not make public the account, nobody knew how much he had grafted. According to the government regulations, the tax rice was lent to the people at a yearly

7. The value of money in June, 1944, had been decreased to one forty-seventh of what it had been in January, 1937. So this sum was equivalent to about 10,600 Mexican dollars, or U.S. $5,300.

interest rate of 20 per cent. But he secretly raised the
rate to 40 per cent. Also, when he was ordered to collect
telegraph poles from the people for military use, he collected more than was needed and "squeezed" more than
fifty of the best poles for himself. Again, when the army
passed through Kunyang, the local government was
ordered to supply rice, firewood, and corn or beans. (The
rice was used to feed the soldiers, while the corn or beans
were used to feed the horses.) Head Ting often collected
more than needed and transported the remainder to his
home in the dead of night. After three years his family
became one of the richest in Kunyang.

When Head Chang accused Magistrate Chao, Head
Ting joined him in the action in Kunming. Hence Head
Ting was discharged by the magistrate from his position.
Later Chao was also removed by the provincial govern-
ment. Head Ting then returned to Kunyang and again
dealt in salt.

In January, 1945, Head Chang resigned his position as
head of the Department of Conscription of the county
and recommended Head Ting as his successor to the
magistrate. The magistrate agreed, because he found
that Head Ting was rich and sociable. Since he was rich,
when the government was in need of money, Head Ting
could advance funds. Though Head Ting was not good
at writing official letters, Magistrate Huang, the successor of Chao, thought that this might be made up for
by assigning an able clerk to assist him.

A schoolteacher told me: "After being appointed as
head of the Department of Conscription of the county
government, Head Ting climbed to the top of the social
ladder in the community. Since he was already rich and

influential, he desired nothing more than good reputation to cover up his past evil deeds. He became mild, pleasant, careful, and righteous. He liked to be flattered and admired. If someone involved in a lawsuit or other trouble asked for help, he was willing to speak a word for him. He voluntarily bought many maps and contributed them to the Central Elementary School of the Urban District. He criticized the low salary of the schoolteachers and the corruption of the officials."

Once I visited him at his home. His house was very large and clean. In the court there were many pots of flowers. Scrolls of painting and handwriting were hung on the walls in the hall and study room. The tables and chairs were made of red sandalwood. In the hall several hams and salted ducks were hung from the ceiling.

Head Ting usually went to bed very late and got up about nine o'clock in the morning. After he got up, his daughter would carry him water to wash his face. His food included fish, pork, ham, egg, salted duck, various vegetables, and rice. His clothes were made of wool of foreign manufacture. He carried a fountain pen which had been imported from the United States and wore a wrist watch and a pair of leather shoes. He also had an overcoat of Western style. His bedding was a wool blanket and satin bedclothes. There was a radio in his bedroom. When he was at home, he would listen every night to get the current market report. Everyone who saw these things would praise him highly. He went to Kunming four or five times a month on business. Sometimes he invited several intimate friends to his home to play mah-jongg, while he himself did not join them. Because he had been very often sick in recent years, he started to smoke opium, thinking that opium could cure the sickness.

Head Ting had a large household. There were eleven persons living together. They were Head Ting's parents, wife, second brother, youngest brother, two sons, and three daughters. All the affairs of the family were under Head Ting's management.

Head Ting's wife was able, clever, and virtuous. She managed the whole family in an orderly fashion. Because of her mildness, industry, and patience, all the members of the family lived together peacefully. She was her husband's right hand. In 1946 the eldest daughter was fourteen and studying in a girl's school in Kunming. The second daughter was nine and had graduated from an elementary school. The third daughter was seven and studying at the Central Elementary School of the Urban District. The elder son was five. The youngest son had just been born. Head Ting intended to let his three daughters complete the education of the middle school and to have his two sons graduate from the university.

The Gangster / Captain Yang

*Captain Yang, differing from the corrupt officials whose stories have preceded this, represents the powerful local gangster who seems throughout Chinese history to have been something of a hero to the peasantry, especially when, as in this case, he tends to prey upon the rich rather than to crush the poor. Yang is accepted up to a certain point by the gentry because they fear him, but he is not strictly gentry at all, since he lacks both the education and the ownership of land which would assure his status. It is notable that his escape from justice for his evil deeds comes partly through entry into the army and partly through cooperation with the local authorities and that, if he had not lacked "sophistication," it is believed that he might have established himself firmly in the government.—*Editor.

"Yang Tui-chiang," or Captain Yang—the captain of a company on investigation—had been assassinated two years before I arrived in Kunyang. The people, however, still talked about him everywhere. I was impressed deeply by several things. First, Commanding Officer

Yang's widow was nicknamed "Lao Mo Ting," or "Old Modern," by the county people. (In China a superficially Westernized girl was often called a *mo ting nu lang*, or a "modern girl," which is somewhat sarcastic.) Though old and illiterate, she was rather clever and could talk freely with any kind of person, a rare thing in the community. Second, Captain Yang's new house formed a striking contrast to the others in the village. Third, when I saw the fine long wooden couplets and huge signboard presented by the magistrate and the gentry in the hall of Captain Yang's house, I could not help sighing and thought to myself: "The owner of the house was a hero of a generation. Where is he now?"

Captain Yang was born in a village named Da Ma Tsun. Because of the short distance from the village to the city and the fertility of the land, most of the villagers engaged in truck gardening. On this land they grew more than thirty kinds of vegetables, including cabbage, squash, turnip, spinach, leek, eggplant, peanut, and many others. The vegetables were sold to the city dwellers and other markets near by. So the villagers had more money than they needed. There were many loafers, opium-smokers, gamblers, and even thieves among the villagers. The villagers were well known for their wantonness and lawlessness.

The village was less than one mile from my residence. During the war an American radio station and a Chinese long-distance telephone station were set up in the village, the two stations co-operating in war work. There were three American soldiers in charge of the radio station and a Chinese officer in charge of the telephone station. The three American boys and their interpreter and the

Chinese officer were living in a temple in the village. All of them became my friends. I went there very often to receive war news. The interpreter rented a room from Captain Yang's wife, so I had plenty of opportunity to visit Captain Yang's house and to talk with the old widow, Captain Yang's wife. The village of my assistant was also less than one mile from Captain Yang's village, and he was acquainted with most of the villagers.

Captain Yang's father, Yang Keng-ju, told my assistant:

"My grandfather, Yang Ping-kan, was an able, clever, tall, strong, and shrewd man. Though he was illiterate, he spoke distinctly and eloquently. He was engaged in agriculture and had 95 *kung* of farmland and a house of seven rooms. He was then the richest man in the village.

"Yang Ping-kan wisely managed his farms. Every night he planned the work for the next day for his brothers and hired men. He himself only worked occasionally. Because of his clever management, all the members of his family inherited a good deal of money.

"Yang Ping-kan went to the city every day and liked to meddle in other men's business. When anyone had a misfortune, he would go and console him; when anyone had good luck, he would go and congratulate him. If there was some question of matters such as someone's ox or horse eating another's soybeans or rice in the field and people quarreling, he would try to mediate the affair. He would look after wedding or funeral arrangements by mortgaging a house or selling a farm. When he mediated quarrels for people, he would convince both sides of the rights and wrongs of the issue. Thus he won the confidence of the people. After he had mediated a quarrel, the people would invite him to have a meal as a reward. He liked to drink wine.

"When Yang Ping-kan was forty years old, he divided the property of his family with his three brothers and obtained 25 *kung* of farmland and two rooms for himself. Since the harvest from the farms barely provided living expenses for his family, he had to work hard. Ten years later, the economic condition of his family having greatly improved, he bought 10 *kung* of farmland.

"Yang Ping-kan was merciless to his children. If a child did something wrong, he would punish him severely. As a result all his children feared him very much. He passed away at the age of sixty-seven.

"My grandmother was able and virtuous. She not only did needlework and entertained guests but also worked in the fields. She gave birth to two sons and two daughters. She loved her children so much that she never scolded or beat them even when they did something wrong. She reasoned with them instead. She died at seventy-one.

"My father, Yang Hou-hsi, was the eldest one of three brothers. He worked very hard as a farmer. During the lull in farming in the winter, he was accustomed to go to the mountains to gather firewood for the whole next year for his household. He rented 10 *kung* of farmland from a landlord. In the busy period of the year the wages of a laborer were much higher than usual, and so he hurried to complete his own work so that he could hire out to others. After five years our family's economic condition was improved. Formerly we had had only one ox, now we had two. Formerly we raised only two pigs, now the number had been doubled. After another five years our family bought 15 *kung* of farmland and built a house with two rooms. All the villagers admired my father's ability.

"When my father, Hou-hsi, was thirty-two, my grandfather, Ping-kan, passed away. Two years later my grandmother died also. Ever since the death of my grandparents, my mother's sisters-in-law began to quarrel, and hence my father's brothers became unhappy. The large family was divided into three small families.

"My father, Yang Hou-hsi, had 10 *kung* of farmland and two rooms. Though the economic condition of our family was improving steadily during the first few years, my father did not increase his property very much. He died at the age of seventy-four. [One of Yang Keng-ju's clan members told me: "Yang Hou-hsi's only son, Yang Keng-ju, was spoiled from boyhood and hence very lazy. Keng-ju did nothing except eat and sleep. Keng-ju's laziness made Hou-hsi unhappy. That was the main reason for the decline of his family."]

"My mother was able, clever, agreeable, and generous. She not only pushed my father to work hard but also led her sisters-in-law and brothers-in-law in efforts for the family's progress. Unfortunately, after the division of the family, she felt that her family could not be prosperous, because her only son was lazy and spent his money unwisely. She grew sad and aged rapidly. She died at the age of sixty-nine."

One of Captain Yang's clan members told my assistant: "Captain Yang's father, Yang Keng-ju, was spoiled by his parents from boyhood. When he was around ten years old, he was already cruel, violent, and mischievous. He bullied all the boys about the same age in the village. When he took his ox to the field to graze, he would tell the other boys to steal turnips or melons in the field to give him to eat. If this event was discovered by the owner, he would throw the blame on the other boys. When he went out to pick up fertilizer, he would tell other boys to pick it for him.

"Yang Keng-ju married at the age of eighteen. After his marriage, he was well dressed and did nothing every day. He liked to gamble. Sometimes he went to other places to gamble; sometimes he assembled the gamesters at his own house.

"When Yang Keng-ju was thirty years old, he lost a great deal of money in gambling. Since he had no way to repay his gambling debts, he had to leave home. He worked as a laborer in Anning and as a tin-miner in Kuo Chiu. After one year, however, he returned home penniless.

"After a year of nomadic life, Yang Keng-ju temporarily changed his way of life. Now he worked very hard. He had then 8 *kung* of farm and 2 *kung* of truck garden. Since the income was not enough for the expenses of his family, he had to work as a temporary laborer for others to increase his income. He was noted for his extraordinary strength. After three years the economic condition of his family was improved, but, because of his habits of gambling and drinking, he did not save much money.

"Yang Keng-ju was noted for his violence and cruelty. When someone offended him, he would gnash his teeth in anger and knock him down. He not only had wounded his brother-in-law [the husband of his wife's sister] but had also killed his own third son. Everyone who saw his fierce face would be afraid of him. He often assaulted others without warning. He was so headstrong that he would never acknowledge himself to be wrong. If you insisted on your opinion and did not flatter him, he would hate you bitterly. If you showed admiration or respect for him, he would be very happy.

"Yang Keng-ju was very austere to his children. If he detected any cowardice in them, he would either scold them severely or beat them. He encouraged them in, or even drove them into, various exploits. If he saw his son showing recklessness or courage, he would be greatly delighted. He admired anyone who could instil fear in others. He passed away at the age of sixty-two in 1944.

"Yang Keng-ju's wife was clever, tricky, and cunning. She and her husband were well matched. Even in her middle age, she still liked to be smartly dressed every day and was lively and animated. Nevertheless, she was meticulous in her housekeeping and worked willingly in the garden and fields. She went to the city to sell vegetables every day. After selling the vegetables, she would return home at once and never bought anything to eat in the street. She was inclined to be jealous and was something of a gossip. She was sixty-one in 1946."

Another clan member of Captain Yang told my assistant: "Captain Yang was Yang Keng-ju's first son. When Captain Yang was born, the economic condition of his family was bad. Hence, he had no opportunity to enter school. Ever since he was a boy, he was crafty, bold, and full of wit. He spent his time swearing, teasing, and plotting against boys whom he did not like. Though later all the boys of his village were under his control, the boys of the other villages at first did not obey him. But he organized all the boys of his village into a group and led them in fights with the boys of the other villages. At last all the boys of the neighboring villages were under his control except those at one village, named Hsao Tien Tsun. He vowed to conquer them and ordered the boys of his own village each to be armed with a club or a stick. He led his group to fight with the boys of Hsao Tien Tsun nearly every day. At last he defeated and controlled them.

"This event was told to Captain Yang's father. Yang Keng-ju praised him highly and encouraged him to be more combative. Moreover, from that time on Yang Keng-ju decided to let his son join the army.

"When Captain Yang was sixteen in 1918, he voluntarily enlisted in the army. After five years he was promoted to be a sergeant. Unfortunately, this troop suffered defeat by the enemy at the border of Szechuan and Yunnan. He left the army and came back home.

"Pending his coming back home, Captain Yang robbed three times to obtain money to travel home. After returning home, he associated with many rascals. There was then a Colonel Lu, who was very strong and knew military arts. Colonel Lu earned his living by plundering. Captain Yang had been a bandit under him.

"Captain Yang married at twenty, but, though he was married, he still spent his time with prostitutes. His wife was tall and wild. Though she was not pretty, she was very clever and finely dressed. She had lost her chastity before her marriage, and this angered her husband. If his wife offended him, he would beat her ruthlessly. When he was thirty, he took a concubine. During this period his wife changed her former attitude and gained her husband's sympathy by means of flattery.

Thus he loved his wife more than his concubine until his death.

"Captain Yang's concubine was the daughter of a merchant in Yu Chi. Captain Yang gathered more than thirty members of his gang and went to Yu Chi to carry her off. When her father discovered where she was, Captain Yang sent some money to him for compensation. The merchant thought that since 'the rice has been boiled,' even though he could claim back his daughter by appealing to the court, it would not be easy to marry her to another. So the merchant was compelled to marry his daughter to Captain Yang as a concubine.

"Captain Yang usually led a dissipated life. He not only gambled but also visited prostitutes. He had a pair of thick, black eyebrows, fierce eyes, and a devilish face. He spoke and acted discreetly. When he walked, he kept his eyes to the front. You could not know his intentions from his facial expression. It was said that he had assaulted several women and that, when he raped a woman, he held a knife in his mouth so that the woman dared not resist or cry out.

"One day in December, 1948, Captain Yang's cousin came to tell him that his cousin had been insulted by a young man. His cousin usually earned his living by bringing persons or transporting goods with his horse to and from Yu Chi and Kunyang. This time a young man hired his horse to go from Yu Chi to Kunyang. When the young man arrived in Kunyang, he discovered that his overcoat was lost. The young man not only refused to pay for hiring the horse but also asked Captain Yang's cousin to return his overcoat. After hearing this, Captain Yang left the teashop immediately and hurried to the east gate to find the young man. When he saw him, Captain Yang boxed his ears and knocked him down. He took off his overcoat and threw it to the young man, saying: 'Son-of-a-bitch! Is this overcoat yours? You take it. Are you the only one to have an overcoat? You must wipe your eyes.' He turned his back and walked away. The young man stood up and ran after him to offer an explanation, but he did not pay any attention to it.

"This young man was the nephew of Colonel Chen in Kunming. After returning to Kunming, the young man told his uncle of the beating by Captain Yang. Colonel Chen was so angry that he sent two sergeants and a group of soldiers with his nephew to Kunyang for revenge. After arriving at Kunyang, they looked for Captain Yang everywhere. At last they found him in a teashop, where someone pointed him out; so that when the two sergeants entered the teashop, they immediately aimed their pistols at him. Captain Yang pretended that he was not Captain Yang and stood up to go away. When he walked to the door of the teashop, the young man, who was waiting outside, shouted: 'He is the man we want! He is the man we want!' Captain Yang was seized by the soldiers who guarded the door. They wanted to bind his arms behind his back, but Capaain Yang submissively said that he would go anywhere and that there was no need to tie his hands up. At that time one of the captain's good friends, who was also an army sergeant and was drinking tea with him, saw that there might be a misunderstanding and went up to see if he could patch up the matter. He was also seized by the soldiers, who then searched Captain Yang and his friend for arms. Since they discovered no arms on either of them, they did not tie their hands, but both were held by men on each side and were compelled to walk down the street.

"The soldiers wanted to shoot Captain Yang at a vacant place. Fortunately, it was a market day and some of the spectators said to them: 'There are too many people here. You had better shoot him outside the north gate of the city.' At this critical moment Captain Yang was in great anxiety. He felt that the most important thing for him was to save his life. The Chinese proverb said: 'One who starts first is the stronger.' Captain Yang complained that his shoe laces were loose and asked the two men who held his arms to let him tie them. They found that his complaint was true and let go of one of his hands. They did not know that it was merely a pretext. Captain Yang bent down, suddenly drew a sharp knife from his stocking, killed the two men, and ran away. Though the other soldiers ran after him with their guns in their hands, they could not catch him. He disappeared among the people, ran out of the street, and hid in a public toilet. There he took off his gown, threw it into the pit, and walked out. When the soldiers who had run after him and could not find him finally came back, he had already climbed over the city wall and run far away. It was unfortunate that his friend was shot instead of him.

"After escaping from the city, Captain Yang hurried home to tell his family of the situation and then went to the home of his sister's father-in-law to hide. After seven days he saw that nothing had happened except that his father had been arrested by the county government of Kunyang. But he felt that, if he did not join the army, he would still be in danger of being arrested. At that time Commander Shu, the commander of a division in Kunming, was on the lookout for a courageous man for his guard. Captain Yang enlisted in the army. Commander Shu was Colonel Chen's superior officer and was informed that Captain Yang had killed the two sergeants under Colonel Chen. Because he wanted to test Captain Yang's courage, Commander Shu purposely asked him if he would like to see Colonel Chen. Captain Yang answered readily: 'Yes, commander. Please give me a visiting card of yours.' Then Captain Yang went to meet Colonel Chen with Commander Shu's visiting card. Since Captain Yang was carrying out Commander Shu's order, Colonel Chen did not mention his past offense and received him politely.

"In time Captain Yang's father was released by the county government. After Captain Yang had paid some indemnity money for the death of the two sergeants, the event was considered to be closed.

"Captain Yang's next younger brother, Yang Peiliang, was illiterate and an evil man. He also enlisted in the army of Commander Shu through his elder brother's help. He was put in charge of provisions for the army, a lucrative post, because one could 'squeeze' money from buying supplies.

"Captain Yang and his brother served in the army for three years. During these years they were in Szechuan and Kwangsi and fought with the enemy dozens of times. Though Captain Yang was noted for his courage and adventurousness, he was selfish and cunning. Since Commander Shu had known him for a long time, he gave some money to Captain Yang and his brother to return home, after he was defeated by his enemy in Kwangsi Province.

"During their stay at home Captain Yang and his young brother made acquaintance with rascals of various sorts and wasted all their money in drinking, gambling, and visiting prostitutes. When they had no more money, they began to rob travelers. Once they killed an ox-dealer and robbed him of all his money.

"Captain Yang's second younger brother, Yang Pei-tsung, was the cleverest and most energetic of the three brothers. His father, however, did not love him, and they often quarreled. When they quarreled, Yang Keng-ju usually declared that he would kill Pei-tsung. One day, both Keng-ju and Pei-tsung were cutting cabbage in their truck garden. Keng-ju scolded Pei-tsung incessantly. When Pei-tsung argued with him, Keng-ju chopped him twice on the head with a knife. Three months later, Pei-tsung died at the age of eighteen. Later, when he was in power, Captain Yang still felt badly for the death of his second younger brother. He often said: 'If Pei-tsung had lived, he would be a very good helper of mine.'

"In 1933 and 1934, bandits were rampant in Kunyang. Captain Yang associated with the gangsters of the neighboring counties of Kunyang. They plundered not only the country but also the city. When they committed robbery in Kunyang, Captain Yang himself would not join the looting openly but secretly arranged the plans for the gang. All the money and goods he received he distributed equally. When they plundered in the other counties, however, Captain Yang would join in. They had a leader in every district. Captain Yang was the leader of Kunyang and called 'Ta Ke,' or 'Elder Brother,' by the members of their organization.[1] He was always followed by several bodyguards.

"Once in the spring of 1935 Captain Yang was informed that his next younger brother was quarreling with a gambler. He immediately went to the gambling house with his bodyguards and drew out his sword to chop off the head of the gambler. The gambler turned his head just in time and was wounded on the face. The gambler wanted to snatch the sword with his right hand. When Captain Yang drew back his sword, the gambler's four fingers were almost cut off. Captain Yang fled away at once and went to Kuo Chiu. The county government of Kunyang arrested Captain Yang's father and put him in jail. After three months Captain Yang's father was released on the condition he should pay some money to the gambler for his medical expenses.

"After arriving in Kuo Chiu, Captain Yang still had nothing to do except gamble. The local authority was searching for Communists. Since Captain Yang had no definite gainful occupation, he was arrested and put in jail. Though he suffered a great deal of torture, he con-

1. The members of the organization are all sworn brothers. The ranks are decided according to the age and ability of each member. The member of the lower rank must obey the member of the higher rank. When one member enters the organization, he must formally swear under the open sky and drink some "chicken's blood-wine." This formality symbolizes that blood is thicker than water. Each swears to be responsible for the happiness or misfortune of the others. Each one must protect every other member and the whole organization. One person is chosen as a leader in every place. When a member arrives in his place, the leader of that place must be responsible for the member's food and lodging. If a member is not loyal to the organization, he will be dismissed and punished by the other members. They have various gestures and secret language, so that they can know each other even if they have not met before. They usually make their living by gambling, robbing, and being hired as assassins.

fessed nothing. After half a year he escaped and came back home.

"After returning home, Captain Yang became more adventurous and swaggered through the streets every day. He associated with the rascals of other counties to do various lawless deeds. Hence, all the people called him 'Ta Yeh,' or 'Great Father.' Captain Yang's men often robbed money or goods from merchants or travelers at the passes between two counties. There was one case of robbery every three or four nights in the city of Kunyang. The rich merchants in the city were extremely afraid of him. They had to stay up all night to watch their property. Captain Yang was noted for his hatred of the rich people. He did not disturb the poor people."

One of the gentry told me: "In 1937 Magistrate Ho came to Kunyang. He saw that the whole county was in chaos and found that public order could be accomplished only by the strategy of "pitting gangsters against gangsters." After inquiring about the organization of the gang, he knew that Captain Yang was the highest leader. He invited Captain Yang to the county government and asked his opinion about the public order of Kunyang. Since the magistrate praised him highly and begged him earnestly to do so, Captain Yang promised to accept an appointment as captain of a company of investigation.

"After taking over this position, Captain Yang appointed all the able robbers under him as members of the company. Indeed, the robberies within the district of Kunyang decreased daily. In the city the cases of robbery disappeared completely. Captain Yang was loyal and grateful to the magistrate and accompanied him every day. Hence, Magistrate Ho regarded Captain Yang as a reformed man and had faith in him. Then Captain Yang suddenly became one of the most powerful men in Kunyang. When the families of the gentry had feasts or banquets, he was always invited as an honorable guest. The magistrate and gentry gave him a eulogy—*chu pao an liang*, or 'getting rid of evil and giving peace to the good.' The richest merchant of Kunyang, Wu Chi-min, took Captain Yang's daughter as a fiancée for his son, because he wanted to receive protection from Captain Yang. When Captain Yang walked in the streets, the common people would bow before him. When he walked into a teashop or restaurant, he was greeted with cordiality by the people and the owner of the shop. Captain Yang's father was called 'Lao Tai Yeh,' or 'Grand Old Gentleman,' by the people. In a word, Captain Yang had climbed from the bottom to the top of the social hierarchy.''

Another one of the gentry told me: ''During these years there were three notorious leaders of a gang in Kunyang. One was Hsiao Ku, who occupied the western district of Kunyang; another one was Mei Heng-chun, who occupied the southern district of Kunyang; the third one was Captain Yang, who occupied the remaining district of Kunyang including the city. They were sworn brothers and associated with each other. The magistrate appointed Mei Heng-chun as the captain of the Company for Suppressing Bandits in the southern district of Kunyang and later ordered him to kill Hsiao Ku. Consequently, Hsiao Ku was assassinated by Mei Heng-chun.

''Several months after the death of Hsiao Ku, the magistrate induced Captain Yang to kill Mei Heng-chun.

In carrying out this order, Captain Yang allotted several of his helpers to watch Mei Heng-chun's going and coming. He himself frequently accompanied Mei Heng-chun to smoke opium and drink wine together in order to show his intimacy with his sworn brother and to avoid being suspected by Mei Heng-chun. One day they went to an opium house to smoke opium on the second floor and lay on the bed face to face. When Mei Heng-chun put his pistol on the bed, Captain Yang immediately said: 'Elder brother, where is that pistol manufactured? It looks very good.' Before finishing his speech, Captain Yang had taken over Mei's pistol. He examined the pistol carefully. When he saw Mei Heng-shun was not on his guard, he aimed at Mei and fired twice. Though Mei Heng-chun was wounded, he still tried to resist Captain Yang. Captain Yang descended the stairs hastily. After a while Mei Heng-chun fainted, and at last Captain Yang went upstairs and killed him.

"During this period, though he did not plunder, Captain Yang found another way of accumulating wealth under the cover of the company on investigation. He often raided the gambling houses and ordered his men to arrest the gamblers. He also searched the opium houses. If the gamblers or the owners of the opium houses were arrested, they would be fined severely. He got a great deal of money from them this way. If he got money, he would distribute part of it to his men. Moreover, he allotted his men at various passes to search the travelers. If opium or guns and bullets were found, all of them would be confiscated. If was estimated that he got about 10,000 *liang*, or *tael*, of opium and more than two hundred pistols in this way. He prepared to use these arms as a foundation to enlarge his power.

"Two years after taking this position, Captain Yang returned to his old vices. He hated the rich and often sent his men to plunder them of their money or goods at night. Captain Yang would pretend to seek out robbers, but all his efforts were naturally in vain.

"Thieves from the local and other counties would visit Captain Yang first if they wanted to be robbers in Kunyang. If a thief had been promised the territory by Captain Yang, he would divide the money or goods which he got with Captain Yang. Otherwise, if he tried to carry on his business in Kunyang, he would lose his life.

"There was a stream flowing from west to east between the village of Da Ma Tsun and Cheng Lei Tsun. It was usually dry, but it filled with water during the rainy season. The people of both villages became hostile through competing for the water. When Captain Yang became the captain of the company on investigation, the people of Cheng Lei Tsun dared not use the water of the stream any more for fear of Captain Yang's powerful influence.

"Captain Yang's special ability was to fire a gun accurately and to use a sword swiftly. He could meet the greatest dangers with the utmost calmness and get out of the difficulty. For example, once after plundering a merchant, Captain Yang and several of his helpers were drinking and eating in the hall of a family. At this time the policemen of the county government came to encircle the house and fired their guns outside the gate. Captain Yang dashed out of the house with two chairs in his hands for cover. Though all the policemen aimed their guns at him, he still escaped with his life. Since he had passed through many dangers, he often said: 'I am not easy to kill. If I had been going to die, I should have died years ago.'

"Through his robberies, Captain Yang acquired a great deal of money. He did not use his money to buy farms but built a large new house.

"Magistrate Ho was informed many times that Captain Yang plundered in the city, but he did not believe it because there was no evidence. Nevertheless, the magistrate began to pay attention to this.

"In January, 1941, Captain Yang secretly opened many gambling houses in the county, while he allotted his men to arrest the gamblers. All the arrested gamblers were fined severely according to their means. In three nights in succession, he got more than $100,000.[2] He kept the money for himself alone. One day, his right-hand man, Fan Piao-meng, wanted to borrow some money. Captain Yang not only refused his request but also scolded him. Henceforth, Fan Piao-meng began to hate him.

"One night Captain Yang asked the magistrate to lend him two ten-round automatics and one hundred bullets. The magistrate asked him what his purpose was. He answered: 'In recent days there are many cases of plundering in the city. I shall use them for searching and arresting the robbers.' The magistrate had a hard time turning down this request. If he lent him the pistols, it might be harmful; if he did not lend the pistols to him,

2. The value of money in January, 1941, had decreased 9 times on the base of January, 1937. So this sum was equivalent to 11,111 silver dollars, or U.S. $5,555.

he might offend him. At last, the magistrate made an excuse that the pistols were not at hand and asked Yang to take fifty bullets with him first.

"The next night Captain Yang took the fifty bullets with him and went to plunder the family of a rich merchant in the city. The neighbor of the rich merchant was a restaurant owner. Captain Yang ordered some dishes at the restaurant in the daytime for their eating at midnight.

"After drinking and eating at midnight, Captain Yang and his men piled the tables and benches on top of each other on the top floor of the restaurant and climbed over to the rich merchant's home. However, when they began to carry out the goods, the rich merchant found them. Captain Yang's brother fired at the merchant's right hand. Hearing the sound of the gun, the policemen came over to arrest the robbers. But when they found that it was Captain Yang, they immediately went back. At this time the family of the rich merchant cried and shouted for help. Captain Yang and his men ran away in great haste. Unfortunately, Captain Yang left the fifty bullets which he had borrowed from the magistrate behind him at the counter in the merchant's shop. The next morning Captain Yang pretended to gather his men to hunt the robbers. But the rich merchant had reported the case of robbery and the fifty bullets to the county government. The magistrate was greatly surprised to recognize the bullets which he had lent to Captain Yang the previous night and became convinced of the truth of the information which the gentry had reported to him.

"Since the magistrate was very worried, he appointed a man in his confidence to make secret inquiry if there was anyone who dared to assassinate Captain Yang. The reward for carrying out this assassination was appointment to the position of commanding officer in the county government and $10,000. Information was obtained that Fan Piao-meng had quarreled with Captain Yang, and he was asked to kill Captain Yang. The magistrate secretly called Piao-meng to the county government and personally asked him to promise to carry out this mission. The magistrate gave Piao-meng a written order to kill Captain Yang within ten days.

"After accepting the order, Piao-meng was struck with fear when he saw Captain Yang and dared not execute the scheme. Later Fan Piao-meng asked someone else to carry out the plan. However, this man was also afraid to act.

"Unexpectedly, on the evening of the sixth day the magistrate's nephew told what was being planned to Captain Yang. After obtaining this information, Captain Yang with five of his men, each of them with pistol in hand, went directly to the bedroom of the magistrate and angrily asked: 'It is said that you are asking someone to kill me. Please tell me how have I offended you?' Though his heart was beating, Magistrate Ho still remained calm and said: 'No such thing! Captain Yang, please don't believe rumors of this sort. I cannot keep my position without you, I need you so much. How could I do that? You know that I have always treated you kindly. It doesn't matter that I am in the position of magistrate. The feeling between you and me is very important. Please take it easy. In the near future, I will make inquiry as to the source of this rumor.' After hearing Magistrate Ho, Captain Yang became calm. The magistrate also asked him to smoke opium.

"Since he had had a narrow escape, Magistrate Ho urged Fan Piao-meng to execute their scheme as soon as possible.

"After this, though puffed up with pride and feeling that no one dared to kill him in Kunyang, Captain Yang planned to move away from Kunyang. The morning of January 23, 1941, he picked up his luggage, fed his horse, and was ready to leave his native county. Before setting out, he went to the teashop to drink some tea. This information was reported to the magistrate. Magistrate Ho thought that, if he did not kill Captain Yang at this time, it would be like releasing a tiger in the mountains. It would mean trouble in the future. Hence the magistrate told the head of the Division of Receiving and Sending Public Letters of the county government, King Cho-jan, to accompany Captain Yang to the teahouse and to order the assassin to kill Captain Yang at once. Fan Piao-meng let the assassin enter the teashop first. After a while Fan Piao-meng himself came to the teashop, ostensibly to drink tea also. While Captain Yang was walking with King Cho-jan and Fan Piao-meng, the assassin suddenly came over with a knife and stabbed Captain Yang several times without warning. Though he was wounded seriously, Captain Yang still tried to get out his pistol to shoot. At this time, Fan Piao-meng hurried to Captain Yang and asked: 'What happened? Elder Brother, give me the pistol!' Captain Yang thought Fan Piao-meng was coming to help him and gave him the pistol. Fan Piao-meng took the pistol and fired twice at Captain Yang. Captain Yang died." (The speaker sighed a deep sigh.)

After pausing a while, the speaker continued: "It was

said that, though he was wounded several dozen times, Captain Yang did not groan once. He was really a brave man.'' (The speaker sighed again.)

My assistant told me: ''Hearing of his elder brother's assassination, Yang Pei-liang immediately hurried to the city with a gun in his hand. When he arrived at the south gate of the city, he was advised not to fall into the trap. Thus he returned to his home in haste.

''The city guard eventually came to the village and encircled Captain Yang's house. They looked for Yang Pei-liang everywhere; but he had escaped from his home before their arrival.

''The other gangsters fled when they heard that the magistrate had hired an assassin to kill Captain Yang. One of them, however, was arrested and shot the next day by the county government police.''

After the death of Captain Yang, his family was mournful and busy. Because they had been advised to hide their things of value, Captain Yang's wife, concubine, and parents transported their goods to another place. Therefore, Captain Yang's home became an empty shell of four walls within a short time. Later, when the magistrate's men came to liquidate Captain Yang's home, they found only some articles of no value.

In the evening the family went to the city to claim Captain Yang's corpse. All of them cried bitterly. Captain Yang's mother cried: ''My clever and talented son, I have repeatedly warned you to be clear-sighted. But you said that you had nothing to fear.'' Captain Yang's wife cried: ''My brave and martial-looking husband, you were a great hero when you were alive; you must be an evil spirit after your death. You must revenge your death in the next world.''

People reacted in various ways to the death of Captain Yang. The rich merchants and gentry considered Captain Yang a troublemaker in Kunyang and felt happy for his death. They said: "If the great thief were not dead, there would be no public order in Kunyang." The peasantry, however, felt that, though he was ill-famed, Captain Yang had never bullied or blackmailed any poor country people, and they sympathized with him and his family. They said: "We admire him because he was a man not afraid of force or oppression."

Once when I talked about Captain Yang with a schoolteacher, I asked him why, although Captain Yang had climbed from the bottom to the top of the social ladder, he was not content with his position as a member of gentry? And since he hated the rich and used much of his money to buy arms instead of buying land, why did he not become a social revolutionist? What were the reasons for Captain Yang's failure? The schoolteacher explained the matter to me as follows:

"Captain Yang could temporarily indulge himself as he did because he was backed by the force of his underground group. The county government did not attempt to arrest and kill him, because to do so might only result in Captain Yang and his men retiring to the mountains as bandits. However, with the coming of Magistrate Ho, the situation changed. The magistrate was a very artful official. He adopted a policy of 'pitting one against another' to annihilate the group. Captain Yang and his fellow-gangsters fell into the magistrate's trap.

For though the gangsters had organization, they were not well organized—with no common ideology and group interest or consciousness. Though Captain Yang might have tried to take advantage of his position to enlarge his strength, he had no idea of political intrigue. The main reason for Captain Yang's failure was his lack of sophistication.

"After becoming the captain of the company on investigation, if he had changed his former ideology and conduct, Captain Yang might have become a member of gentry forever. But after becoming captain, he still hated the rich people and did not use his money to buy land. He was in the position of a member of the ruling class, but he still carried on action against it. 'Because of having no secure property, one could not have a stable mind.'[3] Captain Yang had no firm position. Moreover, since Captain Yang himself and his ancestors had not been educated, they were not fit for the status of gentry. Captain Yang could not pick up a 'brush,' or pen, instead of a sword or gun. Even when Captain Yang was in power, the other members of gentry and the rich people did not really respect him; they just dared not speak out, even though they were angry. These might be the reasons for Captain Yang's discontent with his position as member of the gentry.

"Though the gangsters and gentry belong to different classes, they are just the same in that they do not engage in production and are parasitic on the industrious and virtuous peasantry. The peasants are envious of them for their ease of life. Captain Yang was a leader of the gangsters and feared by the people. He was not respected,

3. From a Mencian saying.

loved, and championed by them. Though sometimes he might appear to be a chivalrous knight-errant whose inclination was to defend the weaker and poorer groups against the rich and powerful gentry, Captain Yang was actually greedy, unscrupulous, and relentless. He would resort to any means to achieve his ends when he was struggling for money and power. Since he did not belong to the peasant group, he could not win the support of the poor peasants. Since he and his group had not won the support of the masses, how could Captain Yang become a social revolutionist?

"Is it true that in the last years before his death, Captain Yang used most of the money which he plundered to buy arms and secretly distributed them to more than five hundred members of his gang, and he might have made some political attempt, because he often said that he wanted to suppress the rich and protest social injustice. Yet, since he himself was illiterate, Captain Yang had no vision of a new society."

One of the neighbors of Captain Yang informed me: "Captain Yang was tall and well knit. He looked calm, silent, and serious but was not to be trusted. He was resolute in action, and, if someone offended him, he would not hesitate to apply force. He usually brought two pistols and knife with him; pistols filled with bullets—the smaller pistol worn under his hat and the larger at his waist. He never forgot to try out his pistols before going out of his home. He was clever at shooting and using a knife.

"Captain Yang was usually well dressed and changed his clothes every day. He generally ate good meals three or four times a day. [The peasants usually eat two meals a day.] But his life was often not regular. Sometimes he stayed awake all night; sometimes he slept all day. His bedding was of good materials, such as British wool blankets. When he went to some rather distant place, he usually rode a big, swift horse or bicycle. His horse was well fed daily. He was very generous to his friends. Though he was noted as an evildoer and 'unreasonable,' he was very kind to the common people."

The Reformer / Liu Tsung-tao

*At first the life of Liu Tsung-tao appears to be that of a modern
revolutionary. Yet he is far from a "Marxian hero," following
a party line and maneuvering popular discontent as directed
by those higher up in party authority. He is rather an indi-
vidualist working, and none too effectively, with little support
except from an unorganized popular feeling, to do away with
what his conscience feels to be wrong and unjust. Thus he may
be rightly seen as corresponding with those Chinese intellectual
rebels of the past who took up the cause of the people against
the imperial power. Less characteristic of the traditional order
than Chairman Wang, he nevertheless represents a form of the
"scholar's conscience" which throughout Chinese history has
from time to time led to direct action against abuses of authority.—*EDITOR.

To celebrate the Midautumnal Festival in 1944, the
principal of the junior middle school of Kunyang gave a
dinner party for all the teachers. Chairman Wang was
there as principal and I as a part-time teacher at the

school. At that time the gentry of Kunyang were going to accuse Magistrate Chao. They talked about the corruption, incompetence, and injustice of the magistrate and the sauciness and ugliness of his wife (she was marked with smallpox). Simultaneously, they talked about the talent, bravery, thoughtfulness, and farsightedness of Mr. Liu Tsung-tao and how he was compelled to be a "bandit" by the magistrate. The atmosphere was full of contempt and admiration, hatred and tenderness. This symbolized the disorganization of the government leaders and the people's longing for drastic reform.

One of my assistants had taught in an elementary school for one year in Liu Tsung-tao's native district and had come to know Liu Tsung-tao well. Later he visited there twice to interview Mr. Liu and others and stayed at Mr. Liu's home for two days. Here are my assistant's reports:

"Liu Tsung-tao was born in 1910 in a small village west of Kunyang. It was thirty-five miles from his native place to the city of Kunyang. The village was at the foot of a mountain, and communication with the outside world was very difficult. Most of the villagers were Lolos. Everyone here engaged in agriculture except a few rich people who had a lumber business. The farms, which were on the slopes of the mountains, were called *ti tien*, or 'ladder farms.' The mountains, covered with thick forests, offered a safe refuge for many bandits."

Liu Tsung-tao told my assistant: "My great grandfather, Liu Shang-kuei, was clever, energetic, and eloquent. Because the economic condition of our family was then pretty good, and he was an only son, he was rather spoiled by his parents. From boyhood on he liked to dress well and make friends, roam about, and gamble or drink in the town market.

"Between the ages of twenty and thirty, Liu Shang-kuei became a real good-for-nothing. Sometimes he did not even go back home once in ten days. Only when he had squandered all his money in the town market would he return home to sell some rice. If his wife interfered with him, he would beat her. He not only gambled but also liked to *wan hsiao ku niang,* or 'patronize unmarried girls.'[1] In the district he did not fear criticisms by others. On the contrary, he often interfered with others' *hua chang,* or 'flower ground.'[2] Nearly all the gay young girls of the region had been entertained by him. His singing was very passionate, and it was said that he could sing folk songs for three days and nights without repeating the same tune. Moreover, he could play various musical instruments very well. His humorous speech often made others laugh. Since his presence was enlivening, he was usually welcome everywhere. He was strong, gentle, lighthearted, and always smiling.

"Shang-kuei was generous. He made friends with both good fellows and bad men. He often went to a restaurant to have dinner with five or six friends and paid for them. Thus, he squandered a great deal of money. As a result, all his friends thought well of him. The wild young men especially upheld and protected him. If anyone criticized

1. This refers to a custom of the Lolos in which men engage girls to go to the mountains at night—usually to sit under the moonlight or around a fire. The men prepare wine, fruits, cookies, etc., as refreshments, and they may play musical instruments, tell stories, dance, or sing love songs. Usually they spend the night in the mountains.

2. The place of assignation.

him, they would defend him. Gradually he became a leader of the loafers; nevertheless, he did not bully anybody. He often said: 'I shall never oppress the common people; I do not fear the influential.'

"But when he was forty years old he learned a bitter lesson. Shang-kuei was forced to sell 20 *kung* out of his 30 *kung* of farmland. Since he could not entertain his old friends any more, they deserted him and despised him. He often said: 'Life must be nourished by money. A man without a job has no way to get on. The result of loafing through life will be more grief than happiness.' He passed away at the age of sixty-eight.

"My great-grandmother was an able and energetic woman. She was painstaking, industrious, and frugal. The wildness of my great-grandfather made her sad. Her earnings of four or five days were not enough even for one meal for her husband. When she tried to stop her husband from selling land, she would get a beating from him. These circumstances made her heartbroken. During her old age she wept very often when she recalled the difficulties of her earlier life. She gave birth to two sons and two daughters. At seventy-four she died.

"My grandfather, Liu Chen-lo, suffered a great deal when a young boy. Because his father did nothing good for his family, he had to assist his mother with chores around the farm when he was only seven years old. He did everything according to his mother's direction and became old for his years. He felt that, though his father was no good, he himself should have the determination to struggle for fame and wealth. If he did not strive when he was young, he felt he would have no future. His mother also felt hopeful for him.

"When Chen-lo was twelve, his father was again going to sell some of his farmland. He and his mother tried to persuade his father from selling it, saying: 'Papa, if you sell all your land, what will we eat in the future? How can you support yourself when you become old?' But his father replied, 'Er sun tzu yu er sun fu, mo wei er sun tao ma niu' ('The descendants will have their own blessing; don't toil like a beast of burden for them').[3] After that Chen-lo became very indifferent to his father, for he felt that his father was not a good man. He and his mother worked hard and asked the people not to buy the farm from his father. Thus, they preserved 10 *kung* of 'level field' and 5 *kung* of 'hilly land.' Though his father turned over a new leaf in his old age, 'the fertile water had flowed to the farm of others.' Chen-lo had a hard time throughout his life.

"Chen-lo was honest, careful, and painstaking. He led his younger brother to work every day. To obtain more income, he rented 10 *kung* of farmland from a farmer named Hsieh Pao-hsin. These farms were originally infertile and the rent was light. He applied more than the usual amount of ferilizer, and, since he could keep two-thirds[4] of the products of the farm, the economic condition of his family improved gradually.

"The improvement of his family's finances encouraged him to work harder still. He bought twenty goats for 8 piculs of rice so as to obtain fertilizer. As a result the harvest from his farm was greatly increased. Moreover, the star of his family was in the ascendant during these years. His production of various kinds of grain rose great-

3. An ancient Chinese saying.

4. The ordinary rent for land in this region was at least half of the produce.

ly, and his domestic animals flourished. When he was fourty-four, he bought the 10 *kung* of farmland which he had rented from Hsieh Pao-hsin. Besides, his family was able to save 8 piculs of rice aside from that used by themselves. He lent the 8 piculs of rice to the villagers at a yearly interest of 70 per cent. Though he was then a rich man in his village, he and his family were so frugal that he would never spend a penny carelessly. When he was sixty, he had bought 15 more *kung* of farmland. Thus, his family had 45 *kung* of farmland altogether. He died at seventy-one.

"My grandmother was ingenious and vivacious, tall and energetic. She did what she had planned without talking about it. She was busy all the time. Her house was well managed, and everything was in good order, both in her household and on the farm. She loved her children so much that she would never scold them, and they were devoted to her. She gave birth to one son and one daughter and died at sixty-five.

"My father, Liu Yen-tau, was an only son. Therefore, his parents loved him as though he were a pearl. He needed to do nothing in the family. His parents often prepared candies and fruit for him, and he had the right clothes for every season. [The village children usually did not have enough clothes to change them every season.] The villagers told my grandfather that Chen-lo was spoiling his son. But Chen-lo said: 'I am willing to be criticized for letting my only son take things easy. No one should interfere with me.'

"While he was in his teens, Yen-tau was very wild. He went to the mountains to hunt every day. When he hunted some bird or beast, he would drink a large quantity of wine. When he wanted to have an affair with a girl, he would never care about the distance he had to go, and he spent his money freely. He also liked to eat dog meat, because the local people considered it as a tonic and preventive of malaria. Though he took care of nothing in the family, the economic condition of his family was still good, owing to his parents' industry and frugality.

"Yen-tau married at the age of seventeen. The marriage was arranged by his parents as usual. [One of Liu Tuang-tao's neighbors told my assistant: "After marriage, Liu Yen-tau and his wife did not love each other, because he felt that 'Chia hua pu ju yeh hua hsiang' ('The domestic flower is not so fragrant as the wild flower').[5] And his wife was also unfaithful to him. Thus, he and his wife did not care for their family, and the responsibility for their family was left to their old parents. He only asked his parents for money when he needed it."] His wife was pretty and intelligent.

"At the age of thirty, however, Yen-tau gradually changed. As he became older, he became more responsible, nor did the young girls care for him any more. Henceforth, he became more affectionate to his wife and began to take care of his family.

"Though not well educated, Yen-tau became careful, and everything he tried to do was well planned. The fortunes of his family were improving steadily. Every year he stored his rice until the following spring and then sold it at a high price. He was always ready to buy more farms.

"When he was fifty, Liu Yen-tau had bought 20 *kung*

5. A Chinese proverb.

of farmland. He had altogether 65 *kung* and was the richest farmer in the village. But, as he became richer, he became more frugal. He wore shabby clothes, and those who did not know him would have thought him a poor man. His only hobby was drinking wine. Every morning he would go to the fields to see to his farm. In the daytime he would look after his children. He did not do any heavy work.

"Yen-tau was very kind to his children. He scarcely ever scolded or beat them. If a child did something wrong, he would give him advice. If a child did well, he would praise him highly. He felt that one's nature could not be changed. One who was clever would not need much education. Though he was illiterate, Yen-tau was bright and reasonable, with a strong character. If he decided on a course of action, he would never change his mind. He could not bear dishonesty. He passed away at sixty-seven.

"My mother was energetic and willing to do any kind of work. She was, however, most stubborn and temperamental. [One of Liu Tsung-tao's neighbors told my assistant: "If Yen-tau offended his wife, she would not speak to him for weeks. She liked to be flattered by others. If anyone criticized her to her face, she would never forget it and hated him secretly. Since her family was rich, she was respected by the villagers."] She had two sons and one daughter. She was sixty-seven in 1946."

One of Liu Tsung-tao's clan members told my assistant: "Liu Tsung-tao was the elder son of Liu Yen-tau. When he was born, his father was already thirty-one years old. His father was very happy and loved him very much. Yen-tau often said: 'Both family and purse should

〚 276 〛

be prosperous. But family is more important than the purse, because the purse is a *sau pao*, or a "dead gem," while the family consists of *huo pao*, or "living gems." ' He undertook all the jobs of housekeeping in order to allow his wife a good rest and time to care for the child."

Tsung-tao's self-centered and domineering tendencies were seen when he was four or five years old. He claimed as his own everything which happened to please him. He threw away anything he had in his hand and cried all day when he lost his temper. His parents and others in the family acceded to his every wish in order to prevent his tantrums. When he played with other children, all his fellow-players had to be under his command. If any-one did not obey his orders, he would knock him down or drive him away. When he wanted to do something, his action could not be checked. His extraordinary stubbornness was probably due to his parents' indul-gence.

Tsung-tao started to study at nine. In his native dis-trict education was backward. Usually there was a single school for more than ten villages. He entered a private school located five miles from his home where he had to reside and board at the school. There were only a few families who could afford to send their children to such schools.

Liu Tsung-tao's father was well disposed and far-sighted. He felt that there would be no future for his family unless he allowed his children to study. But if one of his children were to become an official, there would be fame for his family and ancestors. A farmer was not in a position to develop greatly. He was very glad when his son's teacher told him that Tsung-tao was clever and had a good memory. The teacher also said that, though Tsung-tao liked to play, his record was one of the best.

After eight years in the private school, Tsung-tao came to the city of Kunyang to compete in the entrance examination of the junior normal school of the county. When Yen-tau was informed that his son had been selected as worthy of being a student, he gave a big feast to his relatives, friends, and the local gentry. All of them who came to congratulate him on the success of his son contributed one or two Mexican dollars toward the school expenses.

Liu Tsung-tao told my assistant about his initial journey to the city as follows: "When I was studying in the normal school, I felt very proud of myself, because I thought that, though I was born in a mountainous region, I had now come to the city to study along with the city boys. Since I knew that the other boys of my village could not enter school and I had a golden opportunity to study in the capital of the county, I tried to study very hard and not disappoint my father. At the same time, I really had a sense of inferiority, because the clothes of the other boys were better than mine. I had not eaten what the others had eaten; and I had not seen what the others had seen."

One of Liu Tsung-tao's classmates told me: "When he was studying in the school, Tsung-tao often fought with the others. He had a strong sense of justice. If someone offended him, he would fight with him to the end. But all his classmates liked him, because he had new ideas and was eloquent. His Chinese composition was often praised by the teacher."

Tsung-tao told my assistant: "After four years I

graduated from normal school. Before graduating, I
went to Kunming to compete in the graduating examination given by the Department of Education of the provincial government. I stayed in Kunming for ten days.
The contrast between the social life of Kunming and my
native community greatly puzzled me. I could not help
thinking: 'Why is the city so rich, while the country is
so poor?' "

One of Tsung-tao's clan members told my assistant:
"After returning to his home, Tsung-tao became a
schoolteacher in an elementary school in a market town.
After a year he went to Kunming to attend the elemen-
tary-school teachers' advanced practice class during the
summer vacation. Later he told his friends: 'High officials and rich merchants live in the large cities. The
country becomes poor, because the wealth is concentrated in the city.' "

One of Liu Tsung-tao's colleagues told my assistant:
"During the year of teaching, Tsung-tao visited the *chu*
officials[6] very often. Thus, he became friends with the
head of the district government and the local gentry.
His ability, knowledge, sense of responsibility, and
politeness was highly appreciated by them."

In 1938, when he came back from Kunming, Liu
Tsung-tao was immediately asked by the head of the
chu government to become a staff assistant. He felt much
more interest in administrative work than in teaching.
He was prudent and energetic, enthusiastic and right-

6. Before 1944 the district of Kunyang was divided into five *chu*. After that
year, with the reintroduction of the *pao-chia* system, Kunyang was divided into
eight *hsiang-chen*, or seven *hsiang* and one *chen*.

eous. Little by little he became an outstanding figure in the district.

Though he won the faith of the people and of many of the gentry, he stirred up the jealousies of the other staff members. He often openly criticized their corruption, their lack of a sense of responsibility, and their outward agreement while acting to the contrary, and he gained many enemies among his colleagues. At last he was compelled to resign his position. The intrigues of the administration of the local government impressed him deeply.

After leaving the *chu* government, Liu Tsung-tao won the warm sympathy of many common people and gentry. He bravely stood out and told the people what he would do for their benefit and his native place. Simultaneously, the provincial government ordered the magistrate to do away with the system of *chu* government and enlarge the original *hsiang-chen* instead. Since Liu Tsung-tao found that public opinion was on his side, he took advantage of the opportunity to urge the people to divide their *chu* into two *hsiang*. He encouraged the people to present a petition to the county government. The magistrate, finding that the area of the district was too large and that there were bandits in that *chu*, promised to divide it into two *hsiang* for convenience in administration. The eastern part was named "Nei Tien Hsiang," and the western part "Chu Tu Hsiang." Liu Tsung-tao was chosen as the head of the Chiu Tu Hsiang. He was then twenty-seven years old.

After he was appointed as the head of the *hsiang*, Liu Tsung-tao immediately set up the machinery of the district administrative office. He decided that his staff members should include both able youths and older men of the gentry class. The former would be responsible for action and the latter for supervision. He found the most important principles to be honesty and justice. First of all, the goverment should avoid doing harm to the people. Then the government should try to do some welfare work for the district. He had no desire for wealth but rather for a good reputation. He often said: "Chun tzu mou tao pu mou shih" ("The superior man searches after truth, not after food").[7]

Liu Tsung-tao himself was an able youth. Both his character and his deeds were admired by the gentry and the people. Since the establishment of the *hsiang*, taxes were suddenly decreased. The government was the center of activity of the people of the district. They knew what the government had done and would continue to do. Moreover, Tsung-tao asked his staff members to make public the government expenses once a month. He himself did not charge any fees. If he received any orders from the county government, he explained them to the people. As a consequence, the condition of Chi Tu Hsiang was much better than Nei Tien Hsiang.

After putting the affairs of the *hsiang* in order, Liu Tsung-tao turned his attention to popular education. There was formerly a central elementary school under the *chu* government. After the *chu* was divided into two *hsiang*, the central elementary schools were comparatively few, because there was no junior primary school in most of the villages. Thus he ordered every *pao* to have a junior primary school and the head of the *pao* to be responsible for the compulsory education program. After

7. A Confucian saying.

one year the students were greatly increased. Then he suggested the establishment of a separate central elementary school for his own *hsiang*. Because of transportation difficulties, this was more convenient for the students.

Liu Tsung-tao's most outstanding achievement was the suppression of bandits. Formerly, bandits were so common that persons were being looted or killed almost daily. People dared not walk freely in the daytime and could not sleep tranquilly at night. Then, Liu Tsung-tao secretly befriended the rascally element. He often invited them to drink wine and asked about the conditions of the bandits from them. At last he organized them as a corps for bandit prevention and asked their leaders to be corps leaders. He divided his *hsiang* into three districts and distributed the districts to different leaders and organized still another group under his own command. He often led his corps in fights with the remaining bandits. Because of his bravery and strategy, he was very much feared. Hearing of his determination to get rid of them, the bandits fled away. Thus he kept public order in the whole *hsiang* and won the admiration and support of all the people.

Being in a rather dangerous position, Tsung-tao carried a pistol and a knife with him at all times. He was always on the alert; if someone came to visit him, he would ask his identity before he would receive him. Sometimes he went to a teashop or a restaurant, but he did not stay very long. When he left the *hsiang* offices, he usually rode a big horse and was guarded by four or five attendants. He was very polite to the people.

Liu Tsung-tao had complete control of his *hsiang*.

When he came to the county government to attend meetings, he usually spoke what he thought. Among the heads of the various *hsiang-chen* administrative offices, he was the only one who dared to offend the influential and to speak for the people. If he regarded something as unjust, he would fight it to the end. He often criticized the other officials: "They work merely for the own interest. Fighting for the correct principle means offending the influential. Who wants to take this risk? They are wise men." On the other hand, he was frequently criticized for being too straightforward.

In 1943 Magistrate Chao came to Kunyang. A man from Liu Tsung-tao's native district who was a clerk in the county government and had desired to obtain Liu Tsung-tao's position for a long time bribed the magistrate to appoint him to office. Magistrate Chao dismissed Liu Tsung-tao without any reason. This greatly bewildered the gentry and people of the district. They petitioned the magistrate to rescind the order and simultaneously asked Liu Tsung-tao to hold on to his office under any circumstance. At last the clerk led a group of armed men to the *hsiang* offices to take over the position by force. When they arrived, Liu Tsung-tao ordered his guards to fight them. As a result, two of the clerk's men were killed and four were wounded.

After the incident, Magistrate Chao tried to put an end to the matter, because he feared that it would influence his prestige and position. He sent out a group of armed policemen to arrest Liu Tsung-tao and put him in jail in irons. The people of the *hsiang* were greatly stirred up and refused to allow the clerk to become their head of *hsiang* government. In order to appease the anger of the

people, Magistrate Chao was compelled to choose someone else to take the position. Thus the matter was
solved peacefully. But Liu Tsung-tao was still in jail.
Though the people petitioned the magistrate several
times for his release, Magistrate Chao turned a deaf ear
to their request.

The magistrate hoped that Liu Tsung-tao would bail
himself out and bargained with him every night. But Liu
Tsung-tao was an honest man and had not accumulated
money, though he had been in the position of the head
of the *hsiang* for more than four years. He did not wish
to ask his family for money.

Liu Tsung-tao told my assistant:

"I thought that I would be unable to face my parents
and brother if I dissipated the fortunes of my family for
myself. If I had grafted lots of money without considering the people, it would not have mattered if I gave a
part of the money to Magistrate Chao. But I had never
done anything which was harmful to the people. So I
decided not to present a single cent to him. Nevertheless,
life in jail was cruel. It was so dark that you could not
see a person beyond five feet, even in the daytime. It had
a bad smell and was filled with bugs and lice. We sat
by ourselves on the wet ground. They did not give us
enough food. At last I had to ask my family to get ready
$25,000[8] for bail. My family sold 5 *kung* of farmland in
order to do so. Then I was released."

One of my assistants told me: "After staying in jail for
two and a half months, Liu Tsung-tao became thin and

8. The value of money in March, 1943, had decreased 137 times on the base
of January, 1937. So this sum was equivalent to about 200 Mexican dollars,
or U.S. $100.

weak. He was full of anger at and hatred for the government. He wrote in his diary: 'How dark is society. How absolute is our government. The tyrannous official distorts the truth. Barbarous institutions suppress justice. Money exterminates human nature.' He hugged his anger and complained bitterly of the incapability, corruption, and meanness of the magistrate and vowed vengeance against him."

Being informed of Liu Tsung-tao's bitterness toward him, Magistrate Chao ordered his men to arrest him again. When he got this news, Tsung-tao immediately fled in a mood of desperation, thinking it was time to go to Liang Shan, or the Liang hills.[9] It was a critical moment in the war against Japan. Because Japan had occupied Indochina and Burma, Yunnan was threatened by Japan. Liu Tsung-tao followed the leader of certain Yunnanese bandits into the mountains and joined in fighting a guerrilla war against Japan. He instilled political ideas into the bandits and persuaded them to cooperate with the people. Since guerrilla war could not be carried on without the support of the people, his first motto for them was "never do any harm to the people." But he considered it all right to loot the officials, opium-dealers, and other rich people whose wealth was ill-gotten. After joining the bandits, many of his intimate friends and the youths inspired by him offered their services.

One of Liu Tsung-tao's friends told me: "After Tsung-tao had been with the bandits for a year and a half, Japan surrendered. Tsung-tao felt that, since the war was over, he should not continue in guerrilla warfare. As there was

9. See above, chap. i, n. 5.

no longer any function for him in the mountains, he returned home in December, 1945.'' (Magistrate Chao had been dismissed and a new magistrate had come to Kunyang.)

After his return, Tsung-tao engaged in agriculture. He no longer concerned himself with the local government, became very silent, and only associated with his bosom friends. But the people thought well of him and were respectful to him. When he came to a teashop or restaurant, the people would not charge him anything. His intelligence, courage, and sense of justice were highly admired by the people. In the district even women and children knew the name of Liu Tsung-tao.'' Nobody considered him a ''bandit.''

After remaining home for half a year, Liu Tsung-tao was elected by the people a member of the People's Political Council of the county. They found that he knew what was going on and also dared to speak for the people. So he was considered qualified to be a representative of the people. At first he dared not attend meetings in the city. But, since the people had put their trust in him, he felt he must pluck up courage to do so. He knew, however, that the People's Political Council had no power to carry out what the members suggested. He often said: ''The Nationalist government has been in power for twenty years. During these years they have said all the good words and done all the bad things. Endless talk will result in nothing.'' After the first term of the People's Political Council, he was re-elected a second time.

Liu Tsung-tao was tall and vigorous with a dark complexion and piercing eyes. He was clever in mind and quick in action. Though he was friendly with every kind of people, he often said: "Chun tzu nan yu hsiao jen chiao" ("A perfect gentleman finds it difficult to make friends with a mean man").

Liu Tsung-tao was ambitious for his future. He studied very hard and liked to be with energetic youths. He was always ready to fight against evil and looked for a chance to realize his ideal. His life was very plain and un-adorned. He liked to ride and hunt and could shoot accurately. He also liked to play the Chinese violin and the three-stringed guitar.

Liu Tsung-tao's elder son, Ta-jen, was nine years old in 1946 and was studying in an elementary school. The second son, Li-jen, was four years old. Both of them were very clever. The daughter was then only one year old.

Index

Agricultural production, 110

Authoritarianism, 11, 21, 22, 24; *see also* Government (centralized), authoritarianism in

Bureaucracy, 97

Ch'eng, 95, 96, 100

Chiang Kai-shek, 9

Chih, 59, 60, 61

Chou Kung, 37, 38

City: definitions of, 91–93; function of, 96, 108; modern, 121, 138, 139

Communists, 2, 3, 6, 7, 8, 9, 10, 14, 123; entry of, into Peiping, 2

Comprador, 106

Confucian ideal, 10, 11, 12, 44, 115, 142

Confucius, 22, 35, 36, 37, 38, 39, 40, 41, 42, 44, 45, 46, 47, 48, 49, 50, 56, 59, 60, 61, 65, 66, 67, 68, 69, 70

Conscription, 23, 141

Despotic monarchy, 19

Do-nothingism, 34, 86; *see also* Government (centralized), do-nothingism in

Erosion, social, 127, 131, 137, 140

Fa Chia; see Legalist school

Fei, Hsiao-tung, 14; career of, 1–3; purposes of, 4–5, 13

Fung Yu-lan, 25

Garrison towns, 91, 95, 102, 103, 104, 106, 107

Gentry, 122, 136; as landlords, 7, 12, 13, 97, 98, 112, 114, 117, 124, 126; as leaders, 81, 82, 83, 84, 88, 89; as scholar-officials, 6, 7, 11, 17, 24, 26, 55; and wealth, 99

Government: Communist, 9, 10; local, 81, 82, 84, 85, 87, 88; Nationalist, 2, 3, 14, 136

Government (centralized), 75, 84, 86, 90; authoritarianism in, 18, 19–24, 26–32; do-nothingism in, 10, 26, 31, 76, 78; and local community, 79, 83; popular significance, 9, 57, 58

Government servants, 84

"Grass roots," 129, 130, 131, 132, 133

Han Fei-tzu, 25, 76, 77

Han Yü, 56–58

Handicrafts, 8, 11, 12, 97, 111, 114, 116, 117, 118, 120, 121, 123

Hsien, 79, 92, 95

Hung Kung-sun, 53, 54, 55, 56

Imperial censor, 56, 57

Income, of peasants, 110, 111, 115, 121, 125

Intellectuals: modern, 8, 10, 15, 133, 135, 137; traditional, 59, 64, 65, 67, 68, 70, 72, 73, 74, 132, 133, 136, 139

Jên, 61

Kao-tsu, 20

Kuomintang, 7, 9, 136

Labor force, 112–15

Landlords, 7, 12, 13, 97, 98, 112, 114, 116, 117, 119, 122, 123, 124, 126

Lao-tzu, 21

Legalist school, 25, 76

Li, 62, 66

〖 289 〗